The ANZUS States
and Their Region

The ANZUS States and Their Region

REGIONAL POLICIES OF AUSTRALIA, NEW ZEALAND, AND THE UNITED STATES

EDITED BY Richard W. Baker

Under the auspices of the East-West Center

Westport, Connecticut
London

Library of Congress Cataloging-in-Publication Data

The ANZUS states and their region : regional policies of Australia,
  New Zealand, and the United States / edited by Richard W. Baker.
    p. cm.
    "Under the auspices of the East-West Center."
    Includes bibliographical references and index.
    ISBN 0-275-94693-2 (alk. paper)
    1. ANZUS Council. 2. United States—Relations—Australia. 3. New
Zealand—Relations—United States. 4. Australia—Relations—New
Zealand. 5. New Zealand—Relations—Australia. 6. United States—
Relations—New Zealand. 7. Australia—Relations—United States.
I. Baker, Richard W.   II. East-West Center.
E183.8.A8A74 1994
303.48'27309—dc20   93-14121

British Library Cataloguing in Publication Data is available.

Library of Congress Catalog Card Number: 93-14121
ISBN: 0-275-94693-2

First published in 1994

Praeger Publishers, 88 Post Road West, Westport, CT 06881
An imprint of Greenwood Publishing Group, Inc.

Printed in the United States of America

The paper used in this book complies with the
Permanent Paper Standard issued by the National
Information Standards Organization (Z39.48-1984).

10 9 8 7 6 5 4 3 2 1

To the Memory of

John C. Dorrance
1932–1991

Diplomat, scholar, and tireless exponent
of the common interests of
Australia, New Zealand, and the United States
and of their special interest in the Pacific Islands

Contents

Tables and Map

TABLES

MAP

Preface

This is the final book of a three-volume series containing the findings of a multiyear study of relations between Australia, New Zealand, and the United States during the period of the ANZUS alliance. The project was sponsored by the East-West Center of Honolulu, Hawaii, in conjunction with the Institute of Policy Studies at Victoria University in Wellington and the Australian Institute of International Affairs (AIIA). The project was not a study of the security alliance per se, but rather of the broader interrelationships between the three societies and governments. The objective was to identify the major trends, dynamics, and issues in the relationships over this period, and to consider the implications of these findings for the future relations among the three and for the broader Asia-Pacific region.

The first phase of the project examined sociopolitical trends in the three countries and changes in their national self-images and perceptions of each other. It resulted in the first volume in this series, *Australia, New Zealand, and the United States: Internal Change and Alliance Relations in the ANZUS States,* published by Praeger in 1991. The second phase considered economic trends and relations among the three. It resulted in *ANZUS ECONOMICS: Economic Trends and Relations Among Australia, New Zealand, and the United States,* published in 1992. The third phase, leading to this final volume of the series, looked at the regional policies of the three governments concerning security, economic cooperation, and the Pacific Islands.

In each phase, teams of experts from each country representing various academic and professional specializations were assembled to compile studies of the individual country experiences and then, in a conference, to compare these experiences and identify the major similarities, discontinuities, and implications for other aspects of the relationships. The conference on which this volume is based took place in Canberra in December 1990. Subsequent to the conference, the country studies have been revised and updated, and additional material in each section of the work plus the final section on implications have been prepared, drawing in part on conference discussions. It should be noted in this context that some of the material in the comments at the end of the first three sections as well as the concluding section previously appeared, in somewhat different form, in an overall project summary published by the East-West Center in September 1991.

Regrettably, during the process of preparing the manuscript for publication, a misunderstanding as to the subject matter of the country chapters led to the withdrawal from participation in the volume of the original Australian authors. In this situation, the AIIA did not consider it appropriate to continue as a co-sponsor of this volume. A team of Australian writers was subsequently reconstituted, independent of the AIIA, and their contributions appear in the book.

The editor wishes to express appreciation to all the authors of the country chapters for their efforts in writing and updating their papers, as well as their patience during the time it took to finalize the book. The editor would also like to acknowledge the contributions of other conference participants as well. In each case, the chapters represent the views of the individual authors, but each element has profited from the comments of others.

This volume has also benefited from the assistance of a group of senior advisers from each of the three countries, who have provided overall guidance to the Australia–New Zealand–U.S. Relations Project as well as many individual contributions in each phase. They are: Professor Dame Leonie Kramer, Sir Russel Madigan, and Mr. Bob White from Australia; Mr. Noel V. Lough, CMG, Rt. Hon. Sir Wallace Rowling, KCMG, Rt. Hon. Sir Brian Talboys, CH, and Ms. Sue Wood from New Zealand; and Professor Henry Albinski and Mr. James A. Kelly from the United States. All served in their personal capacities and not as official representatives of any organizations with which they may be affiliated. The project organizers are deeply grateful to all the advisers for their participation in and contributions to the design and implementation of the project.

The editor also wishes to acknowledge the efforts of many other people that made possible the Canberra conference and this volume. Particular appreciation is due in this connection to Mrs. Susan Allica, then executive director of the Australian Institute of International Affairs, and her staff for making all the arrangements for the project's Australian conference; the Australian team at the conference was organized by Dr. Michael McKinley of the Australian National University. Professor Gary Hawke, director of the Institute of Policy Studies, once again organized and anchored the New Zealand participation in this phase of the project, and also provided invaluable assistance during the preparation of the manuscript. At the East-West

Center, Ms. Deborah Forbis copyedited the manuscript of the volume, and Mrs. Dorine McConnell and Ms. Dorothy Villasenor assisted in word processing the text for publication. Finally, special thanks is owed to Dr. Charles Morrison, director of the Program on International Economics and Politics, who originally conceived the Australia–New Zealand–U.S. Relations Project and who participated and provided overall direction to the project throughout.

The ANZUS States
and Their Region

Introduction

The ANZUS alliance, signed by the foreign ministers of Australia, New Zealand, and the United States on 1 September 1951, was a mutual defense pact. It set out the conditions and procedures under which the parties would act to meet threats to any of them "in the Pacific area." Although the treaty dealt only with security cooperation, it drew on a far broader base of shared experience, values, and understanding among the three countries. All three states viewed themselves as representing the heritage and interests of the Western democratic system in the Pacific, interests they had defended in the Second World War and sought to preserve and advance in the postwar peace and the Cold War that quickly ensued. Also, all three had advanced market economies and thus shared a mutual stake in the new arrangements governing the international monetary and trading systems that had been put into place following the Second World War.

Thus the alliance relationships also rested on and assumed the existence of a wider area of commonality in the interests of the three. This did not imply any expectation of complete congruity or across-the-board cooperation; the wartime experience had shown that even in the defense area there could be significant differences of view and robust exchanges without the fundamental enterprise being jeopardized. The area of common perspectives and policy objectives, however, clearly extended beyond defense.

The interest of this volume is to explore whether, over the 40 years since the signing of the ANZUS pact, there has been convergence or divergence in the broader perspectives and policies of the three partners toward the region in which their defense alliance operates. Can we identify a "habit of cooperation" in regional policy that has grown up over these years? Or has the passage of time tended to bring out a greater individuality and stronger differences in the approach of each to their common region? We also want to consider the implications of our findings in this regard for the future of the relationships among the three for the remainder of this decade and into the twenty-first century.

New Zealand's ban on port visits by nuclear-armed or powered ships and the resulting suspension of the U.S. security commitment to New Zealand under the defense treaty in 1986 clearly pointed to a major difference in a policy area of central importance to the alliance relationship. Far less traumatic but nonetheless serious problems in U.S.-Australian relations during the same period, particularly a vituperative dispute over trade policy, similarly indicated areas of growing difference. The more difficult question, and ultimately the more important one, is whether these differences were exceptions to a broader pattern of common perspectives and interests, or were only the most visible symptoms of a wider divergence in approaches among the three.

This volume explores these questions by looking at three specific policy areas: regional security, the Pacific Islands, and regional economic cooperation. Each of these topics offers a window on a different aspect of the relationships among the ANZUS states.

Concerns about regional security were central to the establishment of the alliance, and so the broader security policies of each country within the region are clearly a major area of common interest that also directly affects how each views the alliance. The Pacific Islands are the geographic subregion where the security interests of the three countries most directly and continuously overlap, and so the place of the islands in the foreign policy of each and their relationships with the islands is also a good area in which to test the degree of commonality in their approaches. Finally, the Asia-Pacific region is of growing economic importance to each of the ANZUS states. It is economically the most dynamic region in the world and it appears to be organizing itself institutionally as a region for the first time. The approaches of the three to economic cooperation in the region will be an increasingly important topic in their future relationships with each other.

The volume is organized in four sections. The first three sections present individual essays on the policies of each country in the three subject areas. Each section ends with a commentary drawing together the elements of similarity and difference in the three national approaches in that area. The final section assesses the implications of the conclusions in all three areas for the overall relationships among the three governments.

Each author presents his or her own perspective. Some are more critical of the policies of their government than others. Nevertheless, each chapter provides an explanation of the policies being pursued and an indication of the major lines of debate on that policy area.

It should also be noted that this work is more concerned with the trends and the dynamics in each policy area than with presenting either a comprehensive treatment of the evolution of policy or the most recent and current developments. Thus, some chapters pay more attention to the earlier part of the postwar period than others, and some give greater emphasis to contemporary events. More detailed histories and analyses of the various issues can be found in the extensive bibliography.

SECTION I

Regional Security Policies

In this section we consider the regional security policies of the three ANZUS governments. We are interested in how each government assesses the security outlook and major issues in the Asia-Pacific region in the 1990s; what each sees as its own national roles and priorities in regional security as well as the appropriate roles for the other two countries and the alliance; and what major differences exist within each country on these questions and how these debates might affect the further evolution of national policies.

Stewart Woodman describes the dramatic shift in Australia's security outlook and policies in the years since the signing of the ANZUS treaty. In 1951 Australia saw itself as an insecure European outpost in a threatening Asian environment, critically dependent on the protection of great power allies. Its policy of "forward defense" was based on supporting those allies in meeting any potential dangers as far from its shores as possible. Today Australia takes a more regionally oriented and independent stance in security matters, accepting the challenge of meeting more local threats of various orders closer to home, primarily through reliance on its own forces, while still looking to its alliance with the United States for a variety of supporting services as well as an ultimate trump card in case of need.

Woodman also assesses the challenges posed by Australia's new orientation. These include: the need for a more sophisticated understanding of the security perspectives of regional states and for broadening security relationships beyond traditional exercises and exchanges; the particular problems of accommodating the security needs of the South Pacific states and the requirements and consequences of what is now a bilateral security relationship with New Zealand; and differing requirements of continental defense and regional security and the overall political-budgetary challenge of meeting the costs of a more self-reliant defense capability. But the most critical questions, in his view, are uncertainty about the future U.S. role and security posture in the region, and the potential for tensions between Australia's closer identification with the region and its alliance ties with the United States. He concludes that the future place of the ANZUS relationship in Australian security policy will depend importantly on U.S. sensitivity to regional strategic dynamics and to Australia's specific interests in the emerging Asia-Pacific security environment.

Steve Hoadley first reviews the longer-term background of New Zealand's 1985 split with the United States over nuclear policy, noting, among other things, New Zealand's early bipartisan expressions of concern over the destructiveness of nuclear weapons and its strong support for the goal of nuclear disarmament as well as the exclusion of nuclear weapons from New Zealand's territory. He also stresses that New Zealand's fundamental orientation has always been internationalist, not isolationist, despite its equally consistent record of very low levels of defense spending.

Hoadley compares the 1983 defense review by a National Party government with the Labour government's 1987 review following the break with the United States. He finds remarkable continuity in defense objectives and priorities. These include a progressively greater focus on New Zealand's immediate geographic region; adherence to the ANZUS treaty; cooperation with allies, with the emphasis now on Australia; and at the global level, support for UN peacekeeping activities. One of the differences he identifies is the implicit recognition in the 1987 document that New Zealand and Australia have substantially different strategic outlooks.

Hoadley sees similar continuity reflected in the 1991 review by the National Party, which regained government in the 1990 election. Noting that National had dropped its opposition to Labour's nonnuclear policy earlier in 1990, and that public support for the policy had grown, Hoadley sees little likelihood of any significant change in the nuclear policy at least before the 1993 election. However, Hoadley believes that the damage caused by the rupture has largely been contained, and that continued overall cooperation among the three countries will prove more important for long-term regional security than the dispute.

James Kelly sees American security policy—in this region as elsewhere—in a transitional phase. The organizing principle of the Cold War is gone, but the new reality is more complex and ambiguous and it may take years for a new consensus to be formed. The United States, according to Kelly, needs to find the correct path between "the 'world policeman' shibboleth . . . and the imaginary attractions of isolation." He reviews formal statements on U.S. policy in the Asia-Pacific region by both the Defense and State Departments, concluding that they attempt to address the new conditions but basically perpetuate the previous bilateral alliance approach and do not offer genuinely new thinking. Most critically, the statements say little about how U.S. military, economic, and political interests in the region are to be integrated or how the United States can deal with the perception in the region of reduced U.S. interest and relevance.

Within the context of this larger uncertainty, Kelly believes that U.S.-Australian security cooperation is basically healthy and will continue to be mutually beneficial and complementary. He sees Australia's new regionally oriented defense policy as quite consistent with U.S. interests. Despite the obvious problems, he thinks there has been a slow improvement in U.S.-New Zealand security relations and that a new relationship will ultimately be built which, while not equal to what existed before, will be cooperative and solid, reflecting their common interests. New Zealand's South Pacific focus also meets mutual interests, although he notes that resources may limit what New Zealand actually does.

Finally, in his comment the editor notes that the evolutionary paths of all three countries in security policy, while differing in specific timing and content, have been parallel — that in each case the focus has been narrowed and there is now a more careful prioritization of their defense interests. A comparison of the nature of their participation and cooperation in the Korean, Vietnam, and Persian Gulf wars illustrates the nature of the change. He concurs with Woodman, Hoadley, and Kelly that the basic policies of the countries remain fundamentally complementary, and that practical military cooperation will continue, at least between the United States and Australia and between Australia and New Zealand, and possibly once again between the United States and New Zealand. However, he concludes that the differences in perspectives and priorities are such that, barring major new crises that galvanize common interests and efforts, the future is likely to see a more diverse set of policies and priorities among the three.

1

Toward an Independent Outlook: Australia's Regional Security Policies, 1945-1991

STEWART WOODMAN

Amid the uncertainty and lack of direction in the post–Cold War strategic environment, the apparent confidence of senior Australian defense and security planners that they have the concepts and policies to meet future challenges appears peculiarly out of place. This paradox is even more apparent considering the legacy of suspicion and self-doubt that characterized Australia's strategic outlook for a long period of time. Despite recognition of Australia's isolated geographic location, fears persisted throughout the nineteenth and early twentieth centuries of attack from Russia, China, or Japan. As Frank Anstey skeptically commented after the Japanese defeat of Russia in 1905, "The jingoes must fake an enemy from somewhere" (Dupont 1991: 11). Japanese attacks on Papua New Guinea and on Australia itself during the Second World War only served to reinforce such concerns.

In retrospect, many of those fears appear hardly credible. Henry Parkes' exhortations in 1888 about "the barbarous power, which is so rapidly creating armies and a formidable navy, that it is sufficient at all events to awaken the intelligent attention of a reflecting man" may have had a point in the context of domestic political concerns about Chinese immigration (Dupont 1991: 5–6). They did not reflect a pragmatic appraisal of the strategic situation.

It would, however, be wrong to see Australia's current security policies as simply the consequence of a more realistic strategic outlook. They are the result of a fundamental rethinking of Australia's security priorities. At first, the changing strategic environment and the actions of major allies goaded Australia into action. More recently, however, Australia's own quest for a comprehensive and relevant security framework has been the driving force behind change and innovation.

To appreciate the strengths and possible weaknesses of those policies, it is important to understand the ways in which, and the reasons why, they have evolved. Only on that basis can informed judgments be made about their appropriateness to tackling prospective strategic challenges in the 1990s.

THE ERA OF FORWARD DEFENSE

The 1939–1945 world war and its immediate aftermath threw many of the traditional underpinnings of Australia's security policies into question. The supremacy and availability of the British navy could not be taken for granted following the fall of Singapore, Britain's loss of control over India, and its increasing preoccupation with European security concerns. Japan's aggression and the emergence of an increasingly assertive Communist China meant that Australia could not see the Pacific simply as a secondary theater for conflicts arising in Europe. The legitimacy of colonial regimes faced growing pressure both domestically in South and Southeast Asia, and in the newly formed United Nations. The United States had established itself as the power with the greatest capacity to determine the future strategic balance in the Pacific.

Australia was not, however, in a position to quickly discard the trappings of its former policies, nor was there any suggestion that it should do so. The fundamental defense assessment paper (the "Strategic Basis") for 1946 stated that, "the basic ingredient of Australia's defence must be Empire Cooperation since the size of this country demands for its defence armed forces and an industrial potential quite beyond our present capacity" (Department of Defence 1987a: 303). This sense of dependency, together with a continued close association with British imperial interests, meant that Australia's forces continued to "be so organised and trained that they can fit in as complete units with Empire forces in any theatre, keeping particularly in mind the Pacific theatre" (Department of Defence 1987a: 303).

The Korean War and the emergence of Communist insurgencies in Southeast Asia quickly convinced defense planners that more needed to be done. Australia dispatched troops to Korea, a squadron of transport aircraft to Malaya, and by 1953 had increased defense spending to 5.1 percent of GDP. The government established a five-year program for defense planning. Capability proposals included two regular army brigades, two aircraft carriers and a fleet air arm, six fast anti-submarine frigates, a fleet tanker, and the local production of Canberra, Sabre, and Vampire aircraft (Millar 1968). Sir Robert Menzies concluded in March 1951 that:

The dangers of war have increased considerably. It is my belief that the state of the world is such that we cannot, and must not, give ourselves more than three years in which to get ready to defend ourselves.

Indeed, three years is a liberal estimate. (*House of Representatives Hansard* 7 March 1951: 78)

These potentially threatening developments in the Pacific focused Australian attention much more directly on the future role of the United States. Concerned the United States might agree to a "soft" peace treaty with Japan as a counter to "the global pattern of communist aggression," Australia sought a formal security commitment from the United States (Millar 1968: 266). Despite the initial opposition of senior American officials, including Secretaries of State Acheson and Dulles, the ANZUS treaty was signed on 1 September 1951. While not a binding security commitment, the treaty recognized the common security interests of Australia, New Zealand, and the United States in the Pacific. The parties agreed to consult in the event of a threat to one another and that each would "act to meet the common danger in accordance with its constitutional processes" (Watt 1968: 112–42).

The ANZUS treaty did not, because of American reluctance, meet Australia's concern for a comprehensive security arrangement linking the U.S. presence with the British forces in Malaya and Singapore. That came about two years later after France's problems with maintaining control in Indochina led to the partitioning of Vietnam and a decision to withdraw the remaining French forces. The Southeast Asia Collective Defense Treaty signed in 1953 established the Southeast Asia Treaty Organization (SEATO) comprising the United States, the United Kingdom, France, Australia, New Zealand, Thailand, Pakistan, and the Philippines (Harper 1963; Millar 1968). Like ANZUS, the SEATO treaty bound members to meet the common danger — including aggression by means of armed attack on any of them, or any other states specifically designated — in accordance with their respective constitutional processes.

For Australia, the concept that came to be known as "forward defense" was quite straightforward. The 1952 Strategic Basis paper argued "While Indo-China is held, defence in depth is provided for the Australia-New Zealand main support area" (Department of Defence 1987a: 304). Over the next decade and a half, capability and deployment decisions reflected these priorities. Australia contributed forces to the Commonwealth Strategic Reserve; deployed troops to Malaya in 1955 "to help the Malayan people maintain the internal and external security that would make self-government possible" (Millar 1968: 306); and reorganized the Army as two Pentropic Divisions (each consisting of five self-contained battle groups, providing a high ratio of combat to support troops and great operational flexibility) to allow it to better contribute in Southeast Asia. It first provided military instructors to South Vietnam in 1961, allocated enhanced combat support to Malaysia during confrontation with Indonesia, and sent an army battalion group to Vietnam in 1965 (Harper 1968; Millar 1968). Planners gave little thought to the direct defense of Australia because they considered that

Australia would "have time to build up to meet this threat provided her basic defence structure is sound" (Department of Defence 1987a: 306).

TOWARD SELF-RELIANCE

The scale of Australia's commitment to regional security during the 1960s tended to belie its increasing uncertainty about the value of forward defense. Not only was Australia concerned about the emergence of regional countries, particularly Indonesia, with their own independent military capabilities, but it believed that unless Australia continued to support its ANZUS and SEATO obligations "it will become more difficult to encourage the US to retain an effective military presence in SE [Southeast] Asia and to assist our security in time of need" (Department of Defence 1987a: 307). Britain's commitment was even more doubtful following its loss of control over the Suez Canal, resource pressures on maintaining a global military presence, and growing NATO commitments in Europe (Richardson 1974: 242–44).

Thus, even before the British announced their decision in 1967 to withdraw their forces from Malaysia and Singapore, and President Nixon set out the U.S. doctrine of more limited commitment to the region in 1969, Australia had begun to consider the possibility that it "must be prepared to deal with situations which directly threaten our territorial interests and in which we could not reasonably rely on receiving help from our allies" (Department of Defence 1987a: 308).

Australia also had to consider how it could continue to contribute to the security of Southeast Asia given that it could not step into the military shoes of the United States or the United Kingdom. Singapore had made it clear that if Australia withdrew its forces, it would seek protection from other external powers. Malaysia, on the other hand, wanted specific treaty guarantees that were more binding than Australia wished (Richardson 1974: 244–46).

The resultant compromise was the signing of the Five Power Defence Arrangements (FPDA). Under the FPDA, the parties – the United Kingdom, Australia, New Zealand, Malaysia, and Singapore – agreed to consult in the event of an attack on either Malaysia or Singapore. Australia announced that it would maintain two Mirage fighter squadrons, a naval vessel, and an infantry battalion in the region, and it continued to provide substantial military aid and training (Richardson 1974: 247–49). The emphasis was on enhancing the capacity of Malaysia and Singapore to provide for their own defense. Should they require more substantial assistance, Australia would maintain a "versatile and flexible defence force capable of rapid deployment over a wide range of situations" (Department of Defence 1987a: 310). The importance of economic and other nonmilitary assistance in combating insurgency was also acknowledged.

The election of the Whitlam Labor government in 1972 saw the dismantling of the final remnants of forward defense. It brought the last Australian troops home from Vietnam, withdrew the Singapore battalion, abolished national service, and expedited the independence of Papua New Guinea including transfer of the responsibility and some capability, albeit mismatched, for security. Furthermore, Australia developed a program of defense cooperation with Indonesia. Its aim was to promote Indonesia's capacity for self-defense through technical assistance, consultation, training, and joint exercises (O'Neill 1980). The Labor government firmly believed that "political, economic and social change in Asia will occur and is indeed desirable; we believe that Australia should not intervene militarily even when the contest for power and control over the 'change' leads to violence" (Millar 1991: 334).

THE DEFENSE OF AUSTRALIA

Coming to terms with the defense of Australia itself was to prove a much more difficult exercise. Rather than relying on commitments overseas either to create a strategic shield for Australia or to "buy" allied support in a contingency, Australia accepted that it had now to "assume the primary responsibility for its own defence against any neighborhood or regional threats." The difficulty was that "Not only does Australia lack identifiable future aggressors against whom specific plans can be made but even those who might one day develop hostile intentions would have to invest several years of effort to deliver a major attack" (O'Neill 1980: 15). Defence Minister Lance Barnard distinguished himself by claiming that there was no threat for 10 to 15 years, a judgment well beyond the scope of confident intelligence prediction.

There was, however, no prospect that Australia would become complacent in its approach to security issues. Added to its geographic isolation were the sheer size of the country, its limited population and resource base, the proximity of Southeast Asia, and some recent unsettling experiences — the Malay Emergency, Indonesia's "Confrontation" of Malaysia, and the Vietnam War. During these years the government created a defense intelligence organization; the Tange Report led to major structural changes including the abolition of the single service departments; Millar's recommendations saw the Citizen Military Forces reorganized as the Army Reserve in a "total force" concept; and a comprehensive study was begun of the requirements of continental defense (O'Neill 1980; Mediansky 1980).

Not surprisingly in these circumstances, security planning in the 1970s was preoccupied with hammering out the fundamental tenets of defending Australia. First, the geographic imperatives of size, distance, harsh terrain, limited infrastructure, and the key maritime approaches were set in place. These highlighted the importance of capabilities for comprehensive intelligence and surveillance, maritime and air defense, long-range transport, responses to hostile landings, national defense infrastructure and communications, and industrial, scientific, and technological support (Killen 1976).

Then began the much more difficult task of establishing just what type and level of threat the Australian Defence Force (ADF) should be structured and equipped to meet. The initial concept was that of a "core force" under which the ADF was to be:

> a force able to undertake peacetime tasks, a force sufficiently versatile to deter or cope with a range of low-level contingencies which have sufficient credibility, and a force with relevant skills and equipment capable of timely expansion to deter or meet a developing situation. (Department of Defence 1987a: 313)

However, that approach failed to provide sufficiently clear direction or to define priorities.

Civilian planners gave priority to those lower-level conflicts that could arise within shorter time frames. Not only did the capability exist within regional inventories, but it was less likely that a clear warning would precede a more substantial attack. Many military officers were far less convinced. They emphasized the potential for conflicts to escalate, distrusted the ability of governments to recognize warning indicators, and focused their planning on the need to have a base force capable of expansion in the event of more substantial conflict. Their continued affinity with the structures and capabilities of their British and American colleagues bred a distrust that civilian planners were engaged in little more than a cost-cutting exercise. Planning stagnated, only to be papered over politically by that wonderful euphemism "constructive tension."

It took the commitment and enthusiasm of Kim Beazley as minister for defense to break the deadlock. Frustrated with the lack of agreement within the defense organization, Beazley appointed defense academic Paul Dibb to forge a consensus. Dibb's report (*Review of Australia's Defence Capabilities* 1986) established the principle that Australia should plan up to the level of available regional military capabilities. It was a level that could be measured objectively and went a long way to satisfying military concerns that they might be caught out by surprise developments. Dibb also formulated a possible defense strategy for Australia and outlined a specific blueprint for capability enhancement over the next decade.

Most important, Dibb's report demonstrated that with the right mix of capabilities and the use of technology, Australia could in fact afford a significant level of defense self-reliance. In doing so, it provided a firm basis for sustained defense expenditure on the order of 2.5 to 3 percent of gross domestic product. This was a major achievement given that there was no identifiable threat to generate a political priority for defense spending. Despite the strong anticommunist rhetoric of the Menzies Liberal-Country Party governments in the 1950s and 1960s, Australian defense budgets had only exceeded this level in the mid-1960s when Australia's participation in the Vietnam War was at its height.

Many of Dibb's recommendations were deftly incorporated into an official

White Paper, *The Defence of Australia 1987*. This document remains the key to Australia's present defense policy direction and capability development program.

AUSTRALIA AND THE UNITED STATES

The other significant change during this period was in how Australia saw its relationship with the United States, which by now had replaced Great Britain as Australia's major strategic ally. Here two issues dominated the popular debate during the 1970s and early 1980s. First was the presence on Australian territory of the joint Australian–U.S. defense facilities at Pine Gap in the Northern Territory, Nurrungar in South Australia, and North West Cape in Western Australia. The early warning and monitoring functions of these facilities directly linked Australia into the West's global nuclear deterrent strategy. They carried with them the possibility that Australia might become a target during a nuclear confrontation (Australian Parliament 1981). A policy review ordered by the Hawke Labor government immediately on taking office in 1983 concluded that, on balance, the joint facilities should be retained because of their contribution to global nuclear stability; this represented a significant victory over widespread rank-and-file skepticism (Hayden 1983).

There had long been considerable concern within the Labor Party about the degree of Australia's dependence on the United States for defense and its at least indirect involvement in U.S. nuclear strategy. At the same time, the Hawke government was conscious of the need not to alienate the middle ground of the Australian electorate who continued to see ANZUS as the cornerstone of the nation's security. The importance of the facilities to preventing a preemptive strike by the Soviet Union, to verification of arms control agreements, and to Australia's leverage in international arms control and disarmament efforts were key factors in the government's favorable conclusions (Hayden 1984).

Labor support for participation in wider U.S. strategic planning however, remained more qualified than that of the conservative Liberal-National Party opposition. The government supported rest and recreation visits to Australian ports by U.S. maritime forces, particularly in the Indian Ocean, and allowed low-level navigation training by B-52 aircraft over northern Australia. It also dissociated itself from New Zealand's bans on visits by nuclear-armed or powered warships, arguing that such rights of access were an essential part of alliance obligations (Hayden 1985b). The Hawke government was not, however, prepared to participate in the Strategic Defense Initiative (or "Star Wars") program, which it saw as potentially destabilizing to the global nuclear balance, nor to permit the use of Australian ports to support long-range missile tests in the Pacific (*Australian Foreign Affairs Record* [AFAR] 56 [1985]: 126, 136, 223–24).

The other issue in debate was the circumstances in which, and the conditions under which, Australia might expect support from the United States in a conflict. Security planners soon reached the conclusion that ANZUS did not represent a binding commitment, but would provide a significant disincentive to any potential adversary who would be unsure of the nature, scale, and timing of possible U.S. support (Australian Parliament 1982). They accepted that the threshold for direct U.S. combat support might be quite high. But firm assurances of continued supply and support meant that considerable intelligence and materiel assistance would still be available, the latter greatly relieving the pressure on stockholding requirements. Implicitly, the United States was still considered Australia's ultimate security guarantor in a major conflict (Hayden 1985b).

A new and more politically skillful justification for the security relationship with the United States was developed by Kim Beazley in the 1987 White Paper, *The Defence of Australia 1987*. That document melded the various elements of Australia's security policies into the concept of "self-reliance within the framework of our alliances and regional associations" (*The Defence of Australia 1987:* vii). Drawing on Dibb's emphasis on the importance of intelligence and technology to the defense of Australia, Beazley argued that self-reliance was only a realistic and affordable strategy for Australia because of the direct benefits it gained under the ANZUS alliance in developing its own defense capabilities. These included access to intelligence and advanced technologies, preferred customer status in defense purchasing, scientific and industrial cooperation, and training and exercises with a sophisticated, combat experienced force. Australia's contribution to regional security and its support for the U.S. global deterrent strategy were, given its size, an appropriate exchange for these benefits (*The Defence of Australia 1987:* 3–5). This emphasis on the practical day-to-day benefits to underpin a more independent Australian security posture effectively countered many of the criticisms from both the political left and the right.

At the same time, the alliance relationship was not without its tensions during this period. For its part, the United States was concerned with the apparent retreat into isolationism heralded by the capability proposals of the Dibb *Review,* Australia's reluctance to wholeheartedly support some aspects of U.S. nuclear strategy and of U.S. interventions in Central America, and its promotion of the South Pacific Nuclear Free Zone treaty (despite efforts to ensure that the form of the treaty was as acceptable as possible to the United States) (AFAR 58 [1987]: 91–92). Australia, on the other hand, was critical of apparent U.S. insensitivity to the interests of the small South Pacific Island states, its lack of consultation on some key regional initiatives (such as the recognition of China in 1972 and the introduction of advanced weapons systems including the Harpoon antishipping missile), and U.S. agricultural policies that undermined Australia's export markets and its economic competitiveness (Hayden 1987). Ultimately, many of these differences came down to frictions between the global policy outlook of the United States and Australia's more specific regional concerns. That the alliance has been able to accommodate those strains is a reflection of the fundamental similarity of interests between the two countries and a pragmatic approach to the relationship. However, the strains also provided a warning that consensus cannot be taken for granted in all circumstances.

REDISCOVERING THE REGION

In the early 1970s, the move away from forward defense broke the close linkage that had existed between the defense of Australia and wider regional security concerns. Amid the struggle to establish a coherent basis for defense planning in the absence of a specific threat, Australia gave only limited attention to its security relationship with the region.

A useful program of defense cooperation, focused primarily on materiel assistance, began with several neighboring countries. The most substantial links were with Papua New Guinea, with Malaysia and Singapore under the FPDA, and with Indonesia and New Zealand. Emphasis was on enhancing the capacity of regional nations to provide for their own security, but the limited ability of the developing nations to absorb advanced defense aid, their focus on internal security concerns, and the relatively stable strategic environment gave little urgency to these initiatives. In the South Pacific, the focus was more on national development tasks as economic security became the primary concern of the newly independent island states.

The later 1980s witnessed an important change of emphasis. One lesson that emerged from resolving the key issues about the defense of Australia was that this was only the first step in a comprehensive security policy. Rather than being a recipe for complacency, the lack of an identifiable threat put even greater emphasis on how a nation should seek to ensure that the favorable environment did not deteriorate. This recognition highlighted the importance of three elements:

1. Understanding the strategic environment and having confidence that it would not change unexpectedly;
2. Developing closer defense ties with neighboring countries and appreciating their security concerns and priorities;
3. Using defense capabilities and other instruments of government constructively to promote strategic consensus and stability.

The emphasis now was quite different from the era of forward defense. Under that strategy, defense cooperation was directly linked to the forward deployment of forces and to contingency plans for combined operations to meet a particular threat. The new objective was to develop a more informed and shared understanding of strategic changes and their possible implications; to cooperate in those areas where strategic interests overlap—particularly with respect to the activities of external powers; and to support neighboring countries in developing the capabilities to provide for their own immediate defense (Dibb 1990).

By the late 1980s the new strategic trends that had begun to emerge underlined the importance of playing a constructive role in promoting regional security. There was the prospect of a drawdown in U.S. force levels with pressure on their continued use of bases in the Philippines, calls for a peace dividend flowing from the increasing accommodation with the Soviet Union, and domestic budgetary problems. The role of emerging major powers with a capacity to influence the region's strategic future—notably China, India, and Japan—remained largely undefined. Buoyed by economic prosperity, regional countries themselves were moving away from the emphasis on ground forces for counterinsurgency tasks toward more balanced and technologically advanced force structures, including significant maritime elements. In the South Pacific, problems with the maintenance of law and order and the need to protect the vast new marine and seabed resources available under the Law of the Sea Convention redefined security priorities (Beazley 1990).

Australia's efforts to revitalize its role in regional security affairs began with a series of specific defense initiatives. In the South Pacific there was the Pacific Patrol Boat program under which Australia provided the island governments with a vessel suitable for policing their Exclusive Economic Zones, able to be maintained with available national expertise, and linked into an enhanced aerial surveillance effort by Australian and New Zealand P-3 maritime patrol aircraft (Beazley 1987). In Southeast Asia, cooperation under the Five Power Defence Arrangements gave greater emphasis to Malaysia's and Singapore's emerging maritime and air defense capabilities. Rotational deployments of F/A-18 and F-111 aircraft and a major surface vessel replaced the permanent stationing of fighter aircraft in Malaysia (Beazley 1988). Defense cooperation resumed with Indonesia after a period of considerable coolness brought about by Australian press criticism of Indonesia's leaders. Overall, the emphasis moved away from materiel aid to joint training and exercises, reflecting the substantial advances made by the countries of the Association of Southeast Asian Nations (ASEAN) in their defense capabilities (*Defence Report* 1989/90: 122–23).

Despite the size of its defense budget, its long established security links with the region and the sophistication of its military capabilities, Australia has not found it easy to gain acceptance of this new regional role. In addition to important differences in political and social values, history, and culture, Australia's southern location and its alignment with the West set it apart from the nonaligned ASEAN nations who are concerned primarily with possible threats from the north. In the South Pacific, dependence on

Australian support is frequently tempered by concerns over potential Australian dominance. Expectations of support should internal law and order break down are matched by fears of Australian interventionism. Even within Australia, some groups have characterized the emphasis on regional engagement as a "new Australian militarism," potentially committing Australia to involvement in a range of regional contingencies in which it has no strategic interest (Cheeseman and Kettle 1990).

More recently, the government has incorporated those specific defense initiatives into a much more comprehensive policy framework. That policy statement, entitled *Australia's Regional Security,* was presented to Parliament by Foreign Minister Gareth Evans in December 1989 (Evans 1989). It linked political, economic, social, and cultural ties with existing defense contacts as the basis for "comprehensive engagement" with the nations of Southeast Asia and "constructive commitment" to the South Pacific. While laudable in its objectives, and a very important declaratory policy for Australia, the statement did underline the fragility of Australia's broader security links with the region. It also highlighted the failure to carry through, in any comprehensive way, the nonmilitary aspects of security identified both in the Colombo Plan in the 1950s, and when forward defense ended in the early 1970s.

Australia's endeavors to promote greater economic and security cohesion within the region have also come under criticism from both the ASEAN nations and the United States. Priding themselves on their tradition of dialogue and consensus, the former have resisted any Australian attempt to dictate the future regional agenda to them (*The Canberra Times* 22 April 1991). Initially, the United States was wary that such proposals would allow the Soviet Union greater influence in Pacific affairs (*The Australian* 24 April 1991). With the end of the Cold War and the dissolution of the USSR, U.S. concerns appear to have been more related to the potential of regional associations to cut across its own ability to control developments in the Asia-Pacific region through a web of bilateral relationships (*The Age* 11 April 1991).

AUSTRALIA'S STRATEGIC OUTLOOK

Just as these comprehensive security policies are being put in place, the changing strategic environment is already beginning to raise important challenges for those policies or, at least, the ways in which they are implemented. In the context of reducing the possibility of a global nuclear confrontation, the end of the Cold War has undoubtedly been welcomed by Australia. It has also led to a much more rapidly changing and uncertain strategic environment in the Asia-Pacific region itself. In the past, the rivalry between the United States and the Soviet Union tended to overshadow and, to a certain extent, condition regional relationships and differences. With the removal of that threat and, at least for many regional countries, the diminution of the protective presence of U.S. maritime forces, other factors have assumed much greater weight in the security planning of both Australia and its neighbors.

Much attention has focused on the potential of emerging major powers such as Japan, China, and India to influence regional developments. There are concerns about the increasing technological sophistication of regional forces, the introduction of enhanced air and naval combat capabilities, and the possibility of a flood of arms imports from European manufacturers. While the settlement process in Cambodia has, at least temporarily, stabilized the situation there, tensions remain on the Korean peninsula and there is considerable potential for friction with respect to overlapping marine and seabed resource claims.

However, what these specific issues tend to hide is the lack of clear direction in the security planning of many regional states. Their traditional props in terms of adversarial relationships, political alignments, and the presence of major powers are being taken away. There are few genuine threats on which to focus. The meaning of "security" is being redefined to include economic stability and, potentially, a range of other social and environmental factors. (This is due in no small part to the strength of the economic interdependency created by Japan with many regional nations.) The timing and extent of any drawdown in U.S. forces remains critical, justifying the habits of the past, and serving as a key determinant of both the strategic balance and required national force levels in the future.

The implications of these changes for Australia's regional security policies are many. The government has already recognized some of these in recent initiatives, but others will evolve only as the post–Cold War strategic environment in the Asia-Pacific region becomes more clearly defined.

First, Australia has begun to widen the geographical focus of its regional security outlook beyond Southeast Asia and the South Pacific to understand the potential impact of emerging major powers on the future stability of areas closer to Australia. It is not a question of countries such as Japan, India, and China representing a direct threat to Australia's security, but of how their growing size and military potential may affect regional security perceptions — in relation to weapons acquisitions and collective or individual national alignments, for example — and the resolution of primarily regional issues. It would not be in Australia's best interest for those countries to compete for influence in Southeast Asia or for opportunities to arise that could tempt them to become involved militarily (Beazley 1990).

Accordingly, it is important for Australia to have defense and security contacts that are sufficient for understanding the objectives and the capabilities of those nations and for alerting those nations to any concerns of Australia and its neighbors. Visits of senior defense officials to Japan and the reappointment of a defense attaché to New Delhi have been important developments in this regard. However, the type and level of such defense interchange can be a sensitive matter to Australia's immediate neighbors, especially in areas such as joint exercises. There is also the attendant risk that Australia could be inadvertently drawn into a wider security agenda, much of which would be of limited relevance to Australia's primary interests.

Second, the changing strategic environment requires corresponding adjustments to the means by which Australia seeks to engage its immediate region on security issues. Foreign Minister Evans's concept of comprehensive engagement clearly moves in this direction at least in terms of declared policy, but it does not obscure the fact that Australia has traditionally defined its security linkages with the region in defense terms. It has given little attention to developing a more comprehensive set of working relationships to underpin common security concerns. Australia's advanced military capabilities will continue to offer some leverage and access in the short term. However, the changing nature of regional security concerns and the narrowing gap in terms of defense technologies and maritime and air defense capabilities point to the need for a broader approach. The caution with which the region received Australian initiatives for new economic or security related structures shows that it is far from being accepted as a natural strategic partner. Its motives are suspected as a bid for regional leadership; its assertive style often clashes with the processes of negotiation and consensus that underpin ASEAN solidarity (Fry l991a; *The Australian* 19 September 1991).

Clearly, one important objective is to enhance understanding both in Australia and the region of each other's interests and policies. Exchanges of high-level military officers, including with Indonesia, and other steps serve to reinforce Australia's declaratory policies. Recent experience suggests, however, that Australia will need to broaden its focus away from existing defense contacts such as the Five Power Defence Arrangements with Malaysia and Singapore—a subject of some suspicion, or at least misunderstanding—to other issues of concern to its neighbors. Apart from monitoring arms and technology transfers, these issues include refugees, environmental protection, narcotics, and the role of the media.

It also appears that, in the short term at least, the most effective measures will be those that offer immediate practical benefits—for example, the establishment of a Joint Development Zone with Indonesia in the area of the Timor Sea where Australian and Indonesian maritime boundary claims overlap, and the Cambodian peace initiative—rather than proposals for structural arrangements such as the Conference on Security and Cooperation in Asia (Ball 1991; Hill 1991a; *The Australian Financial Review* 29 April 1991). To the extent that initiatives of the latter type challenge the role of, and the balance between, different nations in Southeast Asia, they could well be counterproductive.

The third, and in many respects the most critical question for Australia will be the future role of the United States in the Asia-Pacific region. Apart from the practical benefits that the alliance has provided to Australia's own defense capabilities, the ANZUS connection has, in the past, significantly enhanced Australia's regional standing both as a technologically advanced nation and as a conduit for U.S. involvement in a nonaligned region. The United States' own strategic interests in the region have also given confidence that, should a substantial military threat arise, assistance would be forthcoming.

Concerned about the possible impact on regional stability of a significant drawdown of U.S. forces in the western Asia-Pacific, Australia's initial reaction has been to encourage a continued U.S. military presence through the offer of training facilities to replace those no longer available in the Philippines. These include use of the high technology air weapons range being developed at Delamere in the Northern Territory, and the underwater exercise range for submarines off the coast of Western Australia. The longer term outlook is, however, considerably more complex.

The changing U.S. posture may affect Australia's interests in several ways. The debate on burdensharing with Japan and on the future role of the Japanese Self Defense Force in regional security may well have an impact on the solidarity and military capabilities of Southeast Asian nations, as well as on Japan's more immediate neighbors. To the extent that the United States finds alternatives for its bases in the Philippines and develops stronger bilateral links with regional countries, Australia's own capability margins and its value to the United States as its key strategic ally in the region may be reduced. There is also the possibility that if the United States is not sensitive to maintaining strategic consensus within ASEAN, as well as across the Asia-Pacific more generally, selective engagement of individual countries may provoke tensions of policy and status, contrary to Australia's own objective of regional strategic cohesion. The initial negative reaction of Singapore's neighbors to the announcement of its offer to provide the United States with alternatives to the facilities in the Philippines well illustrated these sensitivities (*The Age* 17 September 1991; *The Canberra Times* 23 August 1991).

In the past, the United States has not had an unblemished record in consulting with Australia on key security initiatives that impact upon it. Current developments suggest, however, that the clear distinction in purpose and commitment that existed between the ANZUS defense cooperation and U.S. relationships with other regional nations may not be sustained in the future. Australia will continue to receive significant direct benefits for its own defense, although the relative value of these may diminish. It may also draw some comfort from closer direct ties between some of its neighbors and the United States. At the same time, Australia's capacity to influence regional developments may well be further circumscribed by differing U.S. perspectives, and it may be far more difficult to develop a combined regional voice to put forward views either to the United States or other external powers. There is a danger that, without careful management, Australian and

U.S. activities in relation to regional security may become competitive rather than complementary despite the common interests that they share in promoting stability and cohesion.

Fourth, a rather different dilemma for Australia has emerged in the South Pacific. These issues are discussed in more detail in Chapter 4, but several points are appropriate here. The focus of Australian security assistance to Papua New Guinea (PNG) and the other island nations has been primarily to support national development and enhance the islands' capacity to manage external challenges to their sovereignty and interests. Though the threat from Soviet fishing activity has now abated, Australia is devoting substantial effort to maritime surveillance and patrol programs to protect the islands' Exclusive Economic Zones (Alves 1990). Involvement in internal security tasks, which would potentially make Australia's strategic links and access vulnerable to domestic political change, have been avoided as far as possible.

Internal unrest in the South Pacific in recent years has introduced a less comfortable agenda. Situations in which Australia may be asked, or consider it necessary, to become involved militarily have become far more likely. The island nations' expectations of Australian support in any security crisis and, simultaneously, their fear of possible Australian intervention, suggest that both action and inaction would court condemnation. Australia, for its part, is well aware of the importance of internal security to national development and regional stability. It would also be concerned to protect Australia's own direct interests, especially the safety of Australian nationals, their property, and commercial ventures. There remain, however, significant political and economic limits to Australia's capacity to underwrite overall development strategies in the South Pacific (Woodman and Horner 1991: 60-61, 98-108).

The foreign minister has made it clear that military intervention would occur only in unusual and extreme circumstances (Evans 1989: 21-22). Even then, it would not generally be practical for Australia to assume responsibility for maintaining key aspects of law and order for more than a brief period. The experience with Australian helicopters loaned to the PNG Defense Force during the Bougainville crisis (armed and used in combat by the PNG forces despite an explicit condition that they should not be used for this purpose) graphically shows how even indirect support can impact upon both domestic and regional opinion (Fry 1991b: 24-25). Only a rigorous tackling of the root causes of instability will help alleviate the situation, but that itself points, in particular, to tied economic aid and joint projects which the island nations have frequently rejected as a threat to their political independence. While defense cooperation may help to tackle the symptoms of the present problem, it does not address the fundamental causes of instability.

Finally, there continues to be some potential for Australia's close association with the United States to cut across its regional credentials. As the recent congressional report "Problems in Paradise" points out, U.S. disregard for the concerns of the South Pacific — including tuna fishing rights and the refusal to become a party to the South Pacific Nuclear Free Zone treaty—has jeopardized the goodwill generated in the Second World War (U.S. Congress 1990). While Australia has attempted to balance the competing viewpoints, the clash of views at the 1990 meeting of the South Pacific Forum states over the disposal of chemical weapons on Johnston Atoll—in which Australia supported the U.S. position that there was no danger to the regional environment despite island concerns—demonstrated how Australia's credibility and championing of regional causes can be thrown into question.

A fifth issue is the need for Australia to reassess its security relationship with New Zealand. New Zealand's refusal in 1984 to allow nuclear-armed or powered warships to visit its ports shattered the long-held assumption of an identical strategic outlook within the framework of the Western alliance. Despite Australia's rejection of New Zealand's position, it has continued at some cost to maintain bilateral defense ties with both the United States and New Zealand. More recent strategic changes have shown both the value of a joint Australian–New Zealand response to South Pacific developments and New Zealand's increasing inability to meet its security obligations independently (Jennings 1988). During the Gulf War, New Zealand supported Australian deployments through the use of its Skyhawks for air defense training and the provision of underway replenishment (New Zealand Defence Force 1991). This reinforced the potential for its capabilities to contribute to Australia's own defense effort as the costs of maintaining independent national capabilities continue to rise (Ray 1991b: 3).

In consequence, several proposals have been put forward in both countries, including by government ministers, for greater complementarity between the two forces. These range from more combined operations, training, and procurement through the sharing of capabilities to partial or full integration (*The Canberra Times* 2, 9 August 1991; *The West Australian* 9 August 1991). Differences in size, the potential impact on independent national decision-making, and the need to define both joint and separate security interests suggest that fundamental changes will not come quickly. On the other hand, practical benefits such as joint procurement (as in the project to build a common class of "ANZAC" frigates) and combined operations and contingency planning are likely. These might reduce costs and, if carefully managed, increase effectiveness of both national defense and regional security operations.

The U.S. decision in September 1991 to remove all tactical nuclear weapons from its warships, effectively ending the "neither confirm nor deny" policy, may have opened the way for an eventual resumption by New Zealand of a more active role in the Western alliance and wider international security activities (*The Australian* 30 September 1991, 2 October 1991). The changing nature of U.S. policy and force deployments suggests, however, that the primary relevance of revived trilateral ANZUS links would be in the context of the South Pacific and the direct security concerns of Australia and New Zealand. The potentially greater size and sustainability of combined Australia-

New Zealand operations may also create additional options for both countries to contribute to regional security and UN peacekeeping tasks. Much will depend on the range and level of capabilities New Zealand is prepared to maintain on its own behalf.

Finally, apart from these specific challenges, there are the implications of the changing strategic environment for Australia's overall defense planning. Not only is pressure for a "peace dividend" likely to rule out any significant increases in defense funding in the short term, but pursuit of the new regional security agenda will have to compete for resources with existing defense priorities. Defense planning has already recognized the possibility of ADF deployments to the South Pacific as an element in capability definition (*Force Structure Review* 1991: 28). However, the more immediate demand is likely to come from increased training and operational costs to support new regional initiatives and the collection of intelligence on developments in the Asia-Pacific region.

The impact of these new tasks will be more pronounced because of the difficulties of achieving the comprehensive capability acquisition program set out in the 1987 White Paper. Funds have fallen well short of the desired level; the ADF's personnel and operating budgets have already been squeezed significantly; Defence Minister Robert Ray indicated in 1991 that any additional resources or savings would be allocated to the major capital equipment program (*Force Structure Review* 1991: 41). Yet to meet its new regional agenda, the government needs to fund — at a minimum — increased exercises with the region, combined surveillance and patrol operations such as those in the Timor Sea Joint Development Zone, and the peacekeeping commitment to Cambodia.

The new emphasis on current tasks may also have implications for the readiness of particular force elements and, indeed, the priority with which they are expanded or equipped. Specialist capabilities such as engineers and communicators, for example, will be important to many regional security tasks and United Nations commitments. The readiness and sustainability of those forces, however, currently falls outside the push to acquire major combat systems for possible future contingencies (Australian Senate 1991: 121–25). Some of those combat support roles are being transferred to the civil sector, potentially further limiting the flexibility of the ADF for current tasks (*The Defence Force and the Community* 1991).

THE WAY AHEAD

Australia's defense and regional security policies have thus reached an important crossroads. On the one hand, over the last two decades they have developed a comprehensive approach that tackles both the question of possible future hostilities and a constructive commitment to maintaining a favorable strategic environment. Those policies have much greater sensitivity and sophistication than in the era of forward defense. They also have a considerable advantage in that the emphasis on self-reliance and "no threat" planning concepts insulates them against the need for frequent revision in response to strategic change. The regional security policies are at an early stage, however, as is Australia's concept of security as being broader than just defense linkages.

Those strengths largely explain the confidence of Australia's security planners in their current defense and security policies. The critical issue for the future is that those same policies are underpinned by several long-held strategic verities that the changing Asia-Pacific security environment is beginning to throw into question. The existence of a Western military umbrella in Southeast Asia is problematic, despite U.S. assurances to the contrary. Australia's role as the southern anchor of the Western alliance in the Asia-Pacific region appears to be becoming less important. Its capacity to maintain a technological edge in key combat areas can no longer be taken for granted.

Furthermore, the military role on which Australia has based its security influence in the region appears unlikely to sustain Australia's relevance to regional security in the longer term. The clear distinction that Australia has traditionally drawn between the U.S. alliance with its global interests and the more specific regional security agenda has weakened, as has Australia's capacity to balance those two different aspects of the strategic equation in the southern Asia-Pacific region to its own advantage. That has implications for both the relative value of the U.S. "underwriting" of Australia's self-reliant defense policy and potentially the relationship between Australia and the region.

Despite these uncertainties, the strategic changes currently taking place do not make Australia more vulnerable to the threat of military attack. But they do suggest that the direction and extent of change will be difficult to predict beyond the short term, that knowledge and understanding of developments will be critical to determining meaningful security policy options in the future, and that Australia may have to make some increasingly difficult choices. In particular, the balances are already beginning to change:

- Between the defense of Australia and regional security tasks;
- Between regional security commitments and broader U.S.–Western alliance interests;
- Between self-reliance and a range of options for more collective security relationships, including with New Zealand, some form of Southeast Asian collective security organization and even an enhanced United Nations peacekeeping role.

The difficulty for Australia is that it is not clear to what extent, or within which time frames, it may have to make such choices. Australia will certainly be reluctant to abandon key aspects of its comprehensive security policies without clear justification. However, the changing strategic environment suggests it may not always be possible to have such certainty before a decision needs to be made to embrace a revised security agenda. The need for flexibility in planning and capabilities contrasts starkly with the increasing constraints on defense resources. Much will depend on how effectively Australia can impress its concerns upon the United States in the transitional phase. The United States has displayed only a limited capacity to accommodate Australia's security and security-related interests in the past. Unless that situation changes, the shift away from the traditional ANZUS framework as the foundation of Australia's and Western security interests in the southern Asia-Pacific region may well be accelerated.

2

New Zealand's Regional Security Policies

STEVE HOADLEY

• New Zealand is probably the world's most secure country. Its distance from chronic trouble spots, its protective ocean moats, and its unprovocative international posture make the avoidance of power struggles and armed conflict possible to a degree few other countries could contemplate. Nonalignment has been a viable option for New Zealand through much of its history. However, that option has never been exercised. On the contrary, engagement with powerful friends, first Britain and later the United States and Australia, bolstered by collective defense alliances, traditionally have been the principal instruments of New Zealand's security policy.

The question now arises whether the end of the Cold War, progress in arms control in Europe, and public and political party pacifism at home have converged to nudge New Zealand into a new, more distant orbit relative to traditional partners. Other questions follow. Has Labour led New Zealand substantially and irrevocably away from its long-standing relationships with the United States, Australia, Great Britain, and other members of the Western security community? Has security policy sunk to the bottom of the foreign policy agenda? Did the Labour government after 1984 enact a new security paradigm and if so, is the National government from 1990 accepting it or reverting to the traditional one?

To answer these questions, in this chapter we first review New Zealand's traditional security outlook to provide a baseline against which to measure recent changes. We then analyze the Labour government's nonnuclear policies since 1984 and that government's regional security assessment presented in the 1987 defense review and statements by the prime minister and minister of foreign affairs, and assess the consequences of those policies, particularly for relations with the United States and Australia within the ANZUS context. Public opinion as sampled in 1986 is examined with regard to salient security issues. Finally, we examine the security outlook of the National Party as expressed in its 1990 electoral manifestos, and the National government's subsequent policy statements and 1991 defense review, to identify the significant elements of continuity and difference between these and the policies of the Labour government.

TRADITIONAL REGIONAL SECURITY OUTLOOK

The smallest of the empire's dominions was perhaps the most assertive (Gordon 1960). New Zealand governments of the late nineteenth century demanded from Great Britain, and got, mini-colonies of their own in the South Pacific, pledges by the Royal Navy to protect them from putative threats by France, Germany, Russia, and the United States, considerable weaponry (mostly second-hand), and logistic and training support. New Zealand's support of various proposals for a council of the British Dominions in the early twentieth century reflected not submission to the empire, but rather enthusiasm for membership in a powerful forum where New Zealand's small voice could be heard, in which its minuscule power could be amplified. Imperial defense was the favored security concept through which New Zealand, with a modest military contribution, hoped to gain not only protection by a great power but also maximum political influence among world players.

The advent of the first Labour government in 1935 brought a new element to New Zealand's outlook: universal collective security (Bennett 1988; McIntyre 1985). Labour, idealist and internationalist in ideology, seized on the League of Nations as a forum where small states, in concert with large states to which they were equal under the League's Covenant, could curb aggressors. Labour's delegate publicly condemned and requested League sanctions against Mussolini's Italy, Franco's Spain, Hitler's Germany, and Tojo's Japan for their militarist actions at a time when Britain and France were making accommodations and the United States was not a member of the League and was restrained by the Neutrality Acts. Labour Party leaders steadfastly supported the League (and subsequently the United Nations) as necessary instruments for world peace even as they directed their criticism at the lack of political will displayed by leading members. Because New Zealand differed sharply with Great Britain over the failure to act against Mussolini's attack on Abyssinia in 1936, and at the Pacific Defense Conference in Wellington in 1939 questioned Britain's assurances that the Royal Navy could shield New Zealand from Japan, it is possible to date—from this period—an independent New Zealand security policy, in conception if not in substance.

The inaction of the League of Nations, Japan's buildup in the Pacific, and Britain's admission in 1940 that it could not guarantee protection of the dominions led the New Zealand government to look increasingly to the United States as a security partner. It established an embassy in Washington (its first mission overseas besides London and Sydney) and began negotiations that led to New Zealand becoming a rear base and supplying construction corps and pilots in support of United States South Pacific forces. New Zealand, not facing an imminent threat from Japan, and judging that victory in Europe was the key to global security, decided to keep its ground troops in the European theater to support Great Britain while Australia, facing Japanese bombs on Darwin, Japanese submarines off Sydney, and Japanese troops in New Guinea, brought its troops back to the South Pacific theater. This illustrated New Zealand's tendency, as a small country, to rely on global cooperative solutions in contrast to Australia's inclination, borne of its greater capacity, to pursuing more independent policies, although the contrast was one of emphasis rather than of substance.

The turning of the tide of the Second World War focused New Zealand leaders' minds on long-term security planning. In 1944 the tenets of security policy rested on a combination of faith in universal collective security to be exercised by the nascent United Nations, and on regional self-reliance in close association with Australia expressed in the Australian–New Zealand Agreement (called the Canberra Pact in New Zealand, the ANZAC Pact in Australia). The Canberra Pact provided that "within a framework of a general system of world security, a regional zone of defence comprising the South West and South Pacific areas shall be established and that this zone should be based on Australia and New Zealand" (Kay 1972: 142). The two governments agreed to engage in joint defense consultation, planning and exercising, interchange of staff officers, exchange of intelligence, and cooperation in logistics, objectives that were largely achieved. They also undertook the task of looking after the welfare of South Pacific Island peoples and called for a conference of other colonial powers in the region, including the United States, Britain, and France, to coordinate their efforts. This conference evolved in 1947 into the South Pacific Commission that remains a principal regional institution to this day. In the spirit of the Canberra Pact, New Zealand has developed a web of relationships with the independent South Pacific states that includes military surveillance and small-scale assistance as well as aid, trade access, and diplomacy (South Pacific Policy Review Group 1990; Hoadley 1989). These relationships were extended also to Southeast Asia from the 1950s.

By no means was this regional assertion a retreat to isolationism once the war was won, for Australia's and New Zealand's prosperity depended on distant markets and New Zealand leaders were conscious of the lengthening ranges of the instruments of war and the importance of deterrence by collective readiness. The attorney general in the Labour government expressed this eloquently to the Paris Peace Conference in 1946 when he said:

Peace, like war, is indivisible. An act of aggression is but the stone cast into the world's waters causing the ripples which touch with fatal impact the shores of every country of the world. We in New Zealand know that remoteness provided no safeguard, and that failure to resist aggression would mean the loss of the liberties and principles of justice upon which we had built our way of life. (Ministry of Foreign Affairs 1972: 109; this and following quotations are slightly abridged)

The leader of the National Party as prime minister echoed this conception four years later as he reviewed his government's commitment of New Zealand forces under United Nations command to defend South Korea from the North Korean onslaught:

There is no country which lives in greater security than we do today. But we are living in a fool's paradise if we think that the ocean is our security. We must take notice of those who are nearest to the danger, those countries which are better informed than we are. Our security is our ability to defend ourselves, along with like-minded people like those in the United States and the United Kingdom. We must help to build up the resources of the United Nations so that it will be able to enforce its decisions. (Ministry of Foreign Affairs 1972: 240)

Faith in the United Nations waned as the Cold War deepened and the Security Council was emasculated by the veto in the late 1940s. Partial success in halting North Korean aggression aside, the United Nations seemed incapable of addressing to New Zealand's satisfaction the threats of Communist armies in East Europe and China and Communist guerrillas in Southeast Asia, or the potential threat of a rearmed Japan. New Zealand fell back on the concept of regional collective defense as provided for in Article 52 of the United Nations Charter. In 1949 the New Zealand government endorsed the North Atlantic Treaty (Ministry of Foreign Affairs 1972: 195). In 1951 New Zealand entered into the ANZUS Treaty (Kay 1985). In 1954 New Zealand joined the Southeast Asia Collective Defense Treaty and helped to set up the Southeast Asia Treaty Organization (Pearson 1989). These have been the major expressions of New Zealand's collective defense strategy. But they were set firmly in a context of the ideal of global collective security in as much as each treaty committed itself to the principles of the Charter of the United Nations and all were seen as components of a greater whole. New Zealand's representative at the signing of the ANZUS treaty said:

By creating an area of stability in the Pacific this treaty may be expected to reduce world tension and thus prove a reinforcement of, and a contribution to, the general system of international security which is today being erected and make it possible for its parties to play their part elsewhere. The problem that the free world is facing today is a global problem. It is merely the manifestations of that problem which may appear to be local. (Kay 1972: 254)

This suggests that New Zealand's internationalism transcended even the vital relationship with the United States, a transcendence that was to manifest itself prominently again in 1984.

A corollary conception that emerged in the 1950s, linked both to the indivisibility of security globally and the need for practical regional collective defense institutions, was forward defense. In 1955, New Zealand redeployed forces from the Middle East to Malaya under the auspices of the Commonwealth Strategic Reserve, where, in close association with Australian and British units, they saw combat against communist guerrillas during the Malayan Emergency and against Indonesian paramilitary elements during Indonesia's Confrontation campaign against Malaysia (Mullins 1972). When Britain withdrew its forces from Southeast Asia in 1971, New Zealand, with Australia and Great Britain, entered into the Five Power Defence Arrangements with Singapore and Malaysia, and stationed an infantry battalion in Singapore (Kennaway 1972: 52–61). Cooperation with the United States in Asia was less intimate in the 1950s but picked up in the 1960s as a consequence of New Zealand's decision to send an artillery unit to Vietnam and to reequip its air force with American-built aircraft (Glover 1986; Hoadley 1988a). ANZUS exercises, personnel exchanges, intelligence pooling, and logistics arrangements grew and deepened from this period.

Regarding Southeast Asia, as with Korea and NATO Europe, the predominant notion was that New Zealand's first line of defense lay abroad, that it was better to establish a collective deterrent position or, if necessary, fight in Asia rather than closer to home. This was a modern echo of the earlier notion that New Zealand was indefensible in the South Pacific unless Britain survived in the Atlantic.

In the 1950s, two other facets of New Zealand's security conception emerged: nuclear deterrence, and its obverse side, nuclear disarmament. The linkage between the facets was made explicit as early as 1955 by New Zealand Representative to the United Nations Frank Corner (later to become secretary of external affairs) when he addressed the First Committee of the General Assembly. He observed that "nuclear weapons alone make it possible for the West to stand on a basis of equality with the Soviet Union" (Ministry of Foreign Affairs 1972: 414). But he went on to point out that nuclear superiority was a meaningless concept and that nuclear war would destroy human civilization. He strongly advocated negotiations leading to progressive, mutual, and verifiable reductions of nuclear arms in the context of a comprehensive scheme of disarmament. Prime Minister Sydney Holland in a May 1957 broadcast asserted that New Zealand must support British nuclear tests at Christmas Island so as to assure Western security. "The free world is in great danger if it does not possess the means of deterring nuclear attack," he stressed. He went on to say, "Consistent with the defence of the free world, . . . we are ready to support and to work for the complete banning of nuclear tests when other nations do the same, conditional on an adequate system of international inspection" (Ministry of Foreign Affairs 1972: 468–69).

Holland's eventual successor, Keith Holyoake, when deputy prime minister in September 1957 enunciated New Zealand's first nuclear-free policy, which is cited by the National Party today to prove that the Labour Party does not have a monopoly on nuclear virtue: "New Zealand's own defence planning did not contemplate the acquisition of nuclear weapons nor would she become a storage base for them under her other defence arrangements" (Clements 1988: 41). This policy of exclusion of nuclear weapons from New Zealand soil has never been questioned since; controversy has centered instead on the entry into New Zealand waters and ports of nuclear-powered and nuclear-armed vessels.

In summary form, New Zealand's traditional security outlook has been characterized by the following fundamental concepts. The third (1972–75) and fourth (1984–90) Labour governments modified the emphasis or priority of some of them, but the bulk of them remain valid under the National government elected in 1990.

- New Zealand's security was indivisible from global security.
- Universal collective security was the preferable means of achieving global security and thus New Zealand security.
- Even though great power rivalry and the Security Council veto rendered collective security unattainable, New Zealand would continue to back the UN, particularly by contributing to its peacekeeping and disarmament activities.
- New Zealand should accept nuclear deterrence of Soviet and Chinese aggression as an element of free-world defense but at the same time work for comprehensive, mutual, verifiable disarmament.
- New Zealand would not acquire or store nuclear weapons but the potentially nuclear-armed warships of allies would be allowed to call at New Zealand ports.
- Regional collective defense treaties such as NATO, ANZUS, and SEATO, to contain Communist expansion, were vital contributions to global stability as well as to regional security and New Zealand should support them politically and configure its defense establishment so as to be able to participate in them effectively.
- Particular security arrangements such as the FPDA and forward defense to bolster specific partners such as Malaysia, Singapore, and South Vietnam (until 1972), and low level military mutual assistance programs with friendly Southeast Asian states, were to be maintained.
- New Zealand should participate in special security relationships with Australia, the United States, and Great Britain as enshrined in security treaties and other arrangements but these should not infringe New Zealand's sovereignty or compromise her special interests in the South Pacific.

- New Zealand had a special responsibility, which included providing military training, assistance, and surveillance (in coordination with Australia), to look after the South Pacific Island states and to maintain their Western orientations in the face of Soviet initiatives.
- Security had an economic as well as a military dimension, expressed as aid to underdeveloped countries in New Zealand's region of concern, mainly the South Pacific and Southeast Asia.

A final conception was less explicit but nevertheless dominant then as now: that New Zealand should maintain independent armed forces but at the lowest possible level consistent with a credible commitment to the above security policies. Implicit was the belief that the threat was distant, the allies able to cope; that New Zealand's military contribution would never be of more than symbolic value. New Zealand's real roles were to maintain the potential to provide food and an expansion base in the event of major conflict, stabilize its island dependencies and the South Pacific region generally (with Australia) to relieve the United States of the burden of "strategic denial" of hostile outsiders, and to provide moral, political, and token military and economic support to Western alliances and other security arrangements. Accordingly, New Zealand's expenditure on defense, less than 2 percent of GNP, has been among the lowest in the world and the lowest among its allies and security partners. Unlike Japan, it does not compensate by giving large amounts of aid.

LABOUR'S NONNUCLEAR POLICIES

The third Labour government (1972–75) augmented National's nonnuclear policy by sending a navy frigate to Moruroa Atoll to protest French nuclear testing; seeking an International Court of Justice injunction against French nuclear testing; introducing a comprehensive test-ban resolution into the UN General Assembly; and taking the initiative in drafting a nuclear-free-zone treaty for the South Pacific, all in collaboration with Australia. Labour also declined to accept nuclear-powered warship visits, not on the grounds of their potential nuclear arms but rather because of doubts about environmental safety and ambiguities about legal liability in the event of a nuclear accident. These doubts and ambiguities were resolved in 1974, and by 1975 it appeared that Prime Minister Bill Rowling was, at the urging of his military advisers, considering allowing an American nuclear-powered warship to visit (Clements 1988: 84–85). During this period New Zealand participated in ANZUS in other respects as usual.

The National Party won the 1975 election and shelved the South Pacific nuclear-free-zone initiative and invited American nuclear-powered warships to visit. In 1976 a sharp exchange between Prime Minister Robert Muldoon and Leader of the Opposition Rowling polarized the parties' ship-visit policies and from that time Labour pledged to ban nuclear-armed and nuclear-powered vessels. Labour's 1984 electoral victory gave authority to its policy but also evoked warnings from the United States that a strict ship-visit policy would be incompatible with ANZUS obligations. Prime Minister David Lange's attempts to devise a compromise failed in February 1985 when committed Labour backbenchers persuaded the government's cabinet that in the absence of an assurance to the contrary, nuclear weapons-capable ships should be regarded as nuclear-armed ships, and that the *USS Buchanan* therefore should not be allowed to make a proposed visit (Clements 1988: 129–37; Hoadley 1986: 4–8). The United States responded to this refusal by suspending operational military cooperation with New Zealand.

The Labour government then enunciated a nonnuclear security policy by declaring that New Zealand did not wish to be defended by nuclear weapons either directly or indirectly. As David Lange put it on 5 March 1985, "We do not ask to be defended by the nuclear weapons we exclude and we do not ask any nuclear power to deter any enemy of New Zealand by the threatened use of nuclear weapons" (Graham 1989: 45). The government pressed its antinuclear ideals to their logical conclusions by backing the revival of the South Pacific Nuclear Free Zone Treaty (Treaty of Rarotonga) and signing it in 1986. Also in 1986 the government drafted and introduced in Parliament the New Zealand Nuclear Free Zone, Disarmament, and Arms Control Act which contained clauses banning not only nuclear weapons but also nuclear propelled ships. (The act was passed in June 1987.) These initiatives led U.S. Secretary of State George Shultz, in August 1986, to announce the United States' withdrawal of security guarantees from New Zealand and to declare the U.S.–New Zealand leg of the ANZUS alliance inoperative (McMillan 1987: 155).

However opposed Labour government leaders were to allowing nuclear weapons into their own country, they appeared to be ambivalent about the deployment of nuclear weapons in other parts of the world to deter Communist aggression. With reference to the global nuclear deterrent posture of the Western powers, Prime Minister Lange in 1985 called nuclear weapons "a necessary evil, an abhorrent means," but then added, "to a desirable end" (Graham 1989: 56). This seemed to suggest that at a distance such weapons might have utility. His minister of foreign affairs, Russell Marshall, acknowledged further that "nuclear deterrence has played, and continues to play, an important role in those [European collective] security arrangements and the maintenance of peace at the global level" (Graham 1989: 59). But in the later 1980s the dangers of proliferation, accident, and escalation outweighed the alleged benefits in government leaders' minds. By March 1988 David Lange's position had shifted, and he declared, "We do not subscribe to the validity of the nuclear deterrence theory and we do not support it" (Graham 1989: 59). By contrast, his Australian counterpart Bob Hawke, as recently as September 1987, had expressed his view that:

A stable relationship between the United States and the Soviet Union
is the best means currently available of avoiding nuclear war and of
providing the necessary confidence to engage in negotiations to reduce,
and eventually eliminate, the nuclear arsenals. (Graham 1989: 48)

Thus the trans-Tasman allies adopted opposite approaches to the shared
goals of elimination of nuclear weapons, with Australia tending to the United
States view, albeit with reservations, and New Zealand becoming the deviant
member of the ANZUS trio.

Further, Labour's antinuclear scrupulousness and the extravagant rhetoric
of David Lange led many outsiders to wonder if New Zealand was not only
turning away from United States nuclear weapons and deterrence strategy
but also preparing to propagate to other members of the Western security
community its peculiar conception of security through piecemeal avoidance,
thus fracturing the postwar strategic consensus that had been so painfully
crafted (Jamieson 1990). New Zealand officials hastened to assure allies and
partners that New Zealand's nonnuclear policies were particular to New
Zealand's regional and domestic political circumstances. Yet David Lange's
expressions were ambiguous as late as June 1987:

I've always said that the solution of New Zealand is not for export.
You cannot simply export a model based on our particular security
situation. But the analysis of one's security is, I think, transportable
[for example, in] steps people can take by way of a limited measure of
arms control to enhance their own security. (Graham 1989: 107)

The rhetoric cooled substantially after David Lange stepped down and
was succeeded by Geoffrey Palmer in 1989. But the deep aversion to nuclear
weapons, and the feeling that New Zealand has something new to teach the
world that is more important than old alliance obligations, persisted in public
opinion and the convictions of numerous interest group and political party
activists. And abroad the suspicion remained that New Zealand by its example
of nuclear purism and its precedent of weakening a venerable alliance has
let down its allies and friends.

PUBLIC OPINION ON SECURITY ISSUES

The prime minister's Defence Committee of Enquiry supervised a public
opinion poll in 1986 that remains the most comprehensive of its kind done
in this country. Its broad findings were: strong opposition to nuclear weapons
and testing, absence of a sense of conventional military threat, support for
alliances, particularly with Australia, and strong approval of nonmilitary
and peacekeeping roles for the New Zealand armed forces. The poll found
over 90 percent of New Zealanders opposed to the stationing of nuclear

weapons in their country and 66 percent opposed to visits by nuclear-armed ships (*Defence and Security: What New Zealanders Want* 1986).

Only 18 percent of the poll's respondents believed there was a threat of armed invasion of New Zealand and a plurality of 32 percent said no country was a military threat. The Soviet Union was the country thought to pose the greatest military threat in the opinion of 31 percent, but 14 percent thought the United States a threat, and 13 percent feared France; 5 percent expressed a more general fear of the communist bloc.

Nevertheless, New Zealanders wanted alliances by an overwhelming majority, with 82 percent in favor and only 14 percent opposed. Australia was the preferred ally among 68 percent, the United States among 52 percent, Great Britain among 35 percent, and a South Pacific country among 14 percent (respondents could name more than one country). Fully 71 percent supported the ANZUS alliance and only 10 percent opposed it (support by National Party adherents was higher, at 92 percent, than among Labour Party adherents, 58 percent).

The use of the New Zealand armed forces in combat to support Australia if it were attacked was supported by 80 percent of respondents. But hypothetical attacks on nearby South Pacific countries or Southeast Asian allies attracted much less support (54 percent and 46 percent respectively) for an armed response. Far more popular were nonmilitary uses of the armed forces such as international peacekeeping, training of friendly forces, ocean surveillance, search-and-rescue, and disaster relief, attracting from 80 to 99 percent approval.

The key questions pitted New Zealand's nonnuclear policy against ANZUS. The option of membership in ANZUS and admitting nuclear ship visits was chosen by 37 percent. The option of leaving ANZUS and banning nuclear ship visits was chosen by 16 percent. The option of staying in ANZUS but banning nuclear ship visits was the most popular, chosen by 44 percent. However, because that option had been foreclosed by the United States, the latter group were asked to choose between the former two options and their answers redistributed. Combined totals showed that 52 percent wanted New Zealand in ANZUS even if nuclear ship visits were required, whereas 44 percent wanted no nuclear ship visits even if it took New Zealand out of ANZUS. As before, National Party adherents opted more strongly for ANZUS, Labour Party adherents for the ban on nuclear ship visits.

Subsequently, opinion shifted more strongly against nuclear ship visits and, by implication, against ANZUS. In a poll by the Heylen organization in 1985, when asked to choose between breaking defense ties with the United States or allowing nuclear-armed ships to visit, New Zealanders opted to accept nuclear ships by 47 percent to 44 percent, consistent with the Defence Committee of Enquiry's 1986 poll. But by 1989 the same question evoked support for continuing defense ties by only 40 percent, and by 1991, only 39 percent, while opposition to nuclear-armed ships climbed to 52 percent in 1989 and 54 percent in 1991 (Heylen Research Centre 1991). The antinuclear

policy began to look like a permanent feature of public opinion, at the expense
of traditional pro-ANZUS opinion.

THE 1987 DEFENSE REVIEW: CHANGE AND CONTINUITY

The nuclear question aside, to what extent did the fourth Labour government alter the fundamentals of New Zealand's security outlook and policies?
The most authoritative published guide was the government's White Paper
entitled *Defence of New Zealand: Review of Defence Policy 1987,* generally
referred to as the *1987 Defence Review.* The heart of the review was the
"Defence Objectives" section which crystallized the sections on general outlook, threat assessment, special relationships, and defense organization and
hardware. A point-by-point comparison of the defense objectives sections
of the 1987 review with that of the 1983 review shows astonishing continuity,
even verbatim repetition of whole passages, from 1983 to 1987. Even though
references to deterrence and to ANZUS exercises "alongside allied units"
were deleted in 1987 and stronger emphasis given to passages on cooperation with Australia and United Nations peacekeeping, the commitment to
ANZUS and to cooperation with allies and friends remained. Thus, one
may conclude that New Zealand's essential defense objectives remained
remarkably stable in the transition from National to Labour governments in
spite of the upheavals supposedly occasioned by Labour's strict nonnuclear
policy and defection from ANZUS.

Nevertheless, there were some changes of nuance and emphasis between
the two reviews that deserve attention in order to assess trends of regional
security policy. Forward deployment in Southeast Asia was terminated in
favor of concentration on the area of direct strategic concern, the South
Pacific. But cooperation under the Five Power Defence Arrangements and
the Defense Mutual Assistance Program was to continue. In the South Pacific
New Zealand undertook initiatives in setting up the South Pacific nuclear
free zone. But this did not herald any change in New Zealand's traditional
activities or impose any constraints on United States military movements
and visits in the region. New Zealand's traditional idealism was expressed in
vocal opposition to French nuclear testing at Moruroa, sponsorship of New
Caledonian decolonization, and mediation of the conflict between the Papua
New Guinea government and the Bougainville Revolutionary Army. In
1990 a major review of South Pacific policy was undertaken by the prime
minister's office to underscore the renewal of commitment to the region
(South Pacific Policy Review Group 1990).

LABOUR AND THE UNITED STATES

In 1985, the Labour cabinet seems genuinely to have believed New Zealand could institute its strict nonnuclear ship visit policy and still remain a
partner in ANZUS (Clements 1988: 129). The break with the United States

was a shock but the government remained unrepentant. The 1987 defense review stated, "New Zealand continues to adhere to the ANZUS Treaty . . . and will continue to meet Treaty obligations through nonnuclear conventional means." It continued

> Given our limited resources, we can best meet our ANZUS obligations, and make a constructive contribution to Western security, by playing a constructive role in maintaining the peace and promoting the collective security of our own part of the world. It is regrettable that United States actions have made it more difficult for us to carry out this important task. (*Defence of New Zealand* 1987: 18–19)

The remainder of the ANZUS section was devoted to difficulties caused by the drying up of U.S.-processed intelligence and the loss of exercise, training, exchange, and logistics opportunities, and to remedies being sought in intensifying relations with Australia, Britain, and Canada.

Secretary of State James Baker's agreement in February 1990 to meet with Minister of Overseas Trade Mike Moore was heralded by Labour as a breakthrough validating its nonnuclear policy. However, it had the unintended (certainly by the United States) effect of precipitating the National Party's adoption of a strict nonnuclear ship visit policy on the grounds that a New Zealand government could have the policy and also enjoy high-level contacts with United States counterparts. Neither Labour nor National was right; high-level diplomatic contacts continued to be restricted and no easing of other aspects of Washington's policy of no military cooperation followed the Baker-Moore meeting. Secretary Baker's reaction to National Party leader Jim Bolger's suggestion that a National government would reopen a dialogue with the United States to establish a mutually acceptable defense relationship was to reiterate the American policy to "neither confirm nor deny" the presence of nuclear weapons on U.S. Navy ships. He concluded, "Until there can be an understanding on that on the part of New Zealand, there will not be any opportunity to advance the defense and security aspects of our relationship and, indeed, no opportunity for there to be a dialogue" (*New Zealand Herald* 10 October 1990).

The United States did not ask New Zealand, as it did Australia, to join it in Operation Desert Shield in the Persian Gulf in August 1990, and informed the New Zealand government only an hour before Operation Desert Storm began. The National government's contribution of air force transports and army medics to the coalition forces was welcomed by the United States, but little warming of military relations, save intelligence sharing, on Gulf War topics followed.

LABOUR AND AUSTRALIA

The 1987 defense review devoted 14 paragraphs to New Zealand's relations with Australia, compared with 1 paragraph in the 1983 review. It invoked the close historical ties between the two countries in the ANZAC tradition, the Canberra Pact, and the ANZUS alliance. It noted, "the withdrawal of United States military cooperation with New Zealand has made our defence relationship with Australia more important," but cautioned "it has not substantially changed its nature" (*Defence of New Zealand* 1987: 14). The several links of joint exercises, training, exchanges, intelligence and logistics cooperation, and consultations on mutual interests such as the South Pacific were inventoried. The section concluded:

> New Zealand does not look to Australia to replace the United States — nor is it seeking, or would it accept, a dependent relationship with Australia. But New Zealand does recognize that it shares vital strategic interests in the South Pacific with Australia. (*Defence of New Zealand* 1987: 17)

References to New Zealand and Australia constituting a single strategic entity, dating from the prime ministers' meeting in 1976, were omitted in 1987 in recognition that the two countries have substantially different strategic outlooks — New Zealand toward the South Pacific, Australia toward Southeast Asia and the Indian Ocean. Nevertheless there remained substantial strategic overlap. Examples of the close and converging defense relationship included: joint purchase of Australian-made Steyr rifles and light artillery pieces; coordination of surveillance of South Pacific island states' Exclusive Economic Zones (EEZs); cooperation in the aftermath of the New Caledonia, Fiji, and Vanuatu disturbances; New Zealand's decision to participate in a joint project to build ANZAC frigates; the dispatch of the RNZN tanker *Endeavour* to support an exercise in home waters while *HMAS Success* was in the Persian Gulf; and the stationing of a *RNZAF* Skyhawk training squadron in Australia in 1991. Trans-Tasman security links have remained uniquely intimate in spite of political differences on global nuclear deterrence, regional strategic outlook, policy on nuclear ship visits, and relations with the United States.

THE DEFENSE DEBATE AND THE 1990 ELECTION

In assessing differences between the National government elected in October 1990 and its Labour predecessor, one should recall that it was a National government that began the process of formally reorienting defense policy closer to home and defining the area of direct strategic concern as the South Pacific and Australia (Hoadley 1991). This occurred in the 1978 defense review, undertaken in the wake of the collapse of the American position in Vietnam and the rise of the Soviet naval threat in the Pacific. Also, the withdrawal of New Zealand forces from Singapore was foreshadowed even then, though it fell to Labour to complete the redeployment a decade later. National's 1987 election manifesto, *Let's Get New Zealand Right,* contained numerous passages opposing nuclear weapons in New Zealand, opposing nuclear testing, supporting a Comprehensive Test Ban Treaty, and generally supporting arms control and disarmament efforts. In March 1990, National adopted a nuclear ship visit policy identical to Labour's. These observations suggested that National would not alter current policies significantly.

The National Party's 1990 election manifesto welcomed the end of the Cold War but cautioned that potential instability in the South Pacific and renewed tensions in the Middle East required "maintenance of a credible defence capacity" (Bolger and Graham 1990; Kidd 1990). National was critical of Labour for allowing defense capability to erode, but made no commitment to raise spending again, only to carry through acquisition programs already agreed to, principally the purchase of two ANZAC frigates and a logistics support ship, "within the defence vote (budget)." Deterrence, whether nuclear or conventional, was not mentioned, even though National's foreign policy and defense spokesmen Don McKinnon and Warren Cooper were on record as having no problem with the concept; this led to speculation that the National Party had come to share Labour's traditional skepticism as to the utility of deterrence in maintaining a global balance of power.

National's approach to enhancing security with limited resources is "to develop defence and security arrangements with like-minded nations" (Bolger and Graham 1990; Kidd 1990). National committed itself to military cooperation with Australia and the Five Power Defence Arrangements and "to work to establish mutually acceptable defence cooperation with the United States and the United Kingdom." Return to ANZUS, a feature of the 1987 manifesto, was not mentioned in National's 1990 manifesto. Instead, there was a recommitment to international peacekeeping. Support of collective security was implicit throughout the manifesto and explicit, although somewhat roundabout, in the acknowledgement of "the need for a collective approach to defence." Stress was also placed on avoidance of conflict by enhancing stability through cooperation, peacekeeping, and international law and through addressing global issues such as the environment. National supported economic aid but with a concentration on nearby South Pacific Islands, and overall aid spending was not expected to rise above its previous level of approximately 0.2 percent of GNP (one-tenth the level of defense spending).

Allowing for differences of emphasis and ordering, all of these echoed the preceding Labour government's policy and paralleled the Labour Party's 1990 election manifesto. Public debate on foreign policy and defense issues during the campaign was sporadic and superficial. A majority of polled New Zealanders opposed the purchase of the ANZAC frigates, but both major parties upheld the contrary policy. The breakaway New Labour Party, and the Green Party, opposed both ANZUS and the frigate project but got only 10 percent of the vote between them. Voter turn-out was low, indicating public disillusionment, but more likely based on domestic and leadership factors than on security issues. The National government's decision to send noncombatant armed forces to the Gulf was disputed by the Labour opposition, which preferred a nonmilitary contribution or at best a military unit under UN command, but the debate was brief and without significance. The strong feelings and deep divisions on security issues visible among the public, interest groups, and parties in the 1980s had faded by the October 1990 election.

NATIONAL'S REGIONAL SECURITY POLICIES

In office, National's Foreign Minister Don McKinnon publicly dismissed the Labour government's South Pacific Policy Review and focus on South Pacific security as parochial. He announced initiatives to orient New Zealand to the growing economies of East Asia and to work more closely with traditional allies to restore links to the Western security community. Nonetheless, three of McKinnon's early trips abroad were to South Pacific and Southeast Asian states, indicating that New Zealand's long-standing commitment to the security and well-being of its neighboring regions had not altered in spite of rhetoric about a focus on world markets. National leaders, aware of the drift of public opinion and strong commitments by a majority of their caucus, stated they would not sponsor amendments to the nuclear-free act or alter the nuclear-free policy. Disputes within the National Party in government turned on economic questions of mainly domestic consequence. Substantial revision of the nuclear policy and of other aspects of security policy did not appear to be on the National government's political agenda, at least not for the duration of its first term in office.

President Bush's meeting with Prime Minister Bolger in September 1991 and Bush's subsequent announcement that tactical nuclear weapons would be removed from all U.S. Navy ships seemed to clear the way for American warship visits to New Zealand, a resumption of bilateral military relations, and a patching up of ANZUS. However, the United States made it clear that its policy of neither confirming nor denying the presence of nuclear weapons aboard its ships would remain in effect and that the New Zealand Nuclear Free Zone, Disarmament, and Arms Control Act would have to be amended to allow visits by nuclear propelled ships before military relations could be restored.

The New Zealand government appointed a committee of scientists to study safety aspects of nuclear ship propulsion but, when the committee in late 1992 reported that such ships were safe, the prime minister announced that the government would not amend the antinuclear legislation or change its policy until after the general election in October 1993 (*New Zealand Herald* 18 December 1992: 1, 9). The leader of the opposition, Mike Moore, announced that if National rescinded the antinuclear legislation, Labour would reintroduce it and reimpose a ban on nuclear propelled ships; a new coalition of minor parties, the Alliance, indicated a similar intent. In the face of continued political polarization on nuclear policy, U.S. leaders were understandably cautious about reestablishing military links with New Zealand. If, as was thought likely, the Clinton administration, which took office in the United States in January 1993, adopted a similar posture, then the nuclear-military stalemate was set to persist at least until the end of 1993 or until a New Zealand government changed its policy.

THE 1991 DEFENSE REVIEW

National's policies were consolidated in *The Defence of New Zealand 1991: A Policy Paper,* announced by the prime minister in May 1991. The 1991 defense review returned to the analytical and detailed format of the 1983 review and incorporated the thrust of the National Party's 1990 election manifesto, particularly the emphasis on collective defense. It also carried forward many of the policies of Labour's 1987 review, particularly the non-nuclear policy and the acknowledgment of the impossibility of a defense relationship with the United States (although the tone is regretful rather than assertive). The review considered the strategy options of neutrality, nonalignment, home defense, defense in depth, forward defense, regional defense, and alliance defense and eliminated each in turn. It opted instead for the concept of "self-reliance in partnership," a strategy, it said, designed "to protect the sovereignty and advance the well-being of New Zealand by maintaining a level of armed forces sufficient to deal with small contingencies affecting New Zealand and its own region, and capable of contributing to collective efforts where our wider interests are involved" (*The Defence of New Zealand* 1991: 54).

The review also enunciated the objective of "a minimum credible defence force." This was presented as a means to rationalize the tension between wide interests and limited resources. The phrase may be seen, at best, as a restatement of a dilemma endemic to New Zealand for over a century, at worst as an excuse for the reductions suffered by the defense forces in the 1991–92 budget.

The review's summary of defense policy goals is extracted in the appendix to this chapter. The similarity of the concepts, and of their ordering and phrasing, to the 1987 defense review is evident. The origin of many of the entries may be traced back to the 1983 and 1978 reviews and to earlier policy statements. This is particularly true of the reiteration of security cooperation with the United States (although ANZUS is no longer mentioned), Australia, ASEAN, the United Kingdom, the United Nations, and other collective endeavors, recalling the notion of the indivisibility of security broached first in the 1930s and again in the postwar period as sketched above. The 1991 review leaves the reader with an impression of continuity, of incremental adaptation, rather than of innovation or departure. Those familiar with New Zealand's history will recognize it as an official expression of a deep and long-term New Zealand security outlook, different only in circumstances and degree from its predecessors, but similar in its vagueness about how to achieve its laudable objectives.

CONCLUSIONS

The questions posed at the start may now be answered. One may conclude that New Zealand entered the 1990s more distant from the United States and thus from the Western security community than prior to 1984, but not greatly so, and this distance was reduced by the more intimate relationship with Australia. Labour modified the defense relationship with the United States but not New Zealand's security paradigm of cooperation with powerful friends and collective defense organizations except in respect of nuclear deterrence. National carried forward many of Labour's modifications in practice, and Don McKinnon's efforts to persuade his backbenchers to reverse them and restore ANZUS cooperation (and, implicitly, reliance on nuclear deterrence) appeared fruitless. New Zealand's security relations with the United States and Australia, and policies toward the Pacific region, have adapted incrementally over the decades under both parties and neither the continuance of National nor the return of Labour in the 1993 election is likely to alter the commitment to broad cooperation, even if specific defense links may change.

The nonnuclear policy enforced in 1985 by Labour and reaffirmed in 1990 by National precipitated a rupture which was keenly regretted in defense circles in New Zealand. Abroad, a useful framework for high level and intimate security consultation was voided, Australia was placed in an awkward position, and a source of reassurance to friendly regional states was called into question. But thanks to the easing of military tensions in the late 1980s, the rise of economic concerns to the top of the agenda, and moderation in Washington and Canberra, and despite media, academic, and official prognosis to the contrary, the damage caused by the rupture was contained. The break with the United States defense establishment had little effect on the evolution of New Zealand's regional defense outlook, posture, role, and credibility, and no effect at all on the substance of New Zealand's diplomacy, trade, cultural exchange, or other aspects of international intercourse.

Thus, it seems probable that the longer-term perspective of historians on the dispute over the nuclear issue will focus not so much on the disruption, but rather on the survival of so much of the relationship between New Zealand and the United States, including the maintenance of a high degree of compatibility in security policy and even important elements of security cooperation in nonmilitary sectors. The exercise of tolerance and civility by the two governments, and of sympathy and constructive relations by Australia and other Asia-Pacific governments, may prove to be more important for long-term regional security than the substance of the dispute.

APPENDIX

Defense Objectives Compared: 1987–1991

Defence of New Zealand: Review of Defence Policy 1987 (Excerpts)

The Defence of New Zealand 1991: A Policy Paper (Excerpts)

To preserve the security and integrity of New Zealand, our 200 mile EEZ, and the Island states (the Cook Islands, Niue, and Tokelau) for which New Zealand has defence responsibilities.

To preserve the sovereignty and security of New Zealand and its essential interests [and] to maintain the sovereignty and security of the Cook Islands, Niue, and Tokelau.

To promote the security and stable development of the South Pacific by providing practical assistance in defence matters [and] to mount an effective military response to any low level contingency within our area of direct strategic concern.

To contribute to the security of the South Pacific states with which New Zealand shares historical or other interests and to contribute generally to the security and stability of the South Pacific region.

To continue to meet ANZUS obligations in conventional terms.

To work to re-establish an effective defence relationship with traditional partners, especially the United States and the United Kingdom.

To maintain close defence cooperation with Australia, and in particular areas (defence procurement, logistic support, coordination of defence activities in the South Pacific) to develop a closer defence relationship.

To develop further the existing defence cooperation with Australia, including combined planning, operations, logistics, and the industrial base.

To contribute to the maintenance of peace and stability in Southeast Asia by maintaining an active role in the Five Power Defence Arrangements, military assistance, training, and exchange programmes.

To maintain and develop defence cooperation with ASEAN countries, and to preserve the partnership obligations of the Five Power Defence Arrangements.

To provide disaster relief assistance, resource protection, rescue and medical evacuation services to the community in New Zealand and in the South Pacific [and] to maintain an ability to operate in our southern maritime region, and provide logistic support to our activities in Antarctica.

To ensure that the general-purpose forces are capable of supporting non-military interests, including disaster relief assistance, resource protecion, rescue and medical evacuation services to New Zealand and in the South Pacific, and logistic support for activities in the Antarctic.

To promote peace and international security through contributions to United Nations peace-keeping operations.

To support the United Nations by contributing forces for peacekeeping or peacemaking duties [and] to contribute forces to other collective endeavors where New Zealand's national interests are involved.

3

U.S. Security Policies in the Pacific for the 1990s

JAMES A. KELLY

In the aftermath of a forty-five-year Cold War and a forty-five-day Gulf War, the United States looks into its international security relationships around the world with mixed and uncertain feelings. There seems to be little satisfaction from the victories and ample measures of disinterest, distrust, and fatigue.

However, most Americans realize that they are more a part of the world than they were in simpler days. They also realize that no consensus for a "new world order" has been achieved, whether the phrase is favored or not. There is broad acceptance that basic power relationships in the world have changed, yet dangers remain. Needed is a new set (or at least a newly considered set) of foreign and defense policies for the 1990s.

The process is neither quick nor easy. A forty-five-year strategy of containment worked, but it will take years to reach the popular and legislative consensus necessary for a new strategy and the defense structure to sustain it.

Washington's recent foreign policy agenda has been dominated by the dissolution of Eastern Europe and the former Soviet Union, concessions of sovereignty as Europe builds its community, and knotty Middle East issues. Some Americans, particularly on the East Coast, seem to be ready to forget about the Pacific and East Asia. Some Europhiles suggest the fabled Pacific century has ended—a decade before it was to begin.

The discussion that does occur on Asia-Pacific issues is not encouraging. Economic and trade issues, especially with Japan, are often mentioned superficially, but are not well understood. Poorly thought-out statements by both Japanese and American politicians raise antagonisms, and China is viewed in a simplistic fashion. After overenthusiasm in 1986, the inability of the Philippines to reach a formula with the United States for a new military bases agreement has resulted in real danger that an old friend—which happens to be an important Asian country—will be forgotten in Washington.

There is plenty of reason for this uncertainty about American involvement and policy around the world. Both the scope and the pace of the revolutions in Eastern Europe and the USSR almost exceeded our ability to grasp their true weight. The speed of change, less than three years, and the complications of the Gulf War made the process even more difficult. The various bloody ethnic upheavals since have exacerbated the uncertainty.

Some argue, even after the seizure of Kuwait, that security interests are now passé. Economics and trade are now governments' important concerns, the arguments go. Economic factors indeed have become more salient elements in U.S. foreign policies. With the disappearance of the need for global competition with Moscow, economic and financial interests now drive American policies more directly. Sometimes, as with President Bush's early 1992 visit to Australia and Japan, the results are unappealing. Moreover, policymakers have to remember that force and violence continue as immutable factors in international politics. Harsh realities can rapidly assert themselves to dominate any scene. For example:

- Modern weapons are more damaging and despite earnest nonproliferation efforts, more widely distributed, even to less developed countries which might once have been safely ignored.
- Weapons of mass destruction—chemical, nuclear, or fuel-air explosives delivered by ballistic missiles—are viewed by despots as being able to shift military balances quickly.
- Military budgets may be down in the United States, Eastern and Western Europe, and Russia. But they are up in the Middle East, the South Asian subcontinent, China, and throughout Southeast Asia.

The changes in the world with the end of the Cold War have had differing regional effects. In East Asia, the impacts have been quite different from those in Europe because, for one thing, East Asia was in many ways peripheral to the Cold War. Recall that one reason for the lag in the U.S. military response to the 1950 invasion of Korea was that Europe was rapidly reinforced with American divisions out of the fear (now recognized as unfounded) of a multipronged Communist attack (Blair 1987). Had a NATO vs. Warsaw Pact–USSR conflagration occurred over those Cold War years, East Asia and the Pacific would have been a secondary theater. Major forces and vital Western interests would certainly have been involved, particularly in Northeast Asia. Millions of lives would have been at stake. But the conflict could not have been decided in Asia because the focal point and area of decision would have been Europe. This focal point of bipolar confrontation no longer exists.

There are other differences from Europe. First, Chinese, North Korean, and Vietnamese Communist leaderships are determined to retain power and party control. Second, the end of the Cold War may enable old and new

Asian disputes to proceed without the East-West context that would have insured attention and probably triggered outside interference. Finally, old disputes—Cambodia, South China Sea divisions, or Korean unification—remain unsolved and old fears concerning Japan, China, India, and Korea persist.

U.S PERCEPTIONS OF SECURITY: OUTLOOK AND ISSUES

In the wake of all this change, and most important, in facing a world without the central organizing theme that the Cold War and containment strategy provided, American strategy must try to respond to a more ambiguous and complex reality. The response must consider that:

- The worldwide balance of power has much less meaning now, although faster-changing regional balances may still be important. Regional stability is a reasonable objective, but policymakers must understand that such a concept will never draw the understanding and support that the Cold War engendered.

- Predicting how the intensity and seriousness of regional disputes will develop, or the turns that nationalistic or ethnic rivalries will take is similarly uncertain.

- Defining national interests in such situations will be neither obvious nor quickly agreed upon.

- U.S. strategy should determine the kind and size of military force structure to be purchased and maintained, rather than vice versa. That said, the political process of the budget will have much more importance than any strategy in such choices. The sense of what is to be spent will guide Congress and the administration in selecting a finite set of forces and capabilities (Tyler 1992a). But regional disputes can arise and assumptions about interests can change much more rapidly than a force can be rebuilt. Such limitations on national action must be clearly understood by Washington.

- If the system of alliances developed during the Cold War is to serve further, rather than atrophy or be cast aside, a new degree of consultation and cooperation, based more on mutual respect and less on fear of an enemy, is essential.

In Washington, the process of rethinking is beginning and slow movement toward a new American national strategy is taking place. Such national direction is not handed down by presidents or Congress, though leadership is vital. Rather, a new consensus must develop. A process taking years—probably most of the decade—will be needed.

Missteps are likely. In early 1992, press stories about a Pentagon "Defense

Policy Guidance" paper asserted that collective security was being thrust aside, and that the guidance was only a prop to support a larger post–Cold War force structure (Tyler 1992b). The latter point was more persuasive, but the disclosure showed how much farther the new American dialogue needs to progress before any new strategy can earn broad support.

In the Asia-Pacific region, the U.S. government's process of analyzing interests and establishing a strategic framework got off to a faster start than it did elsewhere. This did not occur because of any particular regional attentiveness, but to meet a U.S. Senate requirement. The senators' concern was primarily to respond to complaints that allies (Japan and South Korea) were not contributing sufficiently to their own defense.

The resulting Defense Department report, issued in April 1990 (reissued in 1992), entitled *A Strategic Framework for the Asian Pacific Rim: Looking Toward the 21st Century,* included a pledge that the United States is and will remain an engaged Pacific power. It also confirmed that forward deployed forces, although only a small part of the overall U.S. force structure, will remain as the necessary center of U.S. Asia-Pacific strategy. The report recognized that force reductions are necessary and will take place (and projected a three-phased reduction over the decade), but reaffirmed that forward deployed forces provide flexible response, economy of force, a logistics base, and demonstrate a visible U.S. commitment.

The report continued the Northeast Asian emphasis in U.S. Asia-Pacific defense policy. The United States continues to view Japan as its key relationship, or "linchpin." But the Northeast Asian emphasis is also due to Korea, which is now possibly the world's most serious security problem. The report acknowledged America's close relationships with members of ASEAN and Australia, but it did not identify specific U.S. security interests in either Southeast Asia or Oceania.

The Strategic Framework has stood up well over two-plus years, yet visitors to East Asia and Australia have found that questions and doubt persist about American interests and policies in the region (Vasey, Kelly, and Levin 1992). Lack of dialogue, highly public frictions with Japan, and the continuing trade deficit contribute to these perceptions. The messy and divisive Washington debate over the future U.S. force structure and defense policies, which is colored by the budget deficit (Tyler 1992a), may also be affecting Asian attitudes. Yet the American commitment to East Asia does remain, and was reaffirmed in early 1993 by President Clinton on assuming office.

POST–COLD WAR CONCERNS IN ASIA

American security policy in East Asia and the Pacific is intended to respond to varied problems. Several possibilities that need to be considered in planning for the 1990s are described in the following paragraphs. With the exception of the Korean peninsula, the security situation in East Asia no longer warrants use of the label of "threat" that was appropriate in the Cold War era. Rather, the term now in most instances is "concern." These are conditions that are at a temperature below flashpoint but which have the potential to emerge as focal points of instability and armed confrontation.

The Korean Peninsula

North Korea remains a present and serious threat to regional stability. Politically, it is increasingly isolated and Soviet aid has all but dried up. The rigid party control of every aspect of life continues, making the country unique. "Great Leader" Kim Il-Sung will pass from the scene during the decade of the 1990s, but no one knows how the transition will fare. With the loss of Soviet aid, a dismal economic picture has worsened, and hunger is said to be widespread (Kristof 1992). These difficulties, coupled with an inability to pay for petroleum, have clearly undermined the readiness of North Korea's armed forces to attack the South with conventional weapons. Yet its military forces remain large, well equipped, and menacingly deployed. Openings to the outside, very active dialogues and some agreements with the South, and membership in the UN are all encouraging steps, but none have been matched by any change in internal isolation or rigid control.

There is particular concern over apparent efforts by North Korea to develop nuclear weapons (Fialka 1989; Oberdorfer 1992; and many others). South Korea, Japan, and the United States are all making attempts to convince North Korea that it must not seek to join the "nuclear club." The withdrawal of any U.S. nuclear weapons as a part of President Bush's worldwide reductions in tactical nuclear weapons, announced in September 1991, was clearly intended by the United States to stimulate forward movement on the issue of North Korea's nuclear program. When it did not, Secretary of Defense Dick Cheney emphasized the seriousness with which the United States viewed this situation by temporarily halting the second phase of reductions of U.S. forces in Korea scheduled under the Strategic Framework program (Seib 1992).

North Korea's nuclear aspirations are a most serious concern for Asian stability. Its upgraded Scud missiles could hit Japan as well as anywhere in South Korea. A nuclear armed Korea—on either side of the demilitarized zone (DMZ)—could be expected to force reconsideration of Japan's renunciation of such weapons for itself.

Russia and the Former Soviet Union

Even though the military forces of the former Soviet Union remain powerful, domestic disintegration and the end of the Cold War have had an impact on their capability. The risk that the Russian Republic might again resort to aggressive foreign policies seems remote. Rising nationalism and splits in the republics are greater concerns. Yet thousands of nuclear warheads remain, not all in Russia, and production of modern weaponry, warships, and aircraft continues, though at a diminished pace. Russian military capabilities in the Far East continue to be disparately large, despite severe political and economic upheaval limiting their employment.

Domestic Instability

Domestic problems are the most serious worry in many Asian countries. Economic growth, while rapid, is not uniform. Political leaderships are aging. Institutions of government are not always well defined or mature, particularly with respect to the rule of law. Thus, economic inequities and inevitable political transitions could hazard stability in Indonesia, China, Vietnam, or the Philippines. On the other hand, the example of Thailand's crisis in 1992, in which military leaders were rebuffed and stability apparently enhanced, gives reason for encouragement.

The South China Sea

Maritime boundaries, particularly involving the Spratly Islands, are in conflict among China, Vietnam, Malaysia, the Philippines, and to a lesser degree Indonesia, Thailand, Singapore, and Taiwan. China's claims cover most of the South China Sea and have been reasserted repeatedly (Hamzah 1990). Given the probability of petroleum or gas under much of the disputed seabed, and multiple overlaps among claims, serious conflict could develop. Recognizing this danger, an informal effort has been launched under Indonesian leadership to seek cooperative solutions, with some kind of joint development arrangement being the most widely mooted option.

India

India, racked by Hindu-Muslim conflict, possesses strengthening military, naval, and missile forces. Its determination to be the Indian Ocean and subcontinental hegemon is clear, but the turns and directions this may take are ambiguous, and concern in Southeast Asia and Australia may mount. The situation in Kashmir and differences with Pakistan also continue to be quite serious. As former U.S. Assistant Secretary of Defense Richard Armitage wrote, "For the first time in history, two Third World nations both of which might have nuclear weapons are on the edge of conflict. Both sides have IRBMs and sophisticated aircraft. The problem is exacerbated by the fact that both potential belligerents have relatively weak central governments, making it difficult to be bold in the search for peace" (Armitage 1990).

Cambodia

A "settlement" was agreed, brokered by the five permanent UN Security Council members with important support from Australia and Japan. But the peacekeepers' task, even if adequately supported, is extremely difficult and stability is unlikely anytime soon in that troubled land.

Borders and Sea Boundaries

China's borders with Vietnam and India have both seen serious armed clashes that might recur. The disproportionate size and power of China, with its uncertain ambitions and leadership continuity, make Beijing a source of anxiety despite remarkable economic progress. China's leaders worry about growth of independence sentiment in Taiwan. Elsewhere around China, irredentism or contested territories with Japan, Russia, Mongolia, and Kazakhstan, perhaps prompted by internal disruptions, could be future flashpoints. Recent public legislative reassertions of broad Chinese sovereignty, particularly over the Spratlies and the Senkaku (or Diaoyutai) Islands south of Okinawa are a case in point (Far Eastern Economic Review [FEER] 1992).

U.S. PACIFIC AND EAST ASIAN SECURITY CONCEPTS

Despite the U.S. Defense Department's framework (Department of Defense 1990) and the assurances of President George Bush during his early 1992 visit to the region, there is still concern that the United States may lose interest. As U.S. defense budget reductions develop, there is increasing concern within ASEAN that the United States may match its withdrawal from the Philippines by a process of disengagement from Asia-Pacific regional issues. These concerns are not particularly specific, but reflect a belief held by some that too many Americans are inattentive to their interests in the Pacific and that distraction or isolationism might cause a turning away (Vasey, Kelly, and Levin 1992).

American visitors have found that Asian governments and most security experts want the United States to remain in the region as the "benevolent balancer." In varying forms, the U.S. forward military presence and its security commitments are seen as useful to sustain a benign regional environment. Few in or out of the region have thought through what kind or size of U.S. presence is needed to perform a balancing function, but most agree that some continued presence is important, and that too great a withdrawal might destabilize regional relations to the detriment of both Asian and American interests.

In late 1991, an article in *Foreign Affairs* by Secretary of State James Baker provided an authoritative statement of the official U.S. position (J. Baker 1991). Published just prior to Baker's attendance at the November 1991 Asia-Pacific Economic Cooperation (APEC) meeting in Seoul and President Bush's January 1992 visit to the region, the article reaffirmed a traditional view of the U.S. role in East Asia. Secretary Baker called this view his "Pacific Architecture." The article correctly noted that stability and dynamism have been secured for four decades by a loose structure appropriate to the region and very different from that in Europe. That structure is a varied network of bilateral alliances with the United States, supplemented by varying arrangements with friendly non-allies. Baker described the architecture in visual terms as "a fan spread wide, with its base in North America and radiating wide across the Pacific." Spokes from the fan radiate first and most importantly to Japan, and also to Korea, to ASEAN allies Thailand and the Philippines, and to Australia. He saw this framework as including both economic and security relations. He also noted: "Connecting these spokes is the fabric of shared economic interests now given form by the APEC process."

However, just as some might question whether the Defense Department's framework represented genuinely new post–Cold War thinking, the same reservation might be applied to the State Department's architecture. The hub-and-spoke model served well during the Cold War and may continue to do so with commitment, careful management, and timely adjustments. The structure is malleable, and builds on the ability of America's forward deployed military forces — flexible and capable even at reduced post–Cold War force levels — to provide cooperative security to a diverse group of friends and partners.

The bilateral model's continued success or acceptance is not assured. The factor of fear that the Cold War engendered has dissipated. This is especially so among Southeast Asian states, Australia, and New Zealand. In this new era the most effective means for protecting U.S. interests may not be military strength (although such forces remain essential), but an ability to tailor policies to a broader set of regional political aspirations and economic development objectives.

At the same time, the end of the Cold War permits consideration of multilateral dialogues — even arms control — as a means of improving American regional relationships. What particular form these dialogues will take is unclear, but multilateral talks are beginning around the annual ASEAN Post-Ministerial Conference. Many Americans see no hazard in encouraging this process, given the end of the ideological struggle.

Spurred by some of the successes of the worldwide Intermediate Nuclear Forces agreement of the mid-eighties, and encouraged by Soviet diplomatic and political efforts of that period, considerable interest in various forms of arms control began to emerge, and has continued over the subsequent years. As the overall security scene has changed, and the superpower conflict dissolved, more ambitious proposals have been put forward for cooperative approaches to regional security. The concept advocated, for a time, by Australian Foreign Minister Gareth Evans of an Asia-Pacific counterpart to the Conference on Security and Cooperation in Europe (CSCE) is one of the more ambitious of these.

For some time, official American responses to such proposals ranged from flatly negative to, at best, cautious (Department of Defense 1990). A major reason for U.S. skepticism was that arms control enthusiasts often failed to take into account the fact that in Asia, naval forces are much more important to the United States than to the Soviet Union. U.S. objections also touched on East Asian diversity and complexity, the resulting possibilities of multipolar conflict, and important unilateral measures such as Japan's renunciation of power projection or nuclear forces. Finally, some questioned whether the three classical objectives of arms control—to make war less likely, to make preparing for war less costly, and to make war less destructive if it comes—would be served by entering into broad negotiations in this region.

Such discouraging views did not exclude American support of confidence building measures (CBMs) as steps on the road toward greater regional stability and reduced requirements for military force. Principal examples were the U.S.-Soviet naval incidents agreements, and the obvious potential for CBMs in Korea.

More recent events, which have gone beyond what was even imagined just a few years ago, obviously have reduced some of the past problems of arms control in the Pacific. Unilateral measures have occurred that represent the best kind of arms control, because such measures reflect reduction in the political tensions that caused the armament in the first place. The major examples are Russian cutbacks at Cam Ranh Bay in Vietnam, the American withdrawal from the Philippines, the removal of tactical nuclear weapons from American ships, the presumptive removal of tactical nuclear weapons from South Korea, and the cancellation of U.S.-South Korean military exercises in 1992. There have also been a remarkable, if uneven, series of negotiations between North and South Korea that continue to have potential for dampening the most dangerous regional flashpoint.

With such sweeping changes in the security environment, proposals for multilateral security dialogue and arms control deserve careful review, if only to prompt more unilateral measures. New efforts on the very serious issue of nuclear weapons in Korea may yet bear fruit. Acceptance in principle by China of the missile technology control regime (MTCR) is a good start, and the time may come when China will be willing to enter into arms control talks on strategic weapons. Nonproliferation of nuclear and chemical weapons may be helped by the new emphasis given to these subjects. Finally, there may now be some prospect of organizing talks on transparency of weapons transfers by primary and secondary producers.

These changes have already had a visible impact on official American attitudes. For example, in 1990 the United States attempted to discourage Asian friends from sending observers to Soviet naval exercises. In 1992, the U.S. Navy itself held simple exercises at sea with Russian ships. It cannot be expected—and this writer would not advocate—that the U.S. government will rapidly embrace any sweeping proposals for regional arms reductions, or other initiatives that could undermine the U.S. alliance structure in the region. In the U.S. view, U.S. military power exercised through the network

of alliances remains the strongest practical instrument in the region for bringing effective force to bear in the event of potential challenges. However,
barring a major reversal in the basic security environment, progressively
greater American interest and involvement in such arms control efforts as
confidence-building measures appear very likely. Although the United States
would be extremely cautious in dealing with the more expansive, and open-
ended, concepts such as the idea of an Asian CSCE (a "CSCA"), intermediate
steps providing for improved multilateral dialogue on security issues in the
region are more likely to find support.

OTHER ASPECTS OF AMERICAN POLICY

The argument that the United States is drifting in the region is supported by
the notion that there is an imbalance among the elements of American policy
(Vasey, Kelly, and Levin 1992). The imbalance refers to the contrast between
well-tended U.S. military policies and political and economic exchanges which
some view as sporadic and lacking in vigor. Presumably Washington talent
has been distracted by events in other areas that are in crisis. But in the current environment, military policies, no matter how well based, cannot carry
the whole burden of complex international relationships.

The problem of policy imbalance is most serious in terms of U.S. economic
policies and dialogues in the region. Three problems are particularly evident.

- First, although investment and financial flows are larger and more
  significant, practical emphasis and public attention is focused on
  trade disputes. Many of these are small in real terms, but they are
  acrimoniously fought. Asian markets do have to be opened more,
  but some issues damage public perceptions and raise doubts about
  the relative priorities of American interests.

- Second, efforts of the U.S. government to promote trade-enhancing
  investments seem unfocused and often ineffective. Perhaps this is
  because of notions that investment overseas is synonymous with the
  "export of jobs."

- Third, there is lack of coordination of American economic interests,
  in Washington or in East Asia. In addition to the U.S. State Department, policies for trade involve two agencies, the Commerce Department and the cabinet-rank Special Trade Representative's office.
  The Treasury Department is responsible for financial and exchange
  rate matters. And Agriculture, Transportation, and Energy are each
  the province of turf-conscious and co-equal Washington bureaucracies.

- Last, the political side of American relationships in East Asia needs
  revitalization. At the presidential and secretarial level, those discussions that do take place seem to go well. But there are not enough

such talks to meet the dialogue needs of a much more sophisticated group of Asia-Pacific partners. Modern ambassadors, even very good ones, are not able to carry the authority and intensity of discussion that many governments in the region want.

As the above suggests, this writer is concerned not so much with U.S. policy as stated, but rather with the inadequacy of policy execution. Alliances and friendship require attention, and the concern is that recent levels of attention have seemed low. It is apparent that the historic American policy emphasis toward Northeast Asia is even stronger than it has been. The departure from the Philippines contributes to this notion, but there is more.

The United States has had access to various Southeast Asian and Australian facilities for years. New forms of low-profile access to facilities have been obtained, particularly at Singapore, but also in Malaysia and Indonesia. The forces that will use these welcome places will be smaller, by an order of magnitude, than those that used the Philippine bases. This is not bad. The level of military forces in post–Cold War Southeast Asia should be far less than the level during the days when Cam Ranh Bay was being equipped by the former Soviet Union. But the perception that American forces will withdraw completely needs to be resisted.

Recognizing the distance factor and a relatively peaceful environment, American forces have always been scarce in Oceania. Occasional transits of naval forces to or from the Indian Ocean may have given an appearance of presence, but in the future such visits are likely to be even less frequent. American interests can be maintained by periodic senior diplomatic and military visits, thoughtful consultation at lower levels, and by cooperation with Australia and New Zealand.

U.S. SECURITY RELATIONSHIPS WITH AUSTRALIA AND NEW ZEALAND

ANZUS and Security Cooperation

Since being formalized in 1951, the ANZUS security treaty between Australia, New Zealand, and the United States has been the framework for organizing security cooperation among the three nations. In 1985, New Zealand's participation was effectively downgraded, but the treaty has continued to organize U.S.-Australian and Australia–New Zealand security cooperation.

As already noted by Stewart Woodman (see Chapter 1), ANZUS was not initially an American idea. The treaty just fit so naturally among the panoply of Cold War alliances through the fifties, sixties, and seventies that it was often viewed in Washington as though it had been an American idea. It has endured because it is flexible, and because it is grounded on very basic interests.

The treaty is based on the shared values of democratic nations, influenced by shared language and Western political traditions (Wolfowitz 1984). Other important influences at ANZUS' founding in 1951 were habits of military cooperation built as allies in the two world wars, the break-up of the British Empire, the perceived spread of communism and the Korean War, and uncertainty in the Pacific about Japan's return as a power.

If a commitment to mutual defense has been the formal purpose of ANZUS, the informal cooperation between military forces and between diplomats and officials has been the more practical accompaniment. The heart of the alliance has been the exchanges of views among government leaders at ANZUS Council meetings, now succeeded by Australia–U.S. ministerial meetings and corresponding Australia–New Zealand consultations; the cooperation in military technology and intelligence cooperation; and ongoing regional and world political dialogues. The outlook for the future of alliance relations will depend importantly on whether these types of practical cooperation remain useful, as well as whether such cooperation impedes any other necessary relationships.

U.S.-Australia

Security and political cooperation between the United States and Australia has always been close and valued by both sides. The effects of the post–Cold War world are not likely to change the benefits each draws from cooperation. The two countries' respective locations in the Asia-Pacific region complement each other in many respects.

First, Southeast Asia, the South China Sea, and the eastern Indian Ocean are areas where neither the United States nor Australia has the resources, at all times, to watch out for its interests. The area is of greater importance to Australia, but U.S. interests are also large. Problems arise from time to time in their individual relations with Indonesia, or Malaysia, or the Philippines, and at such times cooperation may be particularly helpful.

Second, Australia has special knowledge of and relationships in the South Pacific. For its part, as noted by Robert Kiste later in this volume (see Chapter 9), the United States long neglected its interests in stable development in the Pacific. In recent years some positive steps have been taken, such as the Free Association arrangements with the Marshalls and the Federated States of Micronesia, a regional fisheries agreement that removed a major irritant in U.S. relations with the island states, and President Bush's Pacific Island Summit of 1990. But despite such starts and better intentions, U.S. government interest in the South Pacific remains marginal. Assistance budgets have never been high and may go lower. Australia's work in its own interest and its voice as an ally can help ensure that Oceania's problems are not completely out of America's mind.

Third, there is a broad intergovernment agenda and a regular dialogue. The Australia–U.S. ministerial series is particularly important. This is an event that focuses the attention of the bureaucracy on problems that may exist, and fosters the kind of familiarity that permits beneficial cooperation in unforeseen ways. A personal relationship between the prime minister and the president can be especially important. The availability of rapid communication and the predisposition of American and Australian leaders to talk on the phone can slice through some kinds of political or economic problems before they become severe.

Fourth, military to military cooperation between the United States and Australia is close and useful to both. The post–Cold War world will not change the benefits that each draws in enhanced operational competence and confidence. U.S. forces will remain in the region even though at reduced levels. The flexible structure and regional orientation of Australia's armed forces is not dependent on a Cold War rationale, and significant changes in force levels are therefore unlikely. So the basic rationale for cooperation will remain.

As pointed out by Stewart Woodman in Chapter 1, other benefits of the military relationship to Australia include access to information, technology and equipment that would be more costly or unavailable to Australia operating on its own. The U.S.–Australian joint defense facilities proved the continuing practical value of this aspect of cooperation through their key role in detecting Scud missile launches during the Gulf War. As missile systems proliferate, the joint defense facilities are likely to remain useful in sensing danger from unpredictable quarters.

U.S.–New Zealand

The outlook for U.S.–New Zealand cooperation is much cloudier. With the decline of the Cold War, the attraction of indignation politics may decline in New Zealand, although the popular antipathy to things nuclear persists. The removal of tactical nuclear weapons from the American surface fleet in 1992 has not (at least as of this writing) resolved the impasse over conditions and procedures for port visits by American ships. To complicate further, New Zealand's location and U.S. force reductions, coupled with the continuing very low levels of New Zealand's own spending on its military forces noted by Steve Hoadley in Chapter 2, will mean that in practice there will be fewer opportunities for ship visits or other forms of military cooperation in any event.

Despite this, slow improvement has occurred in New Zealand's badly deteriorated security relationship with the United States. New Zealand's participation in the allied coalition in the Gulf War was an important milestone in this regard. The new relationship that ultimately emerges will not be what existed before 1984. Old hands will miss the kind of closeness that existed in the earlier period, and many will wonder whether the split was really necessary. But in the 1990s, the conditions in the world and in the Pacific will be different, and a solid working security relationship is likely to be gradually rebuilt as a matter of common interests. Both are interested in stability within the Pacific community, and ways to cooperate will be found.

U.S. Expectations

What security roles would the United States like Australia and New Zealand to play? Any suggested response to this question must recognize that Americans are deeply uncertain of what their own role should be in a post–Cold War world. Much more time will be needed for the United States to find its correct path between overinvolvement, the "world policeman" shibboleth, and the imaginary attractions of isolation. Even if concern were greater for peace and development in Southeast Asia or the Pacific, if Americans cannot agree on their own policies, they can scarcely provide firm advice to an ally.

Such reservations aside, the United States wants Australia and New Zealand to do for collective security what is natural to them. The process that Australia employed through the 1980s to assess its security interests, as described by Stewart Woodman, has turned out to be timely and successful. This planning was not dependent on the Cold War, and so it has not had to be redone. The orientation to problems in the South Pacific, Southeast Asia, and the eastern Indian Ocean makes sense for Australia. Australia's flexible defense forces seem to fit quite reasonably with that planning, even if the lack of a post–Cold War "peace dividend" upsets those who did not follow or agree with the earlier defense planning process. Australia's policies — in its own interests — are quite consistent with U.S. interests.

New Zealand's South Pacific interests seem to meet mutual interests as well, although there may be greater doubt as to the extent to which resources will permit New Zealand to cultivate those interests.

Beyond these basics, from an American perspective, Australia's attention to military cooperation with various ASEAN militaries is beneficial for all involved. Its familiarity with the particular instabilities in places such as Papua New Guinea, Vanuatu, or Fiji has great potential to help those countries if trouble comes. If collective security is to have substance, U.S. military planners always want to be able to have American forces work together in any crisis with an ally's forces. "Interoperability," the planners' term, is the process by which military forces work together with those of another nation through common or compatible procedures in communications, tactics, and logistics. Interoperability is improved by planning and by working together on practice or real problems day-to-day. It is the essence of a working military alliance.

CONCLUSIONS

Nothing suggests that either the world or the Pacific of the 1990s will be serene or without threat of bitter conflict. Australia, New Zealand, and the United States have shared much. Each country is changing but many common interests persist. Advantages continue for each partner from working together, not least because cooperation is convenient and low in cost. From the viewpoint of the southern partners, ties with the United States also appear increasingly unlikely to bring unwanted burdens. Therefore, each can continue to plan for the individual and common good, discuss emerging trends, and occasionally argue about the best solutions to shared problems. If there is any reservation for the future, it is that diversions in Washington can so easily cut into the quality and quantity of policy dialogue. Distractions and crises are the stuff of Washington life, but the alliance must have management that ensures that time is set aside regularly for sharing ideas and consultation.

Comment

RICHARD W. BAKER

The country chapters bring out a number of points of commonality as well as difference among the regional security policies of the three ANZUS states that are of some significance for our overall interest in the evolution of relations among the three during their period of military alliance.

The first and most obvious similarity is that the security policies of all three countries have undergone significant changes during the period, most rapidly and dramatically so in the most recent years. In each case the result has been a narrowing of the focus of security policy, and there is now a much more careful prioritization of defense interests by all three.

A comparison of the nature and rationales of the three countries' participation in Korea, Vietnam, and the Persian Gulf illustrates the nature of the change. The United States went into Korea in response to an invasion and because it saw major Western interests at stake in the context of the global confrontation with communism. Australia and New Zealand both immediately followed suit (before the ANZUS alliance even existed), out of an essentially identical view of the threat as well as the nature of the strategy —collective forward defense—needed to meet the threat. Although the operation was formally conducted under UN auspices, there was never any question that in practice it was a U.S.-led effort of the Western alliance.

In Vietnam, from rather small-scale and limited purpose origins, the United States was drawn progressively into a deeper commitment to a wider and more costly conflict and in parallel with its increasing involvement also escalated its interpretation of the conflict's strategic significance. Australia came in with initial enthusiasm, partly thinking to help lock in the U.S. commitment; New Zealand followed, with a largely symbolic participation but without doubt as to the worthiness of the cause. Enthusiasm for the war waned even more rapidly in Australia and New Zealand than in the United

States. In the early 1970s, new Labo(u)r governments in each country with-drew their remaining units before the formal completion of the American "Vietnamization" withdrawal strategy. When the other regional dominos did not follow the fall of Indochina, all three governments reconsidered the necessity as well as the wisdom of pursuing this kind of open-ended forward defense strategy.

In the Persian Gulf, the United States again played the leading role, but this time (out of considerations both of limited resources and of domestic ambivalence over such military interventions) insisted on participation by a broad coalition of countries and on prior UN sanction of its actions, and dis-engaged as early as possible when the immediate objective had been achieved. Australia (once more under a Labor government) again came in early and contributed (for it) significant resources, principally navy ships to participate in the interdiction of vessels bound for Iraq. However, Australia's prime minister was careful to stress on this occasion that Australia's decision to participate was not based on the U.S. alliance or an American request for support but rather on Australia's own calculation that a stand in the Gulf would make it less likely that some future regional bully would feel free to pick on Australia. New Zealand also ultimately contributed to the Gulf coalition force. However, the Labour government in office at the start of the crisis took the position that it would only participate in an operation under a UN umbrella. When the UN authorized the use of force, the newly elected National government moved quickly to participate but held back from sending combat forces.

As reflected in these examples, the approach of each of the three countries to the ultimate security problem—armed conflict—has changed dramatically over a period of just over 40 years. Further, due in part to the general uncer-tainty of the security environment in the post–Cold War period, it is also clear that in all three cases the new policies are still in flux. All three authors point out issues and internal dilemmas that their national policymakers have not yet adequately addressed.

However, the security policies of the three that have emerged from this evolutionary process now differ significantly, to a far greater degree than was the case at the start of the alliance when the basic concepts of collective security and forward defense were the accepted wisdom. The United States remains focused on global and regionwide considerations. Within the Asia-Pacific region, U.S. attention is centered on Northeast Asia where the other major players and the principal flashpoint are located. At the same time, the United States is trying to meet its regional commitments at a lower cost in both resources and presence. Australia has refocused its thinking on its "area of direct military interest," which in practice means Southeast Asia and the South Pacific. New Zealand is primarily concerned with the Pacific Islands region.

Interestingly, all the authors see these three orientations as fundamentally compatible. Woodman and Kelly both see an important role for U.S.-Australian cooperation, both in terms of practical exchanges of benefits and in terms of common broad interests in regional security. Kelly notes a useful de facto division of labor in terms of the concentration of each on particular subregions. Woodman and Hoadley agree that Australian–New Zealand security relations are now closer than ever, although neither considers actual integration of the two defense establishments as likely, at least any time soon. Even in the case of U.S.-New Zealand security relations, both Hoadley and Kelly believe the fundamental compatibility of the security interests of the two countries will both ensure the continuation of their overall cooperative relationship and lead to the development of a working security relationship as well. Both point to the example of the Persian Gulf conflict as a harbinger in this regard.

Nevertheless, there are elements in the individual policies of the three that are not necessarily compatible. Woodman points to the potential for tensions between Australia's security interests and involvements in Southeast Asia and Australia's role and image as an ally of the United States. Currently, it is very difficult to imagine a specific scenario that would turn this potential dilemma into a reality. However, it is certainly understandable that, to the extent Australia comes to identify itself as an Asian-Pacific country and a member of the Southeast Asian region as well as the South Pacific, its assessments of particular questions and its priorities in dealing with regional security problems will not necessarily be the same as those of the United States.

One relatively recent example of such differences of perspective can be seen in the fact that the Australian Labor government at the end of the 1980s showed far earlier and far greater interest in reaching a regional accommodation with Vietnam and in working with the Hun Sen government on a Cambodian settlement than did the United States. Another result of diverging conceptions and priorities in regional security policy has been the difference between Australian enthusiasm (at least under the Hawke and Keating Labor governments) for regional arms control initiatives and for institutionalizing regional security cooperation, and the distinctly chilly U.S. reaction (at least under the Republican administrations of Reagan and Bush) to most such proposals.

Between Australia and New Zealand, Hoadley notes that New Zealand does not share Australia's primary concern with Southeast Asia. On the other hand, it is clear that in investing significant resources in defense cooperation with New Zealand, the Australian defense establishment anticipates that the two would operate together in most regional situations. Given the limited defense capabilities of both, it is not hard to imagine circumstances where, despite their practical dependence on each other in carrying out some kinds of military operations, there could be quite robust differences over how the joint resources would be employed.

The possibility for incompatibility in defense policy between the United

States and New Zealand has already been all too clearly demonstrated. In many senses this was a classic clash of perspectives; New Zealand's highly subregional orientation allowed it to adopt a stance on nuclear issues that the Americans considered fundamentally incompatible with global U.S. strategy and requirements. It is at least possible that with more skillful management and perhaps different personnel on both sides, the ultimate break could have been avoided. It would be an exaggeration to say that the contradiction was inherent or the split inevitable. Indeed, it is even still possible that the issue may be bridged and full cooperation restored at some point. However, the difference in perceived interests and priorities is clear.

The inference most easily drawn from these trends is that, barring major new crises that galvanize common interests and efforts, the future is likely to see a more diverse set of regional security policies and priorities among the three. For all the reasons stated, cooperation seems certain to continue, both of a practical nature and in the form of mutual involvement in most conceivable crises. However, there is no way of escaping the reality that broader differences in perspective will need to be bridged to make such cooperation work in the future than was the case through most of the Cold War period.

The Pacific Islands

This section is devoted to a particular subset of the regional policies of the three ANZUS states, their relations with and policies toward the Pacific Islands. The island groups of the southern and central Pacific are the geographic area where the interests of the three countries most directly and comprehensively overlap. The security of this area—or at least its denial to potential enemies—has been seen as a critical element in the security of the alliance. Article V of the ANZUS treaty specifically included "the island territories under [each party's] jurisdiction in the Pacific" as falling within the scope of the treaty's security commitments; at the time the treaty was signed, this covered 12 of the 21 political entities that comprise the Pacific Islands region.

It is not possible to provide detailed background information on the island region here (this can be found, for example, in Fairbairn et al. 1991). However, a brief introduction will help set the context for the discussion that follows. The adjoining table and map will identify and locate the major constituent island groups. The island region is also commonly divided into three ethnic-cultural subareas: Micronesia, comprising the small island groups running in an arc from the Northern Marianas in the northwest through Nauru and the Gilbert Island group of Kiribati in the southeast; Melanesia, a string of larger islands lying below Micronesia and consisting of Papua New Guinea, the Solomons, Vanuatu, New Caledonia, and Fiji; and Polynesia, covering a huge triangle from Hawaii in the north through New Zealand in the southwest and Easter Island in the southeast.

The Pacific Islands region was among the last areas of the world to be carved up during the colonial period, but by the early 1900s all of the islands had come under the control of one or another of the colonial powers. (Tonga was not formally a colony, but had a protectorate arrangement with Britain from 1900 until 1970.) With the transfer of the Micronesian states from

Japanese to U.S. jurisdiction as a result of the Second World War, the entire region was controlled by the ANZUS states, Britain, France, and (until the western half of New Guinea was transferred to Indonesia in 1962) the Netherlands. In 1947, and at the initiative of Australia and New Zealand, the six metropolitan powers established the South Pacific Commission (SPC), primarily in order to facilitate consultation on economic and social issues in the islands. The signing of the ANZUS treaty in 1951 formalized the tripartite security umbrella over the region. Within the framework of ANZUS and the SPC, for most of the postwar period the Pacific Islands region was considered a calm "ANZUS lake."

That situation began to change as significant numbers of island countries gained independence in the 1970s. By 1971, five island countries had regained or attained independence: Cook Islands, Fiji, Nauru, Tonga, and Western Samoa. In that year, under the leadership of Fiji, these five countries established the South Pacific Forum (SPF) for the explicit purpose of having a forum for the discussion of political issues that were excluded from the mandate of the SPC. Australia and New Zealand were involved in the South Pacific Forum from the start as observers (and supporters), and shortly became full members. By 1990, all 13 independent or self-governing island countries were members. Also, through a series of incremental reforms, by the mid-1970s the island states gained effective control of the SPC as well. The changing political configuration of the island region presented a new challenge both to policymakers in the three ANZUS governments and to the alliance relationship.

The authors of the country chapters were asked to address a number of fundamental questions in the relations of the three countries with the Pacific Islands as they have evolved over the postwar period. In each case, we are interested in the place of the Pacific Islands in the foreign and regional policies of that government and the significant changes in these policies, particularly in the more recent period. We examine how each government has viewed the problems facing the islands, and what each has seen as its own role and responsibilities in meeting these problems. We also consider what the islanders think the roles of the ANZUS states should be. We look at the major constraints on each government in its relations with the islands and in responding to island interests and needs. Finally, we ask what each considers the appropriate roles of the other two countries.

Stewart Firth describes the current Australian policy toward the islands, labeled "constructive commitment" by the government, as demonstrating the relatively high priority now accorded by Australia to the islands, in political attention, assistance funds, and defense policy. He views the primary constraints on Australia's relations with the islands as being the conflicting interests of Australia's wider policies, and a certain amount of islander suspicion and sensitivity toward Australia as a Western and much larger state. Firth comments that the major prospective questions for Australian policy are whether the current focus on development in the islands will actually lead to political stability and how Australia will actually respond in crises.

John Henderson emphasizes the importance of the islands in New Zealand's regional policy—diplomatic, security, and economic—and some of the practical qualifications and contradictions to the declaratory policies. In this context, he cites declining levels of New Zealand diplomatic representation, economic assistance to the islands, and spending on defense capabilities that could be used in the islands. He stresses the particular dilemmas facing New Zealand in promoting democratic development in the region without raising excessive expectations (or fears) of direct intervention. Henderson notes that of the three ANZUS states, New Zealand by virtue of size, location, and its Maori heritage identifies more with the islands than either of the others, and its position contrasts significantly with that of the United States with its global interests and multiple competing priorities.

Robert Kiste details the historical and prospective conflict between U.S. global priorities and island expectations. He notes that, of the three, U.S. relations with the islands are the most complex, involving at least three distinct groups of islands—the American flag territories, the (former) trust territories, and the other island states. Kiste traces the history of U.S. relations with all three groups from the time they were dominated by security considerations to increasing attention in the last 15 years. The most recent major event was the Summit meeting between President Bush and 11 island leaders in Honolulu in October 1990, which once again raised island expectations of American interest and attention. Again, the challenge to the American side is to live up to these expectations, which Kiste believes to date the United States has not done very well.

In the concluding comment, the editor notes that the political evolution of the Pacific Islands has been accompanied by the development of a more differentiated set of relationships and policies on the part of the three states. Despite substantial parallels in these policies, each government has its own particular historical and other interests in the island region and its own specific policy emphases. The policies of each are also influenced by differing national priorities and agendas. He does not foresee significant conflicts between the three governments over island issues, but concludes that closer coordination of their respective policies is not likely either.

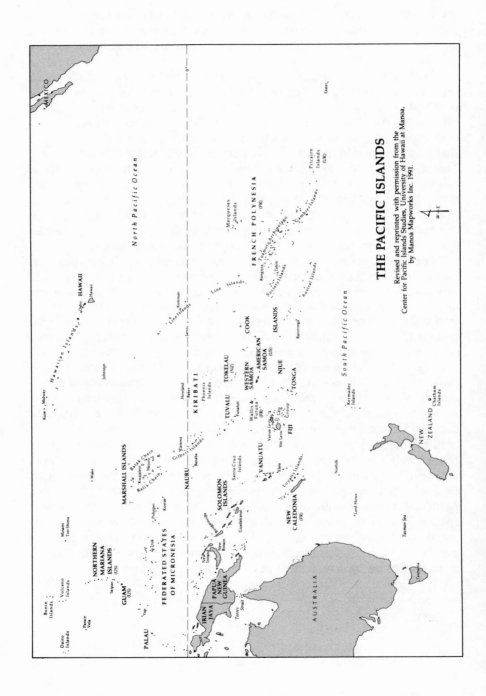

THE PACIFIC ISLANDS

Revised and reprinted with permission from the
Center for Pacific Islands Studies, University of Hawaii at Manoa,
by Manoa Mapworks Inc. 1991.

72

Political Status of Pacific Islands

Current or Former Colonial Power	Independent Nation[a]	Self-governing in Free Association[a]	Continued Dependent Status
New Zealand	*Western Samoa (1962)	Cook Is. (1965) Niue (1974)	Tokelau
United Kingdom	*Fiji (1970) Tonga[b] (1970) Tuvalu (1978) *Solomon Islands (1978) Kiribati (1979) *Vanuatu[c] (1980)		
Australia	Nauru (1968) *Papua New Guinea (1975)		
France	*Vanuatu[c] (1980)		French Polynesia New Caledonia Wallis & Futuna
United States		*Marshall Islands (1986) *Federated States of Micronesia (1986)	American Samoa Guam Commonwealth of No. Mariana Is. Palau

* = United Nations Member

Source: Michael P. Hamnett and Robert C. Kiste, "Issues and Interest Groups in the Pacific Islands," a study commissioned by the U.S. Information Agency (USIA), Research Office, December 1988, p. 10.

a. Years in parentheses indicate dates independence or free association was achieved.

b. Tonga signed a Treaty of Friendship and Protection with the United Kingdom in 1900, but was not administered as a colony. The United Kingdom oversaw Tonga's foreign affairs until 1970 when Tonga reentered the comity of nations.

c. Vanuatu appears twice in the list of independent nations as it was jointly ruled by the United Kingdom and France.

73

4

Australia and the Pacific Islands

STEWART FIRTH

A RISING PRIORITY

In recent years Australia has accorded a new priority to its relations with the countries of the South Pacific. When Senator Gareth Evans became minister for foreign affairs and trade in September 1988, he made his first overseas trip not to Japan, the United States, or Europe, but to the Pacific Islands — with the specific purpose of symbolizing that Australia intended to make its relationship with the region "our most immediate priority" (Fry 1991a: 131). Within weeks he made a major speech on "Australia in the South Pacific" and announced a new policy of "constructive commitment." Early in 1989, after three and a half years of deliberation, the Australian Parliament produced its comprehensive report, *Australia's Relations with the South Pacific*. The report was welcomed by the foreign minister on behalf of the government. It shared his view of the South Pacific as "clearly of the highest strategic significance to Australia" (Department of Foreign Affairs and Trade [DFAT] Cablegram 1989: 3).

Australia's defense White Paper of 1987 — signaling the most significant switch in Australian defense policy since the 1950s — had already included Papua New Guinea (PNG), New Zealand, and countries of the Southwest Pacific in Australia's area of direct military interest. During the following two years, the minister for defense repeatedly suggested that Australia should be prepared to exert its influence in this region, giving broad hints that he was not ruling out the possibility that, under special circumstances, military means might be used to achieve this objective (*The Defence of Australia 1987;* Cheeseman 1991: 87–88).

In December 1989, the foreign minister made a major statement on Australia's regional security in which all these themes were reiterated. Some observers suggested that the impetus for the regional security statement arose from a desire on the part of the Department of Foreign Affairs and

Trade to prevent the Department of Defence from determining the policy agenda on the South Pacific—a case of the diplomats competing with the military within the bureaucracy. But as Greg Fry has pointed out, events in the islands in the late 1980s were of sufficient concern to DFAT to have sparked a response in any case (Fry 1991a: 132). Coups in Fiji, riots in Vanuatu, tensions in New Caledonia, and secessionism in Papua New Guinea were enough to convince the Parliamentary Joint Committee on Foreign Affairs, Defence and Trade that "the Pacific is 'pacific' no more" (Australian Parliament 1989a: xxii).

Whether Evans's concept of constructive commitment represents a significant shift in Australian policy has been the subject of varying interpretations. In announcing the policy, Senator Evans stressed that two approaches to the South Pacific were now to be rejected as belonging to the past. The first was: "To act as the guardian of perceived Western alliance interests to deny access to the region by the Soviet Union or other countries potentially hostile to Australian interests, on the assumption that our interests are indistinguishable from general Western interests;" second: "To seek an independent position of dominance or hegemony as a proximate Western but essentially external power." In place of these outmoded policies of strategic denial and external domination was to come "a partnership with Pacific Island countries which promotes regional stability through economic development and the encouragement of shared perceptions of strategic and security interests" (DFAT *Backgrounder* 28 September 1988).

The Evans formulation did not offer anything new about what Australia wants. Australia has always wanted close relations with Pacific Island countries, effective regional institutions, stable economic development, and a common regional approach to security. On the face of things, though, constructive commitment seemed to augur a new sensitivity on Australia's part to the sovereign rights and claims of the independent Pacific Island states. Even the fact that Australia now had a policy with a name and comprehensively stated goals could be seen as evidence that it would devote more attention to the region.

Yet one critic finds in constructive commitment merely "a less extreme form of the (Australian) Monroe Doctrine" in the Pacific. He asks, who but Australia would have the greatest influence on shared South Pacific perceptions of regional security? Even the idea of regional security, he says, "is itself part of an attempt at Australian leadership or hegemony" (Fry 1991a: 129).

Others have found reason for reservations, not so much in the policy of constructive commitment itself as in its elaboration in the regional security statement of 1989, above all, in the paragraphs dealing with possible Australian military intervention in the South Pacific. These appear to suggest that while Australia's objectives in the South Pacific have not changed, a new element in Australian policy has emerged in the form of a willingness to contemplate military action "in pursuit of security interests not immediately affecting the defence of our national territory" (Evans 1989: para. 88). The issue was raised in the report of the Parliamentary Joint Committee on Foreign Affairs, Defence and Trade, which argued that "Australia is the major power in the South Pacific region, and is looked to by members of the Western alliance to maintain a favourable strategic environment in the region. . . . Should the strategic environment deteriorate, and Western interests be threatened, the ultimate method of influence would be to intervene militarily" (Australian Parliament 1989a: 152).

The committee envisaged the deployment of Australian defense personnel "in a security situation in the region" under two circumstances:

1. In defense of Australian nationals in danger in a country (involvement would be limited to securing their evacuation to safety)
2. Should an external country or group attempt to overthrow the elected government of one of the countries. (Australian Parliament 1989a: 153)

The regional security statement conceded frankly that, in considering the issue of military intervention, "We are effectively looking only at the South Pacific, where our military power is disproportionately large: our ability to undertake such initiatives in the countries of South East Asia will be very limited" (Evans 1989: para. 88; Piper 1990: 128). After disavowing any thought of "an Antipodean Brezhnev Doctrine for the South Pacific," the statement continued:

The use of military force may conceivably be appropriate, however, in unusual and extreme circumstances. While every situation needs to be treated on a case-by-case basis, there are certain cumulative criteria which suggest themselves, viz: the agreement of the recognized domestic authorities (except where an unfriendly government is supporting actions immediately detrimental to Australian nationals, e.g. hostage-taking); a manifestly direct threat to major Australian security interests; a finite time frame for the military operation; a clear and achievable operational objective; and consultation with, and if possible the cooperation and participation of, other states in the region. (Evans 1989: para. 90)

In Parliament, Senator Evans said that Australians "should not be embarrassed about using the military capability we possess, with prudence and sensitivity, to advance both Australia's and the common security of the region" (DFAT *Backgrounder* 15 December 1989).

ISLAND PROBLEMS

Two kinds of Pacific countries are subject to significant Australian and New Zealand influence: the smaller countries and microstates of Polynesia and Micronesia (Western Samoa, Tonga, Niue, the Cook Islands, Tokelau, Tuvalu, and Kiribati); and the countries to the west and in Melanesia with a greater resource base and with better long-term economic prospects (Fiji, Vanuatu, Solomon Islands, and Papua New Guinea).

For the small states, the principal security threats are economic, developmental, and environmental rather than political or military. Here modernization is advancing relentlessly. Work in the subsistence sector of the economy is losing prestige. Fewer and fewer young people are participating in it, and parents want their children to have white-collar employment, which generally means a government job. The effect of the young going to town is to place a heavy burden on those who stay behind in the village. Dependence on imported and processed food proceeds apace: Countries able to produce most of their food are importing most of it instead, and some younger people are going hungry because they do not know how to harvest or catch the traditional foods that surround them. Public funds tend to go to the production of export crops rather than food crops.

Emigration has become part of the way of life of Pacific Islanders in the small states and, through remittances, one of the underpinnings of fragile island economies. Children who go overseas and earn money are seen as the means by which parents can live a better life in the islands. In the Samoas, the Cook Islands, Tonga, Tuvalu, and Kiribati, emigration is almost expected of young people. Kinship groups in these islands have become accustomed to maximizing their economic opportunities in far-flung networks that incorporate New Zealand, Hawaii, California, and the east coast of Australia (Connell 1990). Just as foreign money sustains islanders in the private sphere, so the islanders depend on foreign development assistance in the public sphere. Under such circumstances, the business of governments becomes largely the business of aid: requesting, organizing, distributing, and being held responsible for it (Knapman 1986: 149).

Attempting to conceptualize what has happened in the Pacific microstates in the last 15 years, some scholars have argued that they are MIRAB economies, that is, characterized by *mi*gration, *re*mittances and *a*id, all of which goes to support bloated *b*ureaucracy in the public sector. Others have suggested MURAB might be an acronym that better catches the *u*rban bias of microstate "development," while another, stressing the importance of *g*overnment *e*mployment and the extraordinary artificiality of microstate economies, proposes MIRAGE (Connell 1991: 270). Whatever the preferred label, the microstates clearly face problems of security that derive from their smallness, lack of resources, and potentially permanent dependence on outside sources of support. In addition, those countries that partly or wholly consist of low-lying atolls rising only a few meters above the ocean face the prospect of flooding, contamination of underground water, and—if the most pessimistic predictions of scientists about global warning are borne out—complete inundation at some time in the future. Therefore, it is hardly surprising that the leaders of these countries, such as the former president of Kiribati, Ieremia Tabai, should have resented earlier Australian definitions of regional security that focused on external threats of the kind said to have been posed by the Soviet Union's fishing agreement with Kiribati in 1985–86 (Hegarty 1990: 422–23). Nor is it surprising that the question of fisheries in general should have been so high on the security agenda for the microstates.

Papua New Guinea, Solomon Islands, and Vanuatu are not MIRAB economies but, instead, countries with considerable agricultural, forest, and mineral resources, with the potential for becoming independent of aid. Their security problems, real and potential, are mostly different from those of the microstates.

Papua New Guinea shares a land border with Indonesia (the only land border in the region). In the mid-1980s, it had to deal with an influx of about 10,000 refugees and other border-crossers from the Indonesian province of Irian Jaya. A giant in the South Pacific, Papua New Guinea is a pygmy beside its Asian neighbor and has chosen never to offer assistance or encouragement to the independence movement in Irian Jaya. Cooperation with Indonesia has been the policy of successive governments in Port Moresby, an approach that is now enshrined in the 1987 Treaty of Mutual Respect, Friendship, and Cooperation between the two states. Papua New Guinea signed the Treaty of Amity and Cooperation in Southeast Asia in 1989, extending the same cooperative security approach to its relations with all the ASEAN states. In 1991, it entered a defense cooperation arrangement with Malaysia (Henningham 1991: 19). The 1987 Joint Declaration of Principles guiding relations between Australia and Papua New Guinea has provided a firmer basis than before for defense cooperation between Australia and its former colonial territory. Together, as Edward Wolfers has said, these agreements "constitute a network of commitments, of varying legal force, to mutual respect for national sovereignty, to cooperation, and to peaceful resolution of disputes which Papua New Guinea has constructed in its immediate neighbourhood" (Wolfers 1991: 79).

As Rabbie Namaliu, later prime minister of PNG, presciently observed in 1983, the most likely security risk in the South Pacific would come not from external powers but from domestic internal threats to particular states (Australian Parliament 1989a: 149). His own country has proved him right. In March 1988 the complaints of the traditional landowners at Panguna against Bougainville Copper Limited seemed extravagant but negotiable; by the end of 1988, the landowners' leader, Francis Ona, was leading his followers in a campaign of sabotage against the copper company; by mid-1989, the mine, which at that time accounted for 37 percent of PNG's foreign exchange earnings, had been forced to close; and by the early months of 1990, the Papua New Guinea Defense Force (PNGDF). was in action against the forces of what was now called the Bougainville Revolutionary Army. The PNGDF was flying four Iroquois helicopters in Bougainville, supplied by Australia on condition that they not be used as gunships though, as we now know by the admission of the former military commander in June 1991, the helicopters were, in fact, equipped with machine guns (Australian Broadcasting Corporation 1991). Within a few months the PNGDF withdrew from Bougainville, though not before hardening Bougainvilleans' opinion against the central government by conducting an ill-disciplined series of sorties through parts of the province.

Bougainville declared independence in May 1990. The international community completely ignored it. As people on the island began to suffer from lack of central government health and education services, the Bougainville Revolutionary Army (BRA) leaders were driven to negotiate with the national government in Port Moresby. But two agreements, the first reached in August 1990 and the second in January 1991, failed to settle the fundamental dispute over legal authority on the island. Over the next two years, with talks between the two sides at a stalemate, the PNGDF gradually reoccupied much of the territory previously held by the BRA, and by most accounts many villagers in Buka, north Bougainville, and south Bougainville welcomed the return of the national government and its services. Outside central Bougainville, the site of the copper mine, people seem to have lost their enthusiasm for independence. By 1993 the PNG government, now led by Prime Minister Paias Wingti, was claiming to have captured the rebel stronghold of Arawa, a coastal township close to the copper mine (*Sydney Morning Herald* 16 February 1993). Eager to inflict a final military defeat on the rebels, Wingti was leaving further negotiations over the future of Bougainville until later.

In the meantime, public concern in Australia about the loss of life on Bougainville prompted Canberra to fund a medical relief program for the province and provide assistance to the Red Cross (DFAT *Monthly Record* November-December 1991: 797–98). Senator Evans saw Australia's role in the conflict as one of:

> being helpful but not over-intrusive. The use of Australian materiel on Bougainville, including helicopters—supplied in accordance with the defence cooperation arrangements between the two countries—inevitably generated a hostile reaction from some Bougainvilleans and their supporters. But our attempts to set restraints on the military use of some of that equipment, and our reluctance to become involved in any more direct way, was equally the subject of some criticism from other quarters. (Evans and Grant 1991: 171–72)

Sooner or later, the Bougainville problem will need a political solution, perhaps one that is linked to the Wingti government's plans to reform PNG's unwieldy system of 19 provincial governments.

Bougainville is not PNG's only problem of internal security. Resource projects in other parts of the country, such as the alluvial gold mine at Mt. Kare, have been subject to armed attack, and in the towns lawlessness is on an unprecedented scale. Under an agreement on security cooperation signed by Australia and Papua New Guinea in 1991, Australia is giving PNG extra equipment, training, and infrastructure for both the Royal PNG Constabulary and the PNGDF (DFAT *Backgrounder* 27 September 1991). At the Papua New Guinea–Australian Ministerial Forum in February 1992, the PNG delegation gave assurances of "a renewed commitment by Papua New Guinea to the importance of establishing a coordinated approach to tackling its internal security needs," and Australia announced that it would pay for 150 police houses throughout the country (DFAT *Backgrounder* 28 February 1992).

The political crisis in Vanuatu in May 1988 was sparked by conflict between the national government and an organized group of landowners whose land lies within the capital city of Port Vila. Riots occurred, and the rioters were dispersed with the help of Australian equipment which Father Walter Lini, the prime minister, had requested. In September 1991, Father Lini was defeated in a parliamentary vote of no confidence and replaced as prime minister by his former foreign minister, Donald Kalpokas. While debate raged in Vila over which party was the true Vanua'aku Pati—the organization having split in August 1991—and while police raided the houses of senior public servants and politicians, the transfer of power was accomplished peacefully and constitutionally. There seemed every prospect that the elections for a new Parliament would proceed later in the year with equal respect for the law (Radio Australia South Pacific News Service [RASPNS] 12, 13, 16 September 1991). In the national elections of December 1991 the divided Vanua'aku party presented itself to the electors in two forms, one led by Lini and the other by Kalpokas, and lost office altogether. The new government of Maxime Carlot brought francophone interests to office for the first time and heralded the end of the Vanua'aku party as the dominant force in the country's politics (Steeves 1992: 217–28).

Bougainville, an internal problem, has dominated the security agenda in Papua New Guinea for three years (May and Spriggs 1990). The roots of secessionism in PNG lie not merely in the history of mining investment and local particularism in Bougainville, but, more broadly, in the very construction of PNG as a sovereign state. Papua New Guinea is a highly artificial nation, the product of borders drawn by the colonizers around different parts of the Melanesia culture area, with a weak natural potential for legitimacy on the basis of shared national consciousness. The same is true of Vanuatu, which successfully resisted the attempted secession of the island of Santo at the time of independence in 1980, and of Solomon Islands.

The three independent Melanesian states therefore have a greater potential than other island countries for becoming the Pacific equivalents of Africa's "weak states," where central governments claim authority over territorial areas without actually exercising sovereignty. They may become states that are increasingly sustained from without, both by civil and military aid, while being undermined from within. Yet the problems of the Melanesian countries should be seen in perspective. Papua New Guinea began producing oil in 1992 and at Porgera it has the largest gold mine outside of South Africa. With rich mineral deposits newly discovered, PNG might well stand at the threshold of a new era of prosperity in which Bougainvillean secessionism, tragic though its consequences in loss of life have so far been, will not significantly disrupt the nation's development. Solomon Islands remains a functioning constitutional democracy. The politics of Vanuatu, while robustly conducted, remain within constitutional bounds with no sign of national disintegration or a resurgence of earlier secessionism. Much will depend in all three countries on the degree to which national elites can resist the kind of corruption of which Deputy Prime Minister Ted Diro of PNG was found guilty in 1991, and which threatens to undermine confidence in national government and institutions.

Fiji is a special case. It has the most developed export economy in the South Pacific, the second largest population, the least dependence on development assistance, and — since the military coups of 1987 — the greatest determination to diversify its sources of aid, trade, and investment so as to modify traditional dependence on Australia and New Zealand. For example, in 1991 the Fiji government established the Fiji National Petroleum Company to import oil at what it claimed would be cheaper prices than had been charged for oil from Australia (*Sydney Morning Herald* 30 July 1990; *Pacific Report* 19 September 1991) and announced that it would buy four patrol boats from Israel rather than wait for a resumption of defense links with Australia (RASPNS 2 August 1991). The impetus for this determination derives from the initially hostile reaction to the Fiji coups on the part of Australia and New Zealand (Alley 1990).

With a new constitution designed to ensure that ethnic Fijians dominate, Fiji remains divided not only between ethnic Fijians and Indians, but also between urban and rural dwellers, trade unionists and employers, farmers and the Fiji Sugar Corporation, and Fijians of east and west. For example, 1991 was a year of sugar boycotts by farmers, a six-month strike by workers at the Australian-owned Emperor gold mine, and continuing uncertainty over the operation of the new constitution. However, the election of 1992 confounded those who had predicted a further descent into political intransigence in Fiji. Sitiveni Rabuka, the army officer who mounted the coup of 1987 in order to stop Fiji Indians from holding power, became Prime Minister with the parliamentary support of the thirteen Indian members of the Fiji Labour Party — the same party he had once vowed to frustrate at all costs. In a remarkable volte-face, he promised concessions to organized labor, an extension of land leases, and a review of the constitution. By the end of 1992, he was proposing that the 27 Indian members of Parliament should join him in a government of national unity (*Islands Business* December 1992). Australia welcomed these developments and resumed defense cooperation with Figi.

AUSTRALIAN POLICIES

Security problems of the kind typically confronting the smaller countries and microstates—those defined in economic, developmental and environmental terms—are, in the view of the Australian government, to be approached as in the past: with a traditional mixture of foreign aid, regional cooperation, and where appropriate, diplomatic intervention on the islands' side. Australia's own security can only benefit from such a policy mix, in the Canberra view. "Australian development assistance policies support strategic and defence policy objectives in the region," according to a Defence Department document of 1987: "Where aspirations can be assisted and economic development supported, the ensuing political stability is an important strategic asset. Such considerations are of particular relevance in the South Pacific where strategic considerations are heavily influenced by the economic security of the island countries" (Department of Defence 1987b: 7).

Australia gives far more aid to the South Pacific on a per capita basis than it does to other countries. Its focus on this part of the world dates from the mid-1970s, when Canberra became aware that the process of decolonizing island states held distinct strategic implications. By 1980, nine new sovereign states had come into being in the South Pacific, each capable of determining its own international alignment.

As a direct response to this new situation, Australia became a major aid donor—not only to PNG, something which was to be expected—but to the rest of the South Pacific as well, overtaking first New Zealand in this role and then, in 1983, Britain as well (Australian International Development Assistance Bureau [AIDAB] 1987: 43). The island states benefited from their smallness, which attracts aid, and from their strategic importance. During 1990–91, Australia gave A$453.6 million in aid to the whole of the South Pacific out of a total aid budget, including global programs, of A$1,330 million. As a proportion of Australia's expenditure on country programs of A$772 million, the South Pacific's allocation amounted to 59 percent (*Australia's Overseas Aid Program 1992–93:* 12–13).

No South Pacific country is strategically more vital to Australia than Papua New Guinea. Developments in PNG, as Senator Evans said in 1991, would "continue to have a particular significance for Australia's security, requiring a sustained and sensitive Australian policy response" (DFAT *Monthly Record* July 1991: 400). Australian aid policy has long reflected

Table 4.1. Australian Development Assistance to Papua New Guinea, Fiscal Years 1988–89 to 1992–93 (in A$million and as a percentage of all Australian aid)

Fiscal Year	Total Aid		Country Program Aid[a]	
	Amount	Percentage	Amount	Percentage[b]
1988–89	314.1	26.3	304.2	42
1989–90	337.8	28.8	327.8	44
1990–91	333.1	26.4	322.7	44
1991–92	335.0	25.0	323.3	42
1992–93 (est.)	333.3	24.0	322.3	40.0

Source: *Australia's Overseas Aid Program 1992–93*, pp. 12–13.
a. Excludes aid given via regional organizations.
b. Percentage of total country program aid.

this assessment, with at least one-quarter of all Australia's aid going to its former territory annually. By 1994, Australia's aid to PNG since independence in 1975 will have reached A$5.2 billion, 90 percent of it in the form of a direct, untied subsidy to the PNG national budget. PNG's dependence on this massive bilateral aid flow has gradually diminished as resource projects have come into operation, however, and the Wingti government elected in 1992 has accepted that direct budgetary aid from Australia will be phased out by the year 2000. From now on, the focus in Australian assistance will be increasingly on program aid in education, law enforcement, health, agriculture, and infrastructure, enabling Australia to exercise greater supervision of aid expenditure (DFAT *Insight* 14 December 1992: 12–13). The recent picture of Australian development assistance to PNG is shown in Table 4.1.

Until the mid-1990s, Australian aid to PNG is determined by the Treaty on Development Cooperation of 24 May 1989, which assures PNG of budget support of A$275 million a year until 1993–94, when it will fall to A$260 million (*Australia's Overseas Aid Program 1990–91:* 20). In the very month when the Australian and PNG governments signed the treaty, the Bougainville copper mine was forced to close because of sabotage by the Bougainville Revolutionary Army. At the second Australia–Papua New Guinea ministerial forum, held in Port Moresby in January 1990, the PNG government asked Australia for additional budgetary support after the closure of the mine had led to the devaluation of the kina and a K100 million cut in government expenditure (DFAT *Backgrounder* 26 January 1990). Under the new arrangements, Australia gave PNG an extra A$20 million in the two years 1989–91.

Australia's aid to the rest of the South Pacific, shown in Table 4.2, is much less in absolute terms than that to PNG, but is nevertheless highly significant for small island economies. As well as bilateral country programs,

Table 4.2. Australian Development Assistance to the South Pacific Excluding Papua New Guinea, Fiscal Years 1988-89 to 1992-93 (in A$millions and as a percentage of all Australian aid)

	1988-89	1989-90	1990-91	1991-92	1992-93[a]
Total aid:					
Amount	107.8	108.0	109.0	118.6	120.4
Percentage	9.0	9.2	8.6	8.9	8.7
Country program aid:[b]					
Amount	88.9	84.4	87.9	90.8	91.9
Percentage[c]	12.4	11.3	12.0	11.8	11.5
By country:[d]					
Fiji	16.8	12.8	13.8	14.3	14.4
Solomon Islands	8.6	9.5	10.3	10.6	10.8
Vanuatu	14.1	9.5	10.2	10.1	10.8
Western Samoa	7.8	8.2	8.8	11.4	9.3
Tonga	7.5	7.5	7.7	8.1	8.4
Kiribati	3.1	3.3	2.4	3.5	3.5
Tuvalu	1.3	1.4	1.9	2.3	1.8
Micronesia	0.8	1.0	1.3	1.0	1.4
Cook Islands	0.9	1.0	1.1	1.1	1.2
Niue and Tokelau	0.3	0.5	0.5	0.7	0.6
New Caledonia	0.0	0.0	0.2	0.4	0.6
Total	61.2	54.7	58.2	63.5	62.8

Source: Australia's Overseas Aid Program 1992-93, pp. 12-13, 23.

a. Figures for 1992-93 are estimates.

b. Includes aid given via regional organizations.

c. Percentage of total country program aid.

d. Excludes aid given via regional organizatons.

Australia gives aid on a multicountry basis in areas such as health, education, and environmental monitoring. Under the Special Environmental Assistance Program, for example, Australia is monitoring the possible consequences of the greenhouse effect for South Pacific climates and sea-levels. Australia contributes substantially to almost all the regional organizations now brought under the umbrella of the new South Pacific Organizations Coordinating Committee: the South Pacific Commission, the Forum Secretariat, the Forum Fisheries Agency, the South Pacific Applied Geoscience Commission, the University of the South Pacific, the South Pacific Regional Environment Program, and the Pacific Islands Development Program.

Australia supplements its civil aid with diplomatic initiatives on island issues, and with aid under the defense cooperation program. Probably no regional issue mattered more to Pacific Island nations during the 1980s than fisheries access. The dramatic seizure of the American purse seiner *Jeanette Diana* by Solomon Islands in 1984 was merely the best known expression of widespread concern in the islands about the unwillingness of the United States to recognize the jurisdiction of coastal states over tuna. Australia responded by urging the Americans to take action to restore their damaged reputation in the region and by negotiating alongside other South Pacific Forum countries with the United States. The Multilateral Treaty on Fisheries, which became United States law in 1988, was the successful outcome to these negotiations, providing for American tuna boats to purchase regional fishing licenses and for the U.S. government to give US$10 million annually over five years to 14 of the 17 countries that are parties to the treaty (the other three being Australia, New Zealand, and the United States). The Pacific Patrol Boat Program under which Australia is providing 14 patrol boats to eight South Pacific states represents, among other things, an attempt to arm small island countries with the means of economic defense by enabling them to conduct surveillance of their Exclusive Economic Zones. This is the largest Australian defense assistance project ever undertaken (Australian Parliament 1989a: 156–60).

The security problems of Papua New Guinea, Fiji, and Vanuatu, at least as defined in Canberra, are those that have elicited consideration of new military options in the Australian response to events in the islands. Both the first Fiji coup of 1987 and the Port Vila riots of 1988 prompted Australia to plan military action, to supply equipment for controlling rioters (in the second case), and to place the Operational Deployment Force on alert (Henningham 1991: 23). By the time the regional security statement appeared at the end of 1989, the copper mine in Bougainville had been closed down by secessionist rebels and the Bougainville Revolutionary Army was effectively in control of Papua New Guinea's richest province. Under these circumstances, the regional security statement represented an attempt to articulate a clear policy on possibilities that had been under discussion in Canberra for a couple of years (Fry 1990: 10).

To one body of academic opinion in Australia, the statement seemed to signify a new Australian militarism based on a dangerous misconception of the country's true security needs (Cheeseman and Kettle 1990). Critics in this camp pointed to the fact that the 1986 review of Australia's defense capabilities by Paul Dibb (see Chapter 1) had recommended that the Australian Defence Force be restructured to defend the Australian continent and its maritime surrounds. The old policy of forward defense, expressed in the deployment, for example, of much of Australia's force of F-111 fighter aircraft in Malaysia, was finally to be abandoned and replaced by defense of the continent. In the Dibb review and in the defense White Paper that adopted many of its recommendations — the critics argued — new principles of "defense self-reliance" and "defense in depth" had promised a revolution in Australian defense thinking; yet those same principles were soon being invoked to justify a policy that perpetuated the older tradition of Australian military intervention overseas, with a specific and stated focus on the South Pacific. The critics said it was as if forward defense had been resurrected in a new form and they adduced as evidence the expanded definition that the defense minister of the time, Kim Beazley, was giving to Australia's area of direct military interest. According to Beazley, it was

> an important feature of Australia's strategic circumstances that the forces we need to defend our own territory are well-suited to a broader role if necessary. This is because our area of direct military interest, which defines the ADF's requirements for the defence of Australia, is so large that the capabilities we develop to meet those requirements tend to have sufficient mobility to be deployed widely throughout South-East Asia and the South West Pacific if we wish. (Cheeseman and Kettle 1990: 214)

In the view of the proponents of the "new militarism" thesis, the narrower role envisaged for the Australian Defence Force by Dibb in 1986 had become the broader role of the early 1990s, and the South Pacific was where it would be played. Among the possible outcomes of Australia's new regional policy, Graeme Cheeseman, an analyst with defense department experience, foresaw "the promotion of expensive regional arms races, involvement in third party conflicts, and the undermining of our own force posture" (Cheeseman 1991: 88).

The Australian government has rejected these criticisms. Foreign Minister Evans sees himself not as pushing for new military initiatives in the South Pacific but rather as steering a "balanced middle course" between those who oppose military intervention under any circumstances and those, presumably in the Department of Defence, who "are already comfortable with the idea of Australian military intervention in a range of situations" (Evans 1991a: 149). Far from smoothing the way for use of the military instrument, Senator Evans believes he is placing valuable constraints and limitations on it by defining a policy and urging caution. In a similar vein, one academic observer with foreign policy experience says that Australia in the 1990s will have "appropriate military capabilities which . . . may never be committed in any extensive way, but which should provide some reassurance to PICs [Pacific Island countries] about the maintenance of their sovereignty and resources, and discourage the establishment of alternative security links" (Piper 1991: 229).

In this policy, Australia is working in tandem with New Zealand where, as described in Chapters 2 and 5 of this volume, defense policy specifically shifted to a focus on the South Pacific following the defense review of 1987. Eager to show Washington that its nuclear ship visits ban did not signify diminished commitment to Western interests, New Zealand, under the Labour government of David Lange and his successors, and (since October 1990) the National Party government of Prime Minister Jim Bolger, has articulated an islands-centered defense policy which has brought "an increasing amount of cooperation and consultation (with Australia) . . . concerning possible deployments in the South Pacific" (Fry 1990: 11). The ANZUS crisis and the withdrawal of the U.S. security guarantee to New Zealand has had the effect of encouraging an affinity of approach to military matters in the South Pacific on the part of the two ANZAC countries.

CONSTRAINTS

A number of constraints operate on Australian policy toward the Pacific Islands. One derives from Pacific Island opinion. On issues such as French nuclear testing, fisheries access, driftnetting, and the decolonization of New Caledonia Australia has sought to identify with island opinion and present itself as a country which not only sides with the region but is part of it. The Fiji coups, however, presented Canberra with an issue on which it clearly disagreed both with the interim Fiji government and with other island nations. As a gesture of support for the deposed coalition government of Dr. Timoci Bavadra, Australia blocked the flow of Australian aid to Fiji for almost a year and then attached human rights conditions to a special assistance program. When Senator Gareth Evans criticized Fiji's new constitution in November 1990, he was declared persona non grata in that country, but by mid-1991 he was urging Fiji's opposition parties to participate in the 1992 elections. He said, "What is important is to restore at least a semblance of democratic practice, to take an important step back towards a proper, elected democratic government" (RASPNS 31 July 1991). The rapprochement between Fiji and Australia was symbolized by an invitation from Fiji Prime Minister Ratu Sir Kamisese Mara for Senator Evans to visit his country later in 1991, and has been confirmed since the election of Sitiveni Rabuka as Prime Minister in 1992.

In reacting to developments in Fiji since 1987, Australia has sought, on the one hand, to assert its commitment to democratic principles of government, while at the same time attempting to preserve its influence in the South Pacific by identifying with island opinion. Island leaders were uniformly sympathetic to the Fiji coup, in private if not in public, and their views, according to Senator Evans, formed "a very significant constraint in Australia's response to the evolving situation" (DFAT *Backgrounder* 7 December 1988). Between 1987 and 1993, Australia's position shifted from indignation over the coups to qualified acceptance.

A second kind of constraint arises from conflict between wider foreign policy commitments of Australia, which is more than a Pacific state, and the more immediate concerns of island countries. At the 1990 South Pacific Forum meeting, for example, Australia supported U.S. plans to store and destroy 400 tons of nerve gas on Johnston Atoll against the stated objections of island leaders, for whom the issue was far more one of keeping a clean environment than of taking a step toward global arms control. But Australia, a leading proponent of chemical weapons control, was committed to favoring "peace" over "green" when the two were at odds.

More generally, the ANZUS alliance between Australia and the United States forms the strategic background against which Australian policy is played out. Even those regional issues on which the two countries have disagreed have been handled firmly within the framework of the alliance. While "Australia's interest is not served by perceptions that Australia is acting as a US proxy in the region," as the Department of Foreign Affairs (DFA) observed in 1987 (DFA 1987: 68), Australian policymakers share American views of the kind of regional consensus on security that is desirable. It may be that, on certain issues, Australian policymakers think their expertise in regional sensitivities enables them to protect U.S. interests in the South Pacific better than the Americans themselves. Such was the case when the Australians urged the Americans to do something about their tuna boats in the South Pacific before their regional reputation was further tarnished; so it was, too, with the South Pacific Nuclear Free Zone (SPNFZ) treaty, initiated and negotiated by Australia with the express purpose of channeling "the efforts of the Forum into a constructive program" (U.S. Congress, House Armed Services Committee 1986; quoted in Hamel-Green 1990: 61). Sensing the possible radicalism of South Pacific antinuclear sentiment in the early 1980s, Australia sought to construct a regional treaty that would address the islanders' main concern — French nuclear testing at Moruroa Atoll — without damaging U.S. strategic interests in the process.

A third kind of constraint is electoral and political. Australia championed the SPNFZ treaty with such vigor, partly for domestic political reasons that had nothing to do with the South Pacific. Antinuclear sentiment within the Australian Labor Party (ALP) and in the Australian electorate at large reached its peak during the first and second Hawke Labor governments (1983–87). In the 1984 national election the newly formed Nuclear Disarmament Party gained two seats in the Senate, compelling the ALP to emphasize its own antinuclear credentials so as to shore up its support from the left of the political spectrum. For these reasons and because Australia dominated the treaty-making process, the Melanesian states have not regarded the treaty as a truly regional initiative.

QUESTIONS

A number of questions about Australia's response to the security problems of the islands suggest themselves from this analysis. The first is whether Australia is right to assume that aid or even regional cooperation automatically produces political stability and a shared regional consensus on security. The record of aid in producing economic growth in the island states, after all, is not encouraging. As the Fiji coups showed, even the most sophisticated and economically advanced of Pacific Island countries can be subject to political upheaval that derives from their own unique historical experience. The particularities of island history may produce changes that no standardized categorization of island economies could ever have predicted: The coming of universal suffrage to Western Samoa in 1990 and the growing pressure for democratization in Tonga are possible examples. Beyond that are the political strains that arise from "development" itself, particularly from widening gaps in the distribution of resources. To repeat an old refrain in the Pacific: What is "development" for?

The second question is how Australia ought to respond to developments such as the secessionist movement in Bougainville and, in particular, to requests by Pacific governments for military assistance in internal problems. Senator Evans's "cumulative criteria" of justification for Australian military intervention are an attempt to answer precisely this question but, framed in general terms as they must inevitably be, they have left the real decision to policymakers confronted with a future crisis, as the minister himself recognizes (Evans 1991a: 149). The best that can be said is that the special circumstances of the Pacific might call for what Peter King has called "unconventional wisdom," a willingness to contemplate a compact of free association between Bougainville and PNG if that promises to be a peaceful and stable solution to a seemingly intractable problem (King 1990). As the last place on earth to be visited with the benefits of the sovereign state, Melanesia might have to be among the first to blaze the way for new ideas about semi-sovereignty. Australia should be ready to encourage such solutions.

A final question is whether Australia should so readily identify particular security problems in island countries as general and regional ones. The era of seeing the security problems of the South Pacific as coming essentially from outside the region is over; the era of seeing a regional threat in the internal difficulties of island countries is just beginning. Yet the Fiji coups suggest that one country can change in the region without any of the others changing. It might be appropriate, therefore, to pause and consider the degree to which the South Pacific is not a region, and to contemplate an approach to regional security that does not tempt Australia into unfortunate entanglements.

ACKNOWLEDGMENTS

I would like to acknowledge the generous assistance in preparing this chapter of Robert Tulip, Lindsay Shepherd, and Greg Hancock of the Pacific Regional Team, AIDAB Center for Pacific Development and Training, Mosman, NSW, and of Greg Fry of the Australian National University (ANU). However, none should be held responsible for the opinions, which are my own.

5

New Zealand's Policy toward the Pacific Islands

JOHN HENDERSON

For the purposes of this study, the change of government in New Zealand in 1990 provided a very timely illustration of both the differences in approach and the elements of consensus in present-day national politics on New Zealand's relations with and appropriate policies toward the Pacific Island region. Labour Party governments have generally given considerable emphasis to the need for New Zealand to develop closer relations with its Pacific neighborhood. As the 1990 South Pacific Policy Review report demonstrated, this commitment has been stronger in rhetoric than in action (South Pacific Policy Review Group [SPPR] 1990). The emphasis of past National Party governments has been more on the need to maintain good relations with large traditional allies, especially the United States, United Kingdom, and Australia. However, in practice, National's more pragmatic approach to foreign policy helped New Zealand through the difficult adjustment in regional relationships brought about by the Fiji military coups.

This chapter seeks to put the question of the impact of the change of government into a wider perspective by looking first at the place of the Pacific Islands in New Zealand's foreign policy in recent years. An analysis will then be made of the major issues facing the region, New Zealand's record to date, and future options for helping to meet these problems. Pacific Island attitudes toward New Zealand will also be reviewed. Finally, a brief New Zealand perspective on the appropriate roles in the Pacific Island region for Australia and the United States will be provided.

NEW ZEALAND INTERESTS IN THE PACIFIC ISLANDS

The Pacific Island region is important to New Zealand in several ways. It is important in *diplomatic* terms because it encompasses a neighborhood of

13 independent or self-governing countries. New Zealand is represented by diplomatic missions in 10 of these countries. This represents about one-fifth of New Zealand's overseas representation — in itself a measure of the region's importance. However, the 1990 policy review expressed concern that the number of New Zealand diplomats posted to the region had been cut back from 39 to 34 (SPPR 1990: 29).

In *security* terms the South Pacific was made the official focus of New Zealand's defense policy by the Labour government's 1987 defense review. Although previous reviews had also stressed the importance of the South Pacific, in practice, the focus was with the ANZUS alliance relationship. In this regard, the 1987 review marked a fundamental turning point in New Zealand's defense thinking. No longer would the armed forces be prepared with service in large allied forces primarily in mind. The armed forces now had a mission they could prepare for much closer to home: the security of the South Pacific. While it was acknowledged that this task would be undertaken in cooperation with Australia, New Zealand forces were expected for the first time to develop a self-reliant defense capability.

Developments since the publication of the defense review, such as the Fiji coups, have pointed to the need for New Zealand to acquire and maintain the capabilities necessary to meet the new policy objectives. While the need has grown, the defense budget has been cut, and key items of equipment required to implement the findings of the review, such as the logistic support ship, have been deferred. Meanwhile, the armed forces' limited resources have been further stretched by a number of United Nations peacekeeping operations far beyond the South Pacific.

The *economic* significance of the region is small in terms of New Zealand's overall trading interests. In 1992, exports to the islands amounted to NZ$640.2 million, just 3.57 percent of New Zealand's exports; imports totaled NZ$110 million, or 0.8 percent of overall imports. However, these figures also show that New Zealand enjoys a very favorable balance of trade with the islands. Furthermore, the region's importance in comparative terms should not be underrated. Export earnings from the islands are currently higher than returns from Eastern Europe, including the former Soviet Union, and similar to returns from the Middle East. Exports to Fiji (NZ$178.5 million in 1992) are greater than those to the Philippines or Thailand.

A further indicator of the importance of the region is the amount of development assistance provided by New Zealand. The Pacific Island countries are the major recipients of New Zealand aid. During the 1989–90 period the region received NZ$74 million or over half of total New Zealand overseas development assistance (ODA). But about one-third of this assistance is paid to just three countries, the Cook Islands, Niue, and Tokelau, for which New Zealand continues to retain constitutional responsibility. Also, the level of New Zealand ODA has been declining, and New Zealand's aid to the region is now significantly below that of both Japan and Australia.

These are the basic facts of the relationship. In each case there are signs that problems are being encountered in meeting the expectations fostered by successive New Zealand governments. To understand why this is the case, a closer look will now be taken at the views of New Zealand's politicians and the public, the problems the region faces, and New Zealand's ability to help.

POLITICAL PERSPECTIVES

At the political level there has been strong bipartisan support for according the South Pacific a high priority in New Zealand foreign policy. Labour Party leaders have seen a stronger regional role as an important part of developing a more independent foreign policy. In 1971, Norman Kirk, then leader of the opposition, called for the formation of a Pacific Council made of representatives of the parliaments of the region (Kirk 1971: 13). As prime minister (1972–74), Kirk gave New Zealand foreign policy a more independent and regional focus. David Lange (prime minister 1984–89) spoke warmly of "an identity of interest with our smaller neighbors on issues ranging from nuclear testing to fisheries, decolonization and trade," and proclaimed: "We now not only accept but celebrate what the map tells us—that we are a South Pacific nation" (Lange 1987: 5–6). Mike Moore (Labour prime minister for just two months prior to the October 1990 election and leader of the opposition thereafter) has been a strong supporter of following through on Kirk's suggestion of establishing a Pacific parliament (Moore 1982).

But Labour has not always put into practice this rhetorical enthusiasm. While Labour prime ministers David Lange and Geoffrey Palmer both spent significant periods of time in the region, it is noteworthy that Mike Moore, who served as minister of overseas trade throughout Labour's 1984–90 period in government, only visited the region twice during that period and then for very short periods. Like most of his ministerial and parliamentary colleagues, Moore's preferred destinations were further afield in Europe, North America, and Asia.

The Labour government's lukewarm response to the recommendations of the 1990 South Pacific Policy Review commissioned by Prime Minister Geoffrey Palmer called into question its willingness to go beyond rhetoric and take action. (As the chairperson of the review group, the author admits to a direct interest in this assessment.) The reasons for the Labour government's failure to implement much of the report relate partly to the short time available between the report's presentation in May 1990 and the October election. Much of this time was taken up by the internal party struggles that saw Moore replace Palmer as prime minister two months before the election.

The report was mildly critical of the Ministry of External Relations and Trade, and this may account for the lack of enthusiasm on the part of some officials. The reaction from Pacific Island governments to the report (tabled at the 1990 meeting of the South Pacific Forum in Vanuatu) was, by contrast, very positive. The fact that the review group visited each Pacific Island country to learn their concerns first hand was particularly welcomed. The report was very heavily based on these views of Pacific Island government and community and private sector leadership, which also gave it authority as well as standing with the islanders. But Pacific Island governments were looking for a lead from the New Zealand government before speaking out publicly. This lead was not forthcoming from Prime Minister Palmer.

The New Zealand government did accept the review's recommendation calling for a greater regional approach to resolving environmental problems. These proposals were subsequently endorsed by the South Pacific Forum. But the government took no action on other recommendations that would have given substance to the theme of the report: that New Zealand should play an active role in fostering a Pacific Island community. This would have required endorsement of an active policy of promoting regionalism by strengthening the South Pacific Forum to become the paramount regional organization, and initiating the process that could lead to the establishment of a Pacific parliament. In the expenditure area, the report called for increased levels of diplomatic representation and development assistance and an end to cuts in departmental expenditure (including defense) that had impacted negatively on Pacific Island countries. In the politically difficult area of immigration, the report sought a commitment to maintain traditional levels of immigration from Pacific Island countries.

The most immediately controversial recommendation coming out of the report called for the restoration of ministerial contact with Fiji (which had been broken as a result of the 1987 military coups). Palmer initially accepted this recommendation and agreed to send a junior minister to Fiji, but the plans were not followed through. The reasons appear to be that the announcement generated strong public opposition in New Zealand, and Fiji desired to have a visit from a more senior minister.

Unlike other recent elections that have been dominated by Labour's antinuclear stance, foreign policy issues were hardly featured in the 1990 campaign. National, in effect, had adopted Labour's antinuclear policy, producing, to quote National Leader Jim Bolger, a "new bipartisan commitment to keep nuclear weapons out of New Zealand" (Bolger 1990: 10).

In announcing his party's foreign policy during the election campaign, Bolger made warm reference to the South Pacific, which he referred to as "New Zealand's area of immediate strategic and political concern." He held out the prospect of increased levels of aid. "Under National we will provide help and assistance to the greatest extent possible to our Pacific Island friends. Not only do they live in our strategic area, but because of significant migration from the Pacific to New Zealand, Pacific Islanders are now a significant minority group within New Zealand itself. They are making a contribution to New Zealand in a wide range of areas. Their contribution is most welcome" (Bolger 1990).

Bolger sought to draw a distinction with the Labour government by adding that he rejected the notion that New Zealand was "only a South Pacific nation." (In fact Labour never claimed this to be the case.) "I advance instead the view that we are a Pacific nation which through background, culture and trade has not only Pacific interests, but also global interests" (Bolger 1990: 9).

The same themes were developed in comments made after the election by National Party deputy leader Don McKinnon, who was appointed to the external relations and trade portfolio. McKinnon expressed concern that New Zealand foreign policy had become too "parochial" (*Dominion* 3 November 1980), and that he did not intend to implement the recommendations of Labour's South Pacific policy review, which he dismissed as "philosophical." But of the review's 62 recommendations McKinnon publicly disagreed with only two: liberalizing the provisions on rules of origin under New Zealand's preferential trade agreement with the islands and increasing development assistance. He quickly moved on the key recommendation to restore high level ministerial contact with Fiji, meeting with Prime Minister Ratu Mara and resuming military assistance. He also echoed the review's concern that New Zealand influence in the region is diminishing while the efforts of Australia, Japan, and the United States are increasing (*Christchurch Star* 27 November 1990; McKinnon 1990).

As a tangible indication of his concern for the region, McKinnon made it the subject of his first overseas trip and made a number of subsequent visits. His commitment to the region was apparent in his statement: "As far as I'm concerned that endless debate over whether or not New Zealand is a South Pacific nation is over. This is home" (Henderson 1991: 25).

McKinnon also felt strongly about restoring New Zealand's relations with the United States. In opposition he resigned his shadow defense portfolio in protest at the National Party's change of stance on the nuclear issue. He criticized what he called the former Labour government's "semi-aligned" policy, which he claimed put New Zealand "offside with a number of Pacific Island leaders who would prefer to be co-existing with New Zealand as part of a larger alliance." He also stated that the National government wished to strengthen its role as an intermediary between Pacific Island states and outside powers (*Christchurch Star* 27 November 1990). This is a sensitive area, however, as Pacific Island states are generally wary about having others represent them at international gatherings, and they resent the paternalistic implications of New Zealand, or any other larger country, speaking on their behalf.

It is significant that in his election campaign speech announcing National Party foreign policy, Bolger drew a distinction between defense and foreign policy in relation to the Pacific. "While the emphasis of our foreign policy is more global in its approach, our defence policy, by necessity must be regional in focus." He went on to assert: "National believes New Zealand must have defence forces capable of undertaking an effective role in maintaining peace and security in the South Pacific" (Bolger 1990: 9). In effect Bolger thus endorsed the Labour government's 1987 defense White Paper. There is now bipartisan agreement that New Zealand defense policy should be nonnuclear, have a regional focus involving close cooperation with Australia, and include United Nations peacekeeping duties.

While overall the change of government in New Zealand did not make much difference to relations with the Pacific Island region, there was one important exception. As has been noted, the National government moved quickly to begin the process of normalizing relations with Fiji. The National government had none of Labour's strong emotional attachment to the deposed Fiji coalition government and therefore was free to take the action that is essential not just for the bilateral relationship, but also for New Zealand's regional standing. This move was not intended as, and should not be seen as, an acceptance by New Zealand of the military coups, and the racist constitution that emerged. Rather it is a recognition of the importance of Fiji and the leadership role it plays in Pacific Island affairs.

PUBLIC ATTITUDES

The only systematic data on this subject is now dated, as it was collected as part of the 1986 Defence Committee of Enquiry. Nevertheless it is worth reviewing, particularly because the survey results shed light on public perception of the importance of the Pacific Islands to New Zealand. The data in fact call into question the assertion that New Zealanders think of themselves as Pacific peoples. When asked how well respondents felt they got on with people from various countries, 46 percent replied that they got on very well with people from Australia, and 43 percent with people from the United Kingdom. This was about double the 22 percent of respondents who felt the same way about people from the Pacific Islands. (Other figures were: the United States 31 percent, Japan 19 percent, and the Soviet Union 8 percent.) When asked how much effort New Zealanders should make to be on good terms with other countries, the response for the category "a great deal of effort" was higher for the Pacific Island countries (64 percent), but still less than that for Australia (81 percent) and the United Kingdom (69 percent).

In the security area, while 82 percent of respondents agreed New Zealand should continue its defense responsibilities for the Cook Islands, Niue, and Tokelau, only 14 percent wanted a formal defense alliance with Pacific Island countries, compared with 68 percent for Australia and 52 percent for the United States. In the event of the Pacific Islands being "attacked," just over half of the respondents (54 percent) considered New Zealand should respond with armed forces in "all" or "most" circumstances. Eighty percent of respondents declared themselves in favor of assisting Pacific Island countries to develop their own defense capabilities.

Regarding development assistance to the region, 31 percent of respondents considered present aid levels to be "too high"; 61 percent "about right"; and 3 percent "too low." Seventy-six percent of all respondents favored allowing more young people from Pacific Island countries to attend New Zealand universities. The comparable figure for Southeast Asia was 68 percent (Defence Committee of Enquiry 1986).

Of course there was a time long before the age of the political pollster when, as Maori writer Witi Ihimaera has pointed out, there was no doubt that New Zealand was a Pacific nation. Referring to the indigenous Maori population, Ihimaera wrote: "Like other Pacific peoples we were born in the womb of the Pacific. Our genesis, our mythologies, our histories, were all Pacific-centred" (Ihimaera 1985: 30). European settlement turned the indigenous people into a minority in their own land, and brought a new set of attitudes, which for most of the next century defied the realities of geography.

It is only in recent times that even the small degree of Pacific consciousness evident in the poll began to develop. An American observer, Bernard Gordon, in a book published in 1960 (with a title ahead of its time: *New Zealand Becomes a Pacific Power*) wrote that New Zealand had "just hesitantly begun [to] recognize that while ties of heritage, history, culture and material well-being all draw her to the Western world, the facts of her geography must be faced" (Gordon 1960: 256–57). Gordon correctly predicted that working out the implications would be a slow process. It has taken the major disruptions to New Zealand's external relations of Britain's entry into Europe and the breakup of ANZUS, together with the Maori renaissance at home, to start the process of bringing about a change of attitude.

The need to increase New Zealand's consciousness as a Pacific Island country was a central theme of the report of the 1990 South Pacific Policy Review Group, *Towards a Pacific Island Community*. The choice of the word "towards" in the title recognized that a sense of community consciousness is still a future goal, not a present reality. Witi Ihimaera has some years to wait before he gets the answer he seeks to his statement and question: "While Pakeha New Zealanders now accept, sometimes reluctantly, that ours is a Pacific country, how long must we wait for you to claim as freely as we do that you are Pacific Islanders?" (Ihimaera 1985: 130).

PACIFIC ISLAND PROBLEMS AND
NEW ZEALAND RESPONSES

Compared with other developing areas, the Pacific Islands region has maintained a high level of political stability. The Fiji coups were the exception, and a sharp reminder that the region was not immune from this violent response to very difficult ethnic and economic problems. Indeed, it is likely that there would have been further coups in other Pacific Island countries had they possessed significant military forces. At the moment the only other country in this category is Papua New Guinea, where coups have been widely rumored during the crises generated by Bougainville's attempted secession. There has also been some talk of coups in Tonga, which maintains a small but growing defense force. Vanuatu also has a small self-defense force, and the Solomons are developing paramilitary forces.

Vanuatu and Tonga are examples of two contrary trends of political change sweeping the region. Vanuatu's former Prime Minister Walter Lini talked openly of his doubts about the appropriateness of the parliamentary system he inherited to deal with the many problems his country faces. He suggested that it might be necessary to resurrect more traditional power structures as a means of strengthening the existing parliamentary system. There are signs here of some of the same indigenous sentiments, although in a much milder form, that were behind the Fiji coups.

Tonga is an example of the opposite current: a "peoples" movement pressing for a more democratic political system. There have been allegations of political corruption, and the days when the king can continue to rule without having to be subject to such basic checks as an independent audit of government expenditure are clearly numbered. The minority of directly elected "Peoples Representatives" in the parliament has become increasingly assertive. Unless there is compromise, the existing feudal system will come under more direct challenge—perhaps triggered by an event such as the death of the present monarch, HRH King Taufa'ahau Topou IV. There has also been a move for greater democracy in Western Samoa, as was evident in the passage of the 1990 referendum on introducing universal suffrage.

Given the arbitrary and artificial boundaries determined by the colonial powers, it is not surprising that there have been other examples of challenges to national unity. The most serious has been Bougainville's attempted secession from Papua New Guinea, but there are others as well. Vanuatu faced a secession attempt at the time of its independence, and regional differences underlie current political tensions in that country. Kiribati, covering an area of ocean as large as the continental United States, will continue to face problems of maintaining national unity. So too will other countries, such as the Solomons, where there are strong regional forces based on cultural and linguistic differences.

The region also faces continuing political problems associated with decolonization. Further violence in the remaining French territories is a very real possibility. New Caledonia currently enjoys an uneasy peace established by the Matignon accords, but the accords are likely to come under severe challenge. The independence movement will continue to grow in French Polynesia, although its political aspirations are about a decade behind New Caledonia. The United States has, to date, successfully managed its compact arrangement with the Marshall Islands and the Federated States of Micronesia. But in Palau (Belau) there was resistance, violence occurred, and further trouble may lie ahead.

What can New Zealand do to help the Pacific Island countries deal with these political problems? It is a difficult question, since no New Zealand government will wish to appear to be interfering in the domestic politics of its neighbors. It is important that New Zealand keep up its efforts of consultation with the island states and listening to the concerns of the region. While preaching is likely to be counterproductive, it is nevertheless important that New Zealand's commitment to democratic values be reiterated.

Perhaps the most constructive form of help would be to continue to promote a regional response to the problems of the area. There is scope for developing a mechanism for facilitating the peaceful resolution of security problems, which are more likely to relate to issues of internal stability than to conflict between states. New Zealand's role in providing naval vessels as a neutral venue to facilitate the Bougainville peace talks is an example of what can be achieved. There is scope for enhancing the role of the South Pacific Forum, and particularly the position of the secretary-general, to include a mediation and conflict resolution role.

The most difficult question is what New Zealand's response should be if it was asked by a Pacific Island government to provide military assistance to help restore law and order. This issue was carefully considered by the South Pacific Policy Review Group, and it concluded that as a general rule, New Zealand should defer any decision until consultations had taken place with other Pacific Island governments with a view to devising a regional response (SPPR 1990: 213).

The reasons for this recommendation were twofold. First, it is clearly desirable to avoid a situation where New Zealand, one of the larger and predominantly European states of the region, is open to the charge of "interference" in a neighboring state's domestic problems. A basic test of how acceptable any action is to the region would be to ask other regional governments to join in — even if it is only with police personnel. The most likely contingencies will in any case require a police rather than a military response, so there is scope for wide participation.

The second reason relates to the need for New Zealand to avoid taking on the role of regional policeman. The regular consultations New Zealand has initiated with the region have worked almost too well. There is a danger that the expectation that New Zealand will provide help with military forces, if required, may create a disincentive to a regional government working through an accommodation with the groups seeking political change. As has already been suggested, such change is overdue in some parts of the region.

There are, of course, exceptions to this general rule. In the case of the three countries for which New Zealand retains constitutional responsibility for defense (the Cook Islands, Niue, and Tokelau), there is no question that

New Zealand will honor its obligations. Furthermore, if the lives of New Zealand nationals are threatened, any New Zealand government is likely to take the necessary action to protect those lives.

Despite these exceptions, it is unlikely that this general guideline of no military intervention without regional consultation will be adopted by the New Zealand government. The guideline is seen to be overly restrictive in both Wellington and Canberra, and has been described by senior officials as a surrender of sovereignty. Nevertheless, there remains a need for frank private talks with Pacific Island countries to ensure they understand the circumstances when support is likely to be provided, and that it will not be automatic. In other words, there is a need for a lowering of expectations on the part of Pacific Island governments that they can count on military support from Australia and New Zealand.

Ideally, the policy objective should be to assist Pacific Island governments in developing the capability to resolve their own security problems. Care needs to be taken to ensure that the assistance provided does not result in the excessive militarization of the Pacific Island country. Again, there is a need to facilitate and not freeze the process of political and social change.

ECONOMIC SECURITY

The principal security concerns of Pacific Island governments relate not to military matters, but to economic security. The problems they face are immense. Only about a quarter of the Pacific Island states have the resource base that could provide prospects for economic viability. These are Fiji, Papua New Guinea, the Solomon Islands, and perhaps Vanuatu.

Tonga and Western Samoa fall into a second category. Both are able to maintain a relatively high standard of living based, to a significant extent, on aid and remittances sent home from nationals who have emigrated. The outlook for the smallest of the island states, Kiribati and Tuvalu, is bleak, and like Niue and Tokelau, they are likely to remain heavily dependent on overseas aid. The Cook Islands have demonstrated considerable commercial flair, but will also have an ongoing requirement for development assistance.

There are areas with considerable potential for growth, particularly in tourism and fisheries. In the decades ahead, seabed resources may provide valuable income. The requirement to provide surveillance of the region's vast maritime zones will therefore increase in importance. Assisting with this task is the single most important form of assistance that the New Zealand armed forces can provide.

What else can New Zealand do to help the economies of the region? The South Pacific Regional Trade and Economic Cooperation Agreement (SPARTECA), which gives island countries unrestricted access to New Zealand and Australian markets on a nonreciprocal basis, has provided considerable benefits to the larger countries, such as Fiji, but offers little for the smaller states. The problem for the very small economies such as Kiribati is not so much finding markets as developing products for export. Projects aimed at encouraging New Zealand private sector involvement through the Pacific Islands Industrial Development Scheme (PIIDS) have not enjoyed a high success rate, mainly because the export potential of the projects has not been adequately researched. A liberalization of the current SPARTECA rules of origin provision (requiring that 25 percent of the value of an item originate in an island country, or that it have at least 50 percent island country and New Zealand content combined, for it to qualify for duty-free treatment) would no doubt help, but such a change does not seem likely because, as previously noted, this has been ruled out by the National government.

Development assistance to the region will need to be maintained and expanded, but the direction of this assistance is as important as the amount. In comparative terms, the region is aid-rich and there is a danger that a further influx of aid money may be counterproductive by further expanding the public service, stifling the private sector, or involving heavy recurrent expenditure by the recipient country.

The maintenance and expansion of shipping and air transport is a further key requirement for the region's economic development. The expansion of tourism provides the additional benefit of increasing the air-freight capacity for the export of fresh agricultural produce. There may be scope for joint marketing with New Zealand, making use of New Zealand's experience in the international trade of food products.

Perhaps the most important role New Zealand can play is to keep the concerns and the problems of the region before the larger and rapidly-growing economies around the Pacific Rim. New Zealand can help ensure that the interests of the smaller countries are not overlooked as closer ties are established between the larger developed regional economies. There is resentment in the region that the island country members of the South Pacific Forum have not been more directly involved in the Australian initiative to establish an Asia Pacific Economic Cooperation process.

Development issues are directly related to environmental concerns. While there is recognition throughout the region of the need to promote development on a sustainable basis, there is also a suspicion that environmental concerns, which have become fashionable in the developed economies, are used to hinder the development of Pacific Island economies. Not surprisingly, there is, for instance, some questioning about New Zealand urging the preservation of rain forests in the region, when much of New Zealand's own farming wealth was based on the cutting down of indigenous forests.

But there is nevertheless a very real appreciation of environmental issues that are directly related to the region's well-being and survival. Regional cooperation in seeking to curtail driftnet fishing is an example. There is also serious concern about the predictions that climate change will bring rising sea levels that could render atoll states, such as Kiribati and Tuvalu, uninhabitable. The most helpful response for New Zealand is to continue to urge a regional and international approach to these issues. It is largely as a result of New Zealand's initiative that the South Pacific Regional Environment Program (SPREP) has been strengthened to provide regional leadership on environmental issues.

The region also faces considerable social problems. These relate to the high birthrates and population pressures in most Pacific Island countries. The exception is Niue which, with a resident population of only about 2000 people and falling, faces the problem of depopulation. New Zealand's response has been to funnel significant amounts of development assistance through nongovernment organizations. Women's organizations have a particularly important role to play in this regard, especially in the education and health areas.

It is also very important that New Zealand continue to allow immigration from traditional sources, mainly Western Samoa and Tonga, as well as some additional immigration from Tuvalu and Kiribati. As has been noted, the remittances migrants send home are vital to their home country economies. Immigration also provides a very important safety valve to help prevent the already over-stretched social fabric of countries like Tonga, and to a lesser extent Western Samoa, from bursting. On the other hand, immigration also creates the problems of further reducing already scarce skills. This is particularly the case in the smaller countries, such as Kiribati.

PACIFIC ISLAND ATTITUDES TOWARD NEW ZEALAND

It is helpful to consider Pacific Island attitudes toward New Zealand in a number of categories. The first group are those countries that retain constitutional links with New Zealand—the Cook Islands, Niue, and Tokelau. There is a strong desire for these formal ties to continue, along with economic assistance, a security guarantee, and most important of all, the right to immigrate to New Zealand. It is true that the Cook Islands are also looking further afield cultivating, for example, close relations with France (which makes good sense given the Cook Islanders' very close ethnic ties with the people of French Polynesia). The Cooks still look fundamentally to New Zealand, and have no intention of breaking the constitutional ties that give their people the unrestricted right to settle in New Zealand. There are now more Cook Islanders living in New Zealand than in their home country. To take any action that might jeopardize this free entry to New Zealand would be political suicide for any Cook Islands government.

The second group of states are those mainly Polynesian countries with which New Zealand has close historical and cultural ties. Western Samoa is the most important of these, and looks to New Zealand to provide assistance and advice. The relationship is formalized under a Treaty of Friendship, and should Western Samoa ever require assistance to protect its security, it would expect New Zealand to respond. Tonga is also in this category, although there is no treaty relationship, and Tonga has also fostered a range of other international connections. Many Tongans have made New Zealand their home; in times of trouble it is natural that they should look to New Zealand for assistance.

The third group of states is made up of the larger Pacific Island countries of Papua New Guinea and Fiji, which jealously guard their independence, and are beholden to no other country. However, Papua New Guinea does value its New Zealand ties, and would like New Zealand to play a more visible role, partly as a means of balancing the influence of Australia as the former colonial power. Fiji, especially since the military coups, is in a special category. Despite the reestablishment of bilateral links interrupted after the coup, it will take time for Fiji to again regard New Zealand in the same friendly way as in the pre-coup period.

The Solomons and Vanuatu make up the fourth group. Like Papua New Guinea, they would like a more active presence from New Zealand to balance the influence of Australia. But neither state is as dependent as PNG on Australian aid, nor do they have as much influence in regional political and economic affairs as their larger Melanesian neighbor. New Zealand does have long-standing church and educational ties that provide a positive foundation for a further development of the relationship. Nauru might also fit into this category, although its relative wealth from phosphate makes it a special case. Nauru has also fiercely avoided any affiliation with outside powers or groups. Nauru does not even participate in Commonwealth Heads of Government meetings or the United Nations, and is the only Pacific Island country that has not taken up the offer from New Zealand and Australia to provide surveillance of its Exclusive Economic Zone (EEZ).

The final group is made up of the Micronesian states of the Marshall Islands and the Federated States of Micronesia. These states have attained a large degree of self government from the United States under the "compact" arrangements. However, the dominating influence of the United States remains, and the countries look southward to Australia and New Zealand to provide some sort of balance. Both states would welcome the development of closer ties with New Zealand in all fields, including defense (particularly in the area of surveillance), and the establishment of New Zealand diplomatic missions. A New Zealand embassy has been maintained in the other Micronesian state, Kiribati, despite indications in the early months of the National government that this post might be closed.

CONSTRAINTS ON NEW ZEALAND POLICY

The most important constraint on New Zealand in its relations with the Pacific Island countries, and in responding to their interests and needs, is simply resources. New Zealand has been through an extraordinarily radical and painful period of economic restructuring in recent years. A free-market approach has been adopted, and subsidies removed. But unemployment has grown at alarming rates, and a downturn in agricultural commodity prices added considerably to the problems.

All government departments have been subject to reorganization and budget cuts. The Ministry of External Relations and Trade, and the Ministry of Defence — the two departments most active in the Pacific Island region — have been forced to reduce activities. Other departments as diverse as education, meteorological services, and civil aviation no longer provide the Pacific Island countries with the valuable services they have in the past, assisting with such practical matters as helping administer examinations, providing weather forecasts, and calibration test flights.

Yet at a time when resources are being cut, new requests are being made. For instance, both the Federated States of Micronesia and the Marshall Islands have asked New Zealand to increase the very infrequent surveillance flights over their EEZs. But reduced air force flying hours make it difficult to meet such requests. Policies of charging for educational services have reduced New Zealand's ability to respond to growing requests for help in meeting the region's educational and health needs, although education is a particularly good long-term investment for New Zealand.

The other key constraint is attitude and will. Arguments about policy commitments ultimately boil down to questions of priorities: to a trade-off between policy objectives and resource considerations. As has been noted, the Labour government stopped short of making commitments to the region that would have involved significant additional resources, and the National government considers that Labour accorded the region too high priority. Thus, the outlook is not promising. Calls for New Zealand to increase its role are unlikely to be met. In these circumstances it may well be wise to lower the rhetorical commitment to the region in order to reduce the fallout from the failure to meet heightened expectations.

There is also an attitudinal blockage that prevents New Zealand from playing its strongest card in regional relations: New Zealand's increasingly Polynesian character. A strong case can be made to increase the emphasis on cultural diplomacy, but more traditional attitudes about the way New Zealand should be represented abroad are likely to prevail.

THE ROLES OF AUSTRALIA AND THE UNITED STATES

Although a degree of friendly rivalry inevitably exists, New Zealand has long recognized that the goal of a peaceful and prosperous Pacific Islands region is one best pursued jointly with Australia. Close cooperation exists between New Zealand and Australian diplomatic and defense personnel, both at home and throughout the region.

A controversial and expensive area of cooperation has been the decision by New Zealand to purchase two ANZAC naval frigates, with an option to purchase an additional two. The Labour government argued that the ships were required for the needs of the Pacific Island region. Critics responded that the NZ$2 billion deal (for four ships) was far beyond New Zealand's or the region's needs, and was further proof that New Zealand foreign and defense policy was now being dictated from Canberra, just as it had been from Washington and London in earlier times. (Of course, if this was in fact the case, New Zealand would not have held to its strong antinuclear policy in the face of equally strong opposition from Australia. Nor would New Zealand Prime Minister Geoffrey Palmer have sided with other Pacific Island governments at the 1990 Port Vila Forum meeting in opposing U.S. plans to dispose of chemical weapons on Johnston Island, leaving Australian Prime Minister Bob Hawke to mount a lonely defense of the U.S. position.)

The differences in Australian and New Zealand perspectives on the Pacific Island region are understandable. Australia's most immediate area of concern is Asia to its north. While this does include Papua New Guinea, the immediate focus of attention is Indonesia. New Zealand does not share this same direct concern with Asia, although it has made it clear that it would honor its defense alliance with Australia, and provide assistance in a northern Australian or Papua New Guinea conflict.

Australia also has concerns in the Indian Ocean that are not now shared, to the same extent, by New Zealand or other Pacific Island countries. This may change. India is an emerging major power, whose growing naval strength may well have implications should racial strife recur in Fiji in the early years of the next century.

Finally, Australia has global concerns as an active ally of the United States. Australian forces quickly joined the U.S.–dominated multilateral force amassed to counter Iraq's invasion of Kuwait. While the National government made only a very modest (and noncombatant) contribution of transport and medical units to the multilateral Gulf force, it has given much greater prominence to relations with the United States than did its Labour predecessor. It also acknowledged, however, that adherence to a nonnuclear policy means there can be no quick restoration of the ANZUS alliance.

In short, there is a different emphasis in New Zealand and Australian attitudes toward the region. Both regard the Pacific as important and both acknowledge that their interests overlap. But New Zealand's proximity, size, and demographics provide a sense of identity not shared by Australia, which has wider concerns. For these reasons New Zealand has tried and is likely to continue to try to exercise some restraint on what are seen as Australian overreactions on security issues. New Zealand, for example, helped calm Australian fears of Libyan involvement in the region.

From New Zealand's perspective, especially that of a National government, U.S. involvement in the region is welcomed. There is wide scope for the United States to help with the economic development of the region, and particularly with fostering the private sector. But New Zealand recognizes that U.S. interests will remain global, and that the Pacific Islands region is likely to remain low among U.S. priorities.

In the political sphere, outside its own territories, any push for a greatly enhanced U.S. role is likely to cause wider ripples that could themselves be destabilizing. There are immense difficulties to overcome for a superpower to act constructively in a region of small and microstates. It is in the U.S. and regional interests that the political problems of the area be solved by the countries themselves, which includes a special role for Australia and New Zealand.

The most positive action the United States could take would be to recognize the intensity of feeling in the region on nuclear and environmental issues. Adherence to the protocols of the South Pacific Nuclear Free Zone would be a major step in this direction. Pacific Island concerns over the use of their ocean for the disposal of waste from the developed world, and the testing and destruction of weapon systems is likely to grow. Issues such as U.S. use of Johnston Island for the destruction of chemical weapons will make it difficult for the United States to improve its standing in the region.

As a general matter, the United States needs to listen carefully to what the region is saying. The 1990 summit meeting between President George Bush and Pacific Island leaders was a positive development in this regard. However, from the New Zealand (and presumably also the Australian) perspective, the exclusion of New Zealand and Australia, both South Pacific Forum members, from the meeting set an unfortunate precedent. Any suggestion that the United States, Australia, and New Zealand are competing for influence with the islands is clearly in the interest of none of the three and should be avoided.

Of the three ANZUS countries, it is New Zealand that must give most attention to its Pacific Island policies. By virtue of its island geography, its relatively small size, and the significant number of Polynesian people making up its population, New Zealand is an integral part of the region in a way the United States and even Australia are not. As a result, New Zealand has special responsibilities to other Pacific Island countries in its own neighborhood and should act accordingly.

6

The United States and the Pacific Islands

ROBERT C. KISTE

HISTORICAL BACKGROUND

At the close of the Second World War, the entire Pacific Islands region was divided among and administered by six metropolitan powers. Five of the six remain major players in the region. Of the five, the U.S. relationships with island states are the most varied and complex. The United States has deep historical ties with a half-dozen island entities. Three are U.S. possessions—American Samoa, the Commonwealth of the Northern Marianas, and Guam. Two other countries—the Federated States of Micronesia and the Republic of the Marshall Islands—are self-governing in free association with America, and Belau (formerly Palau) is the last remnant of the U.S.-administered Trust Territory of the Pacific Islands (TTPI). In addition, particularly during the last two decades, the United States has had to manage its relations with the other countries of the region.

Historically, U.S. involvement in the Pacific Islands region has been driven primarily by strategic and security interests. Around the turn of the century, the United States acquired Guam, Hawaii, and the eastern part of Samoa. The three territories represented strategically important possessions with their locations in the northwestern, northeastern, and southern Pacific. In part, the annexation of Hawaii was motivated by economic interests (mainly the sugar industry), but the importance of Pearl Harbor has long been recognized. American Samoa and Guam were valued as coaling stations for the U.S. Navy.

During the first four decades of the century, the Pacific Islands were a relatively calm and unimportant backwater of the world. The strategic requirements of the United States had been met, and it had little other interest in or knowledge of the rest of the region. As one consequence, the United

States was caught unprepared by the outbreak of the Second World War — ignorance had its costs. In the course of the war, however, the United States regained possession of Guam and occupied most of the other islands of Micronesia, the mandated territory administered by Japan under the defunct League of Nations.

With the close of hostilities, the United States adopted a "never again" policy of "strategic denial" (Dorrance 1992: 61) for Micronesia, and there were strong sentiments in Washington, D.C. that favored outright annexation. However, the acquisition of new possessions was not acceptable in the political climate of the postwar era, and in 1947 the United States settled for control of the islands as a United Nations "strategic" trust territory. Strategic denial was extended to include all potentially hostile powers, notably the Soviet Union and its satellites, and became a cornerstone of U.S. policy for the entire region.

With Micronesia firmly within the U.S. sphere of influence, the Pacific was without unwanted interlopers. The United States controlled the northern Pacific, and its Western allies were firmly in charge of the islands south of the equator. All was secure, and like the prewar era, U.S. attention to the region declined. The period that followed has been characterized as one of "benign neglect" (Dorrance 1992: xv).

In the immediate postwar years, the Department of War (later Defense) was satisfied with the status quo, and the island countries had no other constituency in the United States. The islands were far distant from the U.S. mainland, and American economic interests in the region were nil.

An American myth also shaped attitudes and actions toward the Pacific. Americans have never thought of their nation as a colonial power and deny that it has ever had such ambitions. When Micronesia came under U.S. control, the Secretary of War argued that the acquisition of the islands "does not represent an attempt at colonialism." He claimed that "They [the islands] were not colonies; they are outposts," necessary for the security of the Pacific and the future of the free world (quotes from Goodman and Moos 1981: 68). At a conference on the decolonization of the Pacific at Australian National University in 1982, the American official responsible for negotiating the future political status of the TTPI argued that the United States had never been a colonial power because it always gave its territories the option of independence (the Philippines) or integration with the United States (Alaska and Hawaii).

The myth has been carried forward into the present. The report of a congressional delegation that visited the region in 1989 distinguished between the colonial powers (Australia, New Zealand, Great Britain, and France) that maintained South Pacific colonies after the war and the United States, which had acquired Micronesia as a UN trust territory (U.S. Congress 1990: 3). In contrast, and in an unusual statement for an American diplomat, at the Pacific Islands Conference sponsored by the East-West Center in April

1990, the deputy assistant secretary of state with responsibility for Pacific Islands matters noted that "during our colonial era, the United States acquired the Philippines and Guam from Spain and, at that same time, divided Samoa's territory with Germany" (Meyers 1990).

Americans' denial of their colonial heritage had consequences for the administration of its Pacific territories. As a nation that did not conceive of itself as a colonial power, the United States neither created a colonial service nor developed a colonial policy. Aside from perceived strategic and security needs, there was a policy vacuum and a lack of general direction for the future of the U.S. territories. With regard to the rest of the Pacific Islands, decolonization was primarily the business of other metropolitan powers and was best left to them. From the American point of view, there was little if any reason for concern or intervention.

THE UNITED STATES AND THE SOUTH PACIFIC

The Second World War undermined much of the rationale for the old colonial order, and the following two and one-half decades brought enormous social and political changes to the region. Decolonization formally began with the independence of Western Samoa in 1962. Within less than a decade, the South Pacific Forum was founded in 1971. By the latter part of the 1970s, eight other Pacific states had become or were in the process of becoming independent and sovereign states, and two others had achieved self-government in free association with their former colonial ruler.

As a consequence, the United States was no longer able to ignore developments in the Pacific. The existence of independent and self-governing states demanded recognition. At least seven were eventually to gain membership in the United Nations, and the prospect that the new states would soon exercise control over the 200-mile Exclusive Economic Zones (EEZs) surrounding their borders had both strategic and economic implications. Further, with its overture (albeit unsuccessful) to Tonga in 1976, the Soviet Union began attempts to establish a presence and gain influence in the region.

In July 1978, the United States articulated, for the first time, an explicit policy toward the Pacific. Assistant Secretary of State for East Asian and Pacific Affairs Richard Holbrooke outlined the policy for a Senate subcommittee. He began by acknowledging: "The region . . . has been relatively overlooked since the end of the Second World War, but is now emerging into a new and important role in the world. . . . There is a reservoir of great goodwill towards the United States among the peoples of the South Pacific and this enhances the prospects for cooperative relations between them and the United States" (Holbrooke 1978: 3–6).

The policy outlined by Holbrooke had several general elements: (1) understanding and sympathy for the political aspirations of Pacific Islanders; (2) support for regional cooperation; and (3) continued and close cooperation with the other four metropolitan powers in the region in support of the progress of South Pacific nations. More specifically, Holbrooke indicated that the United States would (1) give particular attention to establishing a larger and more effective U.S. presence in the islands; (2) participate actively in regional organizations; and (3) pursue the Micronesian status negotiations to achieve an agreement of free association and termination of the trusteeship by 1981. He also explicitly noted that the United States did not wish to usurp the leadership role that Australia and New Zealand played in the region.

Other initiatives followed. In 1979, treaties of friendship were signed with the region's two most recently independent nations—Kiribati and Tuvalu. The United States renounced antiquated (and doubtful) claims to certain islands in both nations. All three signatories pledged to promote a secure and peaceful Pacific, and it was agreed that the two island states would consult with the United States before granting access to their lands for military uses by any third party. Last, U.S. vessels and vessels supplying canneries in American Samoa were assured of nondiscriminatory access to fisheries resources.

In the following year, two other treaties of friendship were negotiated. One directly involved the Cook Islands and the second pertained to Tokelau but was negotiated with New Zealand. Both were essentially treaties defining maritime boundaries with American Samoa. In the second treaty, Tokelau relinquished its claim to Swains Island in favor of American Samoa.

The four treaties were an indication that the United States was broadening its horizons and wished to improve its image in the region. The first two reflected U.S. strategic and security concerns, and deliberations in the Senate over ratification made it clear that fear of a Soviet presence in the region was a major concern. All four treaties were obviously designed to protect the economic interests of American Samoa.

The statement of U.S. policy as enunciated by Holbrooke in 1978 has not been amended. Subsequent statements on policy have been elaborations on Holbrooke's, and evidence suggests that it continues to provide the basic orientation for U.S. actions in the region. Three major initiatives were derived from the 1978 position; all were launched in that same year.

1. An Office of Pacific Island Affairs was created for the first time within the Department of State. (Previously, the islands were included in a single office along with Australia and New Zealand affairs.) Today, the office has a complement of three foreign service officers — a director and two deputies. It reports to a deputy assistant secretary of state in the Bureau of East Asian and Pacific Affairs, who also has responsibility for Australian and New Zealand affairs.

2. There were staff increases in the two U.S. embassies south of the equator, and a resident American ambassador was placed in Fiji for the first time. (The Fiji embassy had previously been administered

by a chargé d'affaires; a resident ambassador had been appointed to Port Moresby on Papua New Guinea's independence in 1975.) In 1988, one-person embassies administered by chargés d'affaires were opened in the Solomons and Western Samoa. Small embassies with resident ambassadors have also been created in the Federated States of Micronesia and the Republic of the Marshall Islands.

3. An assistance program was launched for the first time. A regional office of the U.S. Agency for International Development (USAID) was opened in Fiji; initially USAID programs were mainly multilateral in scope, although some funds were allocated to support the programs of private volunteer organizations. Subsequently, a country USAID office has been opened in Papua New Guinea, and bilateral programs have been initiated for Fiji and Papua New Guinea. In line with the 1978 policy statement, USAID funding has been modest. The figure for 1978 was approximately $3 million. By 1988 it had been increased to about $12 million annually. Decreases occurred over the next two years, and funding in 1990 was a little more than one-half that of 1988. These figures do not include the financial commitments to the freely associated states in Micronesia or the funding of the fishing treaty discussed below. The United States is one of the smaller aid donors to the region, ranking behind Australia, Japan, the European Community, New Zealand, and Great Britain (Dorrance 1992: 34).

These initiatives represented a greater attentiveness to the South Pacific and were clear attempts to replenish the reservoir of goodwill toward the United States that largely stemmed from the Second World War. Nonetheless, a commonly held perception among island countries is that the United States continues to lack sufficient familiarity with and has only a low level of interest in the region. While it is understood that the United States is a superpower with global responsibilities and commitments, there is a general feeling that the United States could give greater priority to the region. That an Office of Pacific Island Affairs now exists in Washington has little meaning or visibility in the region itself. Resident American diplomats are few in number, and their impact is limited outside the countries that house their missions. Multilateral assistance has relatively low visibility and thus less impact than bilateral programs. The modest USAID budget and the fact that it has declined in recent years are viewed as demonstrating a lack of commitment.

Other U.S. policies and actions have also harmed its image in the region and been interpreted as indicators that the United States clearly has higher priorities elsewhere. There are three major cases in point, one of which has been resolved.

1. For a long time, U.S. policy regarding fishing rights was a major point of contention and source of mistrust and considerable ill will. The United States is not a signatory to the Law of the Sea Convention, and until recently, it did not recognize the right of nations to control stocks of migratory fish, particularly tuna, within their 200-mile EEZs.[1] Serious confrontations with Papua New Guinea and the Solomon Islands (over the seizure of American tuna boats) and Soviet fishing agreements with Kiribati and Vanuatu were required to precipitate an American response acceptable to the Pacific Island countries.

    In 1987, after lengthy negotiations, a South Pacific Regional Fisheries Treaty was concluded between the United States and 16 countries (the 13 island members of the South Pacific Forum plus Belau, Australia, and New Zealand). It had a duration of five years, and provided for annual payments of $10 million for economic assistance, and $2 million in license fees and private funding. The treaty also provided for annual review. A 10-year extension of the treaty, including a 40 percent increase in U.S. payments, was negotiated in 1992. The treaty removed fisheries as an issue between the United States and the islands. The American response was long in the making, however, and the United States could have avoided damage to itself had it been more aware and sensitive to the concerns of island nations at an earlier date.

2. The history of U.S. nuclear testing in the Marshall Islands and the continued nuclear test program of France in French Polynesia have fueled a strong and influential antinuclear movement in the region. The U.S. refusal to sign the protocols for the nuclear powers of the South Pacific Nuclear Free Zone (SPNFZ) treaty was interpreted in the islands as reflecting U.S. support for the development of France's nuclear force de frappe. The issue was a particularly sore point because the treaty was specifically designed by Australia and Fiji to accommodate U.S. interests and nuclear policies.

3. More recently, the plan to destroy old and deteriorating stockpiles of chemical weapons at the Johnston Atoll Chemical Agent Disposal System (JACADS) on Johnston Island south of the Hawaiian Islands has caused alarm and concern in the State of Hawaii as well as elsewhere in the Pacific. The concerns center on fears that JACADS may cause yet unknown harm to the environment and human health in the island region. The program was developed without consultation with Pacific nations, and the inclusion of materials from Europe in addition to those in the Pacific was a particular irritant. Australia's defense of the JACADS scheme at the August 1990 meeting of the South Pacific Forum in Vanuatu was viewed by most islanders as

an unconvincing attempt to smooth over a potentially injurious fait accompli.

In 1989 a U.S. congressional delegation (CODEL) headed by Congressman Stephen J. Solarz, chairman of the House Foreign Affairs Subcommittee on Asian and Pacific Affairs, visited seven countries in the South Pacific — Fiji, Kiribati, New Caledonia, Papua New Guinea, Solomon Islands, Vanuatu, and Western Samoa. The report of the Solarz CODEL supported, but went beyond, the 1978 policy statement; it was both more specific and extensive in the way of recommendations, but much of the document had a familiar ring (U.S. Congress 1990).

The report expressed concern about the diminishing reservoir of goodwill for America, and characterized the postwar era as one of neglect in which the United States was slow to respond to the decolonization of the region. The CODEL called for a rediscovery of, a greater sensitivity to, and the development of a new comprehensive strategy for the Pacific.

The delegation concluded that there was a greater potential than in the past for political instability in the islands, and that in some instances (Fiji, Papua New Guinea, and Vanuatu), recent political disturbances caused immediate concern. More generally and in the longer term, however, it suggested that the lack of economic development may well lead to unrest. Developments internal to the Soviet Union and the end of the Cold War notwithstanding, the report viewed Soviet intervention as a continuing potential danger that required vigilance.

The CODEL identified and suggested that there were two major areas that required attention. First, the congressmen were struck by the importance that island leaders place on environmental issues. These include: the depletion of marine resources by driftnet fishing; the dangers posed by nuclear activities and contamination; the threat of global warming and rising sea levels, especially to atoll nations; and the dumping of toxic and industrial waste materials. Second, island countries stressed the need for greater assistance in the development of their economies. While higher levels of aid were desired, the need was also expressed for substantive development measures in the form of more investment, increased trade, and expanded tourism.

The policy recommendations of the Solarz delegation included:

1. That the United States should project a higher profile in the region. This would include higher levels of diplomatic representation and increased participation in regional institutions, a greater diplomatic presence in the islands, and a realignment of existing diplomatic missions.

2. That there should be more bilateral aid programs, a strategy to promote investment, trade, and tourism, and an increase in the presence of the Peace Corps in the region.

3. That regional environmental issues should be addressed by ratifying the Wellington Convention banning driftnet fishing, the South Pacific Nuclear Free Zone Treaty, and the Convention for the Protection of the Natural Resources and Environment of the South Pacific Region. (The latter is a far-ranging treaty that includes a prohibition on the dumping of toxic wastes.)

Other recommendations suggested creating a scholarship program for Pacific Islanders, improving Voice of America service in the region, and expanding high-level contact between U.S. and Pacific Island officials. As described above, certain initiatives that were already in motion at the time of the CODEL mission were in accord with much of the first two sets of recommendations.

There were and are some points of difference, however. Concerning U.S. representation in regional institutions, the record is mixed. On the one hand, the United States has been represented by high-ranking diplomats at the "Post-Forum Dialogue" meetings, at which Forum members meet with representatives of major external powers, at Kiribati in 1989, Vanuatu in 1990, the Federated States of Micronesia in 1991, and the Solomon Islands in 1992. On the other hand, U.S. representation at the annual conferences of the South Pacific Commission (SPC) has continued to be below the policy-making level and of uneven quality, and the United States accumulated arrears of over $400,000 in its annual financial assessments to the SPC. While that sum may appear relatively small, it is significant in terms of the commission's budget, and the debt is an embarrassment to the United States, raising questions about its commitment to regional organizations and their programs.[2]

There has been some movement on environmental issues. On 25 September 1990, President Bush signed the regional environmental treaty and forwarded it to the Senate for ratification (East-West Center 1990: 8). In October 1990, the president directed the American ambassador to New Zealand to sign the Wellington Convention on driftnet fishing. The SPNFZ, however, has fared less well. Upon the CODEL's return to Washington, a resolution favoring the ratification of the SPNFZ protocols was introduced by Congressman Solarz and passed by the U.S. House of Representatives. However, as yet, there has been no action on this matter by either the Senate or the executive branch.

Independently of concerns directly related to the Pacific, the U.S. Congress has been committed to expanding the presence of the Peace Corps on a global basis, and the number of volunteers in the region has increased accordingly. Some 400 are now serving in 13 Pacific Island countries (Meyers 1990).

THE TTPI AND THE AMERICAN FLAG ISLANDS

Paralleling the earlier lack of interest in the South Pacific, the first 15 years of U.S. administration of the TTPI has also been characterized as an era of "benign neglect." Congressionally imposed ceilings limited annual budgets to $7 million, and even that level was seldom reached. The operation was strictly caretaker in nature. Strategic denial applied to all outsiders, and security clearances were even required of American citizens not officially linked with the administration. The strategic options were exercised in the eastern and northwestern portions of the territory where nuclear and missile tests (Marshall Islands) and CIA training programs (northern Mariana Islands) were conducted. Otherwise, the territory was allowed to drift without direction and with no clear plans for the future.

In the early 1960s, the United States was severely criticized by the United Nations for the lack of development in the territory. In typical American fashion, the United States responded to the criticism by initiating massive spending programs intended to improve education, increase the health and welfare of Micronesians, and stimulate economic development. Annual budgets were increased to well over $100 million by the late 1970s. During the Johnson administration, the territory became eligible for the vast array of new federal programs designed to create the "Great Society." The results generally fell far short of expectations and were disappointing. The end product was a massive welfare state hopelessly dependent upon the United States (Kiste 1986: 127–30).

Stimulated by the decolonization of the Pacific Islands that had begun in the early 1960s, the Congress of Micronesia (a territorywide legislative body created in the mid-1960s) established a political status commission to explore possible options for the future. Discussions with the United States began in 1969.

At the outset, the Micronesians were attracted to the new political status of "free association" that had been negotiated by the Cook Islands and New Zealand in 1965. That arrangement provided the Cook Islands with internal self-government, New Zealand citizenship, and financial subsidization while New Zealand handled defense and foreign affairs as requested. The United States, however, rejected such a loose political affiliation and proposed commonwealth status — integration with the United States. Eventually, the United States agreed to consider some variety of free association, but many difficulties ensued. A long stalemate began, and the next 15 years witnessed the longest and most tortuous set of negotiations in the entire history of decolonization in the Pacific.

As the negotiations wore on, divisions surfaced among the Micronesians based on differences in cultural traditions, languages, and histories as well as political squabbles of the moment. In the early 1970s, the identification of potential U.S. military needs in Belau, the Northern Marianas, and the Marshalls further divided the islands into the "haves" and "have nots" and accelerated the processes of political fragmentation. The three island groups with strategic value to the United States gained new bargaining power while others — Yap, Truk, Pohnpei, and Kosrae — did not. Eventually, the latter four were to become the Federated States of Micronesia (FSM).

For reasons unique to its own long colonial history, the Northern Marianas opted for commonwealth status in 1975. It was incorporated into the United States as the Commonwealth of the Northern Mariana Islands (CNMI), and its people became American citizens.

Compacts of free association were eventually negotiated for Belau, the FSM, and the Marshall Islands. The compacts are lengthy, legalistic, and complex documents that define the relationship between the islands and the United States. In brief, the island states are self-governing with regard to both internal and external affairs. At the same time, they grant the United States extensive strategic prerogatives in exchange for financial subsidies, the provision of certain services (not unlike those enjoyed by the American states), and free entry into the United States (though not citizenship). The United States is also responsible for the defense of the islands, has the option to establish military bases and to use the islands for military exercises, and has the right of strategic denial to any third party. The United States is allowed the ultimate right to determine what constitutes a defense matter, and that right could allow the United States to intervene in either the internal or external affairs of the island states. The compacts for the FSM and the Marshalls have a duration of fifteen years; that for Belau fifty years. In the final analysis, the compacts of free association guarantee the United States the right to intervene substantially in the affairs of the Micronesian states for years to come (Kiste 1983).

Plebiscites were held in 1983, and in all three countries the compacts were approved by majorities. For the FSM and the Marshalls, congressional approval came in 1985, and in the following year President Reagan decreed that the agreements were in effect and had been implemented.

The case of Belau has been quite different. Belau's constitution conflicted with the strategic provisions of the compact. The latter would allow the transit of nuclear powered vessels and nuclear weapons through the country, but Belau's constitution contained a prohibition on all nuclear, chemical, gas, or biological weapons without "the express approval of three-fourths of the votes cast in a referendum submitted on this specific question" (Ranney and Penniman 1985: 28). Between 1983 and 1991, Belau held seven plebiscites on the compact. All seven resulted in majority approvals for the compact agreement, but none achieved the necessary three-quarters (the range was 60 to 72 percent in favor of approval). An eighth referendum in 1992 succeeded in amending the constitution, but as of the end of 1992 it remained unclear whether or when this would lead to the final resolution of the issue. In the meantime, Belau remains in limbo, the last remnant of the TTPI.

Compared with the size of Pacific Island economies, it is an understatement to say that the magnitude of the Micronesian financial packages is enormous. However, because the costs of services provided by the United States cannot be calculated with any certainty, it is difficult to arrive at any precise figure. For the FSM and the Marshalls, the Solarz CODEL reported

$154.5 million for the fiscal year 1989 alone. The CODEL further commented that when this figure is compared with American assistance to the South Pacific, "it is not hard to understand why U.S. assistance levels are a source of some bitterness in the region" (U.S. Congress 1990: 5).

Within the international community, termination of the TTPI was plagued by complications. The other 10 trusteeships created at the close of the Second World War were ended with the sanction of the UN Trusteeship Council. In 1986, the same year that Reagan ordered the implementation of the compacts of free association, the Trusteeship Council also approved the newly negotiated political arrangements in Micronesia.

The case of the TTPI, however, has been unique. Of the 11 trusteeships, it alone was designated as a "strategic" trust. Article 83 of the UN Charter clearly states that all functions of the United Nations relating to strategic areas "including the approval of the terms of the trusteeship agreements and of their alteration or amendment, shall be exercised by the Security Council."

Because of concern over the open-ended nature of the UN Charter provisions and fear of a Soviet veto, the United States declined to seek the sanction of the Security Council after the Trusteeship Council's approval. As a consequence, there was widespread opinion among UN members that the trusteeship had not been legally terminated. Countering such sentiment, the United States maintained that because of the TTPI's uniqueness, there was no precedent for the termination of a strategic trust. It further argued that the United States and the Micronesian states had the privilege of ending the trusteeship themselves.

Such arguments notwithstanding, and using behind the scenes diplomacy, the United States and the two freely associated Micronesian states lobbied to secure a Soviet promise not to exercise its veto power. The termination of the trusteeship for the FSM, the Marshalls, and the Northern Marianas was taken to the Security Council just before Christmas in 1990. Reflecting both the radical changes within the USSR and its new position in global affairs, the Soviet representative to the Security Council noted that the Micronesians have "freely exercised their right of self-determination," and approval was achieved on 22 December 1990 (in United Nations Security Council Resolution 683). According to a U.S. spokesman, the Americans and Soviets had decided to "clear away the underbrush of the Cold War" (Williams 1991: 10).

Within a year, more of the underbrush was removed. On 17 September 1991, the Federated States of Micronesia and the Republic of the Marshall Islands were admitted to the United Nations along with North and South Korea and the Baltic states of Estonia, Latvia, and Lithuania—an event that "would have been unthinkable at the height of the Cold War" (*Honolulu Star-Bulletin* 17 September 1991).

The free association agreements have caused reverberations elsewhere. The U.S. possessions—American Samoa, Guam, and more recently the CNMI, commonly referred to (along with the state of Hawaii) as the "American flag islands"—have raised a number of concerns about their relationship with the United States. Guam and the CNMI have been the most vociferous.

The nature of Guam's territorial relationship with the United States has been a source of discontent for some time. As early as 1974, the Guam legislature formed a political status commission which recommended commonwealth status. In 1980, a Commission on Self-Determination concurred, and two years later, Guam's voters approved the recommendation. In 1988, the Guam legislature submitted a Draft Commonwealth Act to Congress, and in response congressional hearings were held in Honolulu in December 1989. Guamanians were disappointed with the results, and the Commission on Self-Determination continues to meet (Guam Commission on Self-Determination 1990; see also Van Dyke 1990).

Commonwealth status is no panacea for all political aspirations, however, and the people of Guam would be well advised to consider the experience of their fellow Chamorros (the common ethnic group) in the CNMI. While eagerly sought in the 1970s, commonwealth status for the Northern Marianas has not been without its disappointments and involves political and legal consequences (including limits on local autonomy) that were not fully understood or appreciated.

In comparison with the freely associated states, the people of Guam and the CNMI are keenly aware of their lack of autonomy and are envious of the financial packages of the FSM and Marshalls. From their vantage point, they are treated as second class citizens, many federal regulations are not appropriate for island societies, and far too much authority is wielded by far distant Washington, D.C. There is a desire for more control over local affairs, over regulations pertaining to air and surface transportation, over economic relations with the United States and foreign nations, and in the case of Guam, more control over immigration policies. Both the CNMI and Guam want consultations regarding Department of Defense actions that have local impacts.

Some of the same sentiments are shared by American Samoans (who, unlike the peoples of Guam and the CNMI, do not have U.S. citizenship). In October 1990, American Samoa's governor surprised federal officials by calling for a review of his territory's political status (Takeuchi 1990). While the governor's views were not widely shared at home, and he subsequently failed to win reelection as governor, it does appear that the United States is entering into a new era in its relationships with the flag islands.

THE PACIFIC SUMMIT

With relatively short notice, President Bush invited the 13 island state members of the South Pacific Forum (Australia and New Zealand were not included) to a meeting in Honolulu on 27 October 1990. The unprecedented move was billed as The Summit of the United States and the Pacific Island Nations. The event was met with some skepticism as it coincided with a presidential campaign visit to Hawaii for upcoming congressional elections. Nonetheless, the islanders' general response was that the opportunity was not to be missed, and ultimately 11 nations were represented, nine by heads of government (East-West Center 1990: 2–4).

President Bush opened the summit and focused on two main areas. They were environmental concerns and issues related to assistance and economic development.

With regard to the first, Bush indicated that the United States shared the region's environmental concerns. He specifically addressed the anxieties generated by JACADS and offered three assurances: (1) the destruction of chemical weapons would occur "only under extremely stringent environmental controls and protections;" (2) JACADS would only be used to dispose of obsolete munitions already in the Pacific and those being shipped from Germany; and (3) the United States had no further plans to use Johnston Atoll for chemical weapon or other hazardous waste disposal.

As for other environmental matters, Bush reported that he had instructed his ambassador to New Zealand to sign the Wellington Convention, and that he himself had signed the regional environment treaty (the previous month) and sent it to the Senate for ratification. He made no mention of the SPNFZ.

Concerning assistance and economic development, Bush appeared to have taken a page from the CODEL report. He indicated that the United States desired to establish a Joint Commercial Commission (JCC) to meet annually at senior government levels. He said the commission would focus on cooperation in the areas of: (1) trade and investment; (2) tourism; (3) fisheries and the environment; and (4) human resource development.

Also in the area of economic development, Bush announced the U.S. Overseas Private Investment Corporation (OPIC) would establish an Asian-Pacific Growth Fund with $200 million in venture capital and a $100 million Environmental Investment Fund for developing economies for sustainable natural resource development. He also said OPIC would lead a mission of American investors to Pacific Island countries in 1991. Last, new U.S. Agency for International Development and U.S. Information Agency (USIA) programs emphasizing private sector development were promised.

Details of the new initiatives were not provided. By and large, the response of the Forum leaders was one of appreciation for the meeting but a "let's wait and see" attitude with regard to the President's proposals. Prime Minister of the Cook Islands Geoffrey Henry gave concluding remarks on behalf of the island leaders. He noted they were "grateful for the chance to be able to go eyeball-to-eyeball with the president of the United States [and that he had] begun to replenish the pool of goodwill between the Pacific Islands and the United States that had begun to dry up since the last war." He then added, pointedly, "Don't allow it to dry up. Let's get together again" (East-West Center 1990: 13).

Unfortunately, few tangible results followed the summit, raising doubts about the value of the exercise and leading to increasing embarrassment for the United States. For reasons that are not entirely clear, the OPIC mission did not take place until 1992. More important to the islanders, the JCC proposal languished. The Department of Commerce, the agency primarily responsible for the initiative, did not allocate funds to support the JCC. Island leaders at the Post-Forum Dialogue on Pohnpei in July 1991 were both surprised and disappointed when the U.S representatives suggested that the island nations should help finance the JCC. The lack of funding by the Department of Commerce caused fears in other federal agencies, particularly the Agency for International Development, that they might be called upon to rescue the JCC. An agreement on the structure and functioning of the JCC was finally reached only in January 1993. Nothing more has been heard about the Asian-Pacific Growth Fund.

OTHER INITIATIVES

The renewed national-level interest in the Pacific region in the late 1970s and throughout the decade of the 1980s served as a catalyst for other initiatives. Two are of particular importance with regard to U.S. involvement with the region; both began as conferences held in Honolulu in 1980 and resulted in new regional organizations.

In January 1980, a Pacific Basin Development Conference was held, with support from federal agencies, particularly the Department of Commerce. As a spinoff, within the same year the Pacific Basin Development Council (PBDC) was formed as an American club with headquarters in Honolulu. The PBDC is composed of the governors of the four American flag islands — American Samoa, the Commonwealth of the Northern Marianas, Guam, and Hawaii. The PBDC promotes economic development, serves as a liaison among its members, and assists with the coordination of their relations with the Congress and federal agencies in Washington. The PBDC has created some sense of unity and common cause among the four governors. PBDC members have also held discussions with representatives of Asian countries about future economic efforts in the region.

The PBDC is incorporated as a private, nonprofit, tax exempt educational organization. Most of its operating costs are provided by member contributions; other funds are derived from federal and other granting agencies.

In March 1980, the East-West Center (EWC) initiated the Pacific Islands Conference (PIC). The conference brought together heads of island governments and was projected to meet every fifth year. Rarotonga was the site of the second PIC in 1985, and the third was held in Kona, Hawaii, in early

1990. On the latter occasion, the island leaders' commitment to the PIC was made evident when they decided to have it convened every third year.

The major result of the PIC was the founding of the Pacific Islands Development Program (PIDP). While it sponsors occasional short term educational and training programs, the PIDP is primarily a research unit. The research agenda is set by a standing committee composed of 11 heads of government that meets annually. Research projects have included aquaculture, government systems, disaster preparedness, tourism, fisheries, and private sector development. Over 90 percent of the EWC's funding is provided by the U.S. Congress through USIA, and the bulk of PIDP's funding is a line item in the EWC's budget. In addition, country contributions are received from the Pacific member-countries as well as Japan, Australia, and New Zealand. The PIDP is considered by the islanders as a regional organization and is a charter member of the umbrella South Pacific Organizations Coordinating Committee (SPOCC) established in 1988.

CONCLUSION

Historically, America's primary interest in the Pacific Islands region has been strategic. That interest dates back to the end of the last century when the United States acquired its first island possessions and was behind the establishment of the TTPI at the close of the Second World War. The same interest has been evident in subsequent U.S. policy and actions.

Since the late 1970s, the United States has evidenced a greater awareness and concern about the Pacific Islands than at any other time since the Second World War. The heightened awareness of the islands was precipitated by the decolonization of the region and the concomitant emergence of independent and self-governing nations, processes initiated by the island nations themselves and the other metropolitan powers in the region. Purposely and with the articulation of an explicit policy in 1978, the United States has increased its profile in the region. That policy has been consistent with U.S. strategic interests and has been accompanied by several new initiatives. The most visible of the latter have been an enlarged diplomatic presence, the USAID assistance program, congressional visitations, and last but certainly not least, the summit meeting with President Bush in late 1990. There has been substantial continuity in U.S. policy over this time.

A heightened profile in the Pacific Islands has inevitably been accompanied by a greater vulnerability for the United States. For a world superpower and a nation that had played such a prominent role in the region during the Second World War, a renewed and expanded presence was inescapably fraught with pitfalls. It necessarily created greater expectations and, perhaps also inevitably, disappointments.

In part, the U.S. perception of its global role and responsibilities has made it evident that U.S. priorities elsewhere are more important to it than the Pacific Islands. The U.S. positions on SPNFZ and JACADS are cases in point. The primacy of defense interests was manifest both during the U.S. administration of the TTPI and in the arrangements for its termination. The regional fisheries treaty was concluded only after a perceived Soviet threat to the region was judged of sufficient importance to warrant the effort to negotiate a resolution to the dispute with the islanders and the investment of U.S. government funds in the settlement. The relatively modest scale of U.S. assistance to the region (especially when compared to the assistance provided to the two freely associated states in Micronesia) and the U.S. arrears to the South Pacific Commission are disappointments to the islanders and are interpreted as a lack of real U.S. commitment to the region. In this historical context, and if tangible results do not materialize, the expectations raised by the Pacific Summit may well do the American image in the islands more harm than good.

These overall conclusions also shed light on the question of how the United States views the roles of its ANZUS partners in the islands. A couple of basic points stand out. First, the U.S. government clearly recognizes, and supports, the close ties of Australia and New Zealand with the island states, and the important assistance provided by the other two ANZUS countries in this region. It hopes that they will continue to play important roles in the islands. American officials readily acknowledge the breadth of Australian and New Zealand contacts with the islands and the greater expertise of the other two governments on many aspects of island affairs.

At the same time, and contrary to much conventional wisdom, it is not possible to identify a conscious U.S. policy of "delegating" care of the South Pacific "ANZUS Lake" to Australia and New Zealand. Basically, U.S. neglect of the islands region for much of the postwar period was essentially that — neglect. Certainly the involvement and interest in the islands of Australia and New Zealand (as well as that of France and, while it lasted, Britain), helped ensure stability and a pro-Western orientation and thereby made it easier for Washington to ignore the region. But the real bottom line was that the region did not seem to demand particular attention.

When that situation changed, first because of complaints over U.S. stewardship of the TTPI and later when the Soviets started making overtures to the independent island states, the United States took direct (if not always appropriate or adequate) action. The increase in U.S. attention paralleled that of Australia and New Zealand (and the other Western states), but for the most part this appears to have reflected common perceptions of national interest rather than any explicit division of labor or coordinated approach.

In the cases of the Trust Territory and the flag islands, there was no question that there was a direct, unilateral American responsibility. However, essentially the same approach has been followed with the independent island states. Most recently, the Americans clearly felt no need to include Australia and New Zealand in the 1990 summit meeting with the island members of the Forum, an action which (as pointed out by John Henderson in the preceding chapter) was considered an unfortunate if not deliberate oversight by many in the Antipodes.

Somewhat more surprisingly, the record shows some remarkable instances of a lack of consultation by the United States with its ANZUS partners on matters affecting the islands. JACADS was a significant and sensitive activity in the region on which the United States apparently felt no need for advance consultations even with its regional allies. In the case of SPNFZ, the U.S. decision not to accede came as a surprise as well as a distinct disappointment to Australia, which had been the primary sponsor of the initiative and had made concerted efforts to accommodate the stated American conditions for acceptable nuclear free zones. Whether or not the initial expectations of the Australians were realistic, clearly the turndown itself was not preceded by any detailed explanations of U.S. thinking.

In sum, while the United States recognizes the shared interests of all three ANZUS states in the Pacific Islands, it does not appear to have any very firm or explicit conception of what their respective roles should be. This is yet another example of an overall U.S. approach to dealing with the islands region that has been characterized more by incrementalism and natural evolution than by the formulation and implementation of cohesive long-term policies.

ACKNOWLEDGMENTS

The late John C. Dorrance, to whom this volume is dedicated, critiqued earlier drafts of this chapter and provided numerous suggestions that greatly improved the end result. John Dorrance was the first U.S. Foreign Service Officer who developed a special interest in the Pacific Islands. My many contacts with him over the last twelve years led to a friendship that enhanced my own understanding of American involvement in the island world. He is missed.

Sections of the manuscript concerning their respective organizations were reviewed by: Dr. James Osborn, assistant director, and Ms. Amy Nolan Osborn, regional program officer, Regional Development Office/South Pacific, U.S. Agency for International Development, Suva, Fiji; Mr. Jerry Norris, director, Pacific Basin Development Council, Honolulu, Hawaii; and Dr. Sitiveni Halapua, director, Pacific Islands Development Program, East-West Center, Honolulu, Hawaii. Their comments and suggestions are appreciated.

NOTES

1. In late 1990, the U.S. Congress amended the Magnuson Act to recognize EEZ state jurisdiction over migratory species; thus, the juridical basis of the dispute has now been eliminated.

2. The arrears to the SPC were only one instance of a larger problem. Because of

a shortfall in congressional appropriations, the United States has similar arrearages to all international organizations, including the United Nations. In late 1990, Congress passed legislation that provides for paying off such indebtedness over a period of five years beginning in 1991 (Dorrance 1991). In terms of U.S. credibility, however, this action essentially amounts only to closing the barn door after the horse has been stolen; the damage has been done.

Comment

RICHARD W. BAKER

There is a clear common pattern in the evolution of the relations between all three countries and the Pacific Islands. As the political status of the islands has changed over the postwar period, the involvements and concerns of the three powers in the region have broadened and deepened. The trends of recent years are likely to continue. The island states will develop an even wider range of international relationships; they will face intractable problems of economic development, and there will be increased stress on their inherited political systems. A degree of instability appears likely to be a regular feature of this landscape. The relationships of the three ANZUS states with the islands thus seem likely to become even more complex.

The three countries also face a common dilemma in their relations with the islands. This is how to deal with the gap between their own rather expansive declaratory policies and the correspondingly high expectations of the island states, on the one hand, and their actual resource priorities, capabilities, and willingness to engage in the islands, on the other.

As pointed out by both Stewart Firth and John Henderson, Australia and New Zealand share the particular problem of how to deal with expectations on the part of a number of island governments that they will provide military assistance or even direct support in the event of domestic disorder or violent opposition. They may well be faced with some very difficult decisions in this regard. The United States has not raised expectations in the area of internal security, but faces a comparable and possibly even broader problem of living up to the heightened expectations of generalized U.S. attention and sensitivity to the islands created by the 1990 summit meeting. All three have severe resource constraints, stressed most specifically by Henderson in the case of New Zealand where the government departments facing increased demands for assistance from the islands are for the most part undergoing significant reductions in personnel and programs.

Beyond these generalities, a closer reading of the three stories shows how very different the specific relationships of each ANZUS state are in the islands. First, each country has special links with individual states—Australia with Papua New Guinea, New Zealand with the Cook Islands and Niue. New Zealand tends to have closer relations with the Polynesian islands generally due both to geography and the fact that New Zealand's Maori people are Polynesian. The United States still accords vastly more attention and resources to the three flag territories and the freely associated states than it does to the independent island countries. Though in part complementary, these differential ties in the islands also contribute to a unique outlook and approach by each of the governments.

The islanders also view each of the ANZUS states somewhat differently. Australia and New Zealand have a special yet somewhat ambivalent position in the islands. They are charter members of the major regional political grouping, the South Pacific Forum, but are also donor and former colonial states. There are significant value differences between the two European-origin states and the islands, particularly as to political institutions and processes. These were brought out most starkly in the case of the 1987 Fiji coup, which Australia and New Zealand condemned as a violation of constitutional institutions and democratic principles, but with which the island governments basically sympathized as a legitimate defense of indigenous political primacy against the threat of control by immigrant groups.

In its relations with the islands, the United States has all the problems of the giant in Lilliput. Island perceptions of what the United States can and should do in the region can easily be exaggerated, and the United States for its part has been guilty alternately of neglect of the islands (its own territories as well as non-U.S. entities) and of overwhelming attention (as when the Great Society welfare programs were rather uncritically applied to the U.S. Trust Territory in the 1970s, with the perverse effect of virtually destroying local economic initiative.) The 1990 summit may well have begun another cycle. There is always the danger of clumsiness and unintended insensitivity in this relationship, as in the construction of the chemical weapons destruction facility (JACADS) on Johnston Island without prior briefing of the island governments despite the known sensitivities of the island states on such matters.

As to their respective roles in the island region, all three governments clearly and sincerely welcome the presence and contributions of the others. Henderson affirms that New Zealand welcomes U.S. involvement in the region, particularly in the economic sphere. Kiste points out that in his 1978 statement on U.S. islands policy, Assistant Secretary Holbrooke explicitly said that the U.S. government did not wish to usurp the leadership role that Australia and New Zealand played in the region. Firth notes that Australian islands policy remains within the framework of the alliance and a shared view with the United States on regional security objectives. Both Firth and Henderson cite close cooperation between Australia and New Zealand on military matters in the South Pacific.

However, despite the acknowledgment of common interests and of a certain need for mutual consideration and coordination, there is, in practice, relatively little formal collaboration among the three on policy in the islands. They participate in the annual discussions of assistance programs in the islands at the South Pacific Conference. Prior to the U.S.–New Zealand breach, the situation in the islands region was one of the regular topics at the annual ANZUS Council meetings, and it now features in the annual bilateral Australia–U.S. ministerial talks and in separate exchanges with New Zealand by both Australia and the United States. At certain times the intensity of such consultations has increased, such as at the time of the first Soviet overtures to the independent states in the latter 1970s or a brief foray by Libya into the region in the early 1980s, or following the Fiji coups in 1987. However, it is difficult to identify any detailed agreements on strategy or division of labor having emerged from these discussions.

There are a number of reasons for the relative lack of formal policy coordination with respect to the islands. First, the perspectives and priorities of each of the three countries differ significantly. Henderson sees New Zealand as having a different perspective and special responsibilities in the islands because neither Australia nor the United States are "an integral part of the region" in the same way as New Zealand. He cites as a prime example the JACADS issue, on which New Zealand sided with the islanders and against Australia, and comments that New Zealand tries to restrain what it sees as Australian overreactions to security issues in the islands. Henderson notes that it is not in the interest of the three to be seen as competing for influence in the islands, but believes that certain U.S. actions (for example, the exclusion of Australia and New Zealand from the 1990 Summit) do convey this suggestion.

Both Firth and Henderson suggest that Australia and New Zealand may have a better sense of American interests in the islands than the U.S. government does. Henderson points out that issues like JACADS and support for French nuclear testing will make it hard for the United States to improve its standing in the region, and believes it is in U.S. interests that Australia and New Zealand have a special role in helping regional states solve their own political problems. Firth cites the fisheries treaty and SPNFZ as instances in which Australian confidence in its understanding of U.S. interests led to differences between the two.

As Kiste notes, Assistant Secretary Holbrooke was careful to deny any challenge to the Australian and New Zealand leadership roles in the region when he unveiled a more activist U.S. policy in 1978. However, this did not mean that the U.S. government looked to the other two as its surrogates in the islands; as put most explicitly in the statement of Australian Foreign Minister Evans quoted by Firth, Australia and New Zealand would in any event not wish to be placed in such a position. Correspondingly, neither does the United States appear to accord any special deference to the leadership or judgments of Australia and New Zealand on sensitive issues relating to the islands, at least where other immediate U.S. interests are involved. The three specific cases cited by Kiste—the South Pacific Nuclear Free Zone treaty, the 1990 U.S.-Pacific Islands summit meeting, and the Johnston Island chemical weapons destruction facility—provide ample demonstration of this point.

A further reason for a relative lack of formal or close coordination among the three on island policy is the attitude of the islanders. The islands would resent and resist any appearance of a concerted approach with its implications of neocolonial diktat. Australian Foreign Minister Evans clearly had this in mind in his statement that Australia's interest is not served by being perceived as a U.S. proxy. Henderson comments that New Zealand Foreign Minister McKinnon's expressed desire to strengthen New Zealand's role as an intermediary between the islands and outside powers is sensitive because islanders resent the paternalistic implications of any larger country performing such a function. In fact, as Henderson also notes, island interests are served by maintaining a balance among the influence of the three ANZUS states—for example, PNG, the Solomons, and Vanuatu look to New Zealand to balance Australian influence, and the Marshalls and FSM look to Australia and New Zealand to help balance U.S. influence—and so, undoubtedly, they prefer to deal with each of the three separately.

There will always be areas in which consultation among the three governments on island developments is appropriate and useful—such as to exchange information and assessments or to minimize duplication of activities in these very small entities. However, without a truly major crisis or security challenge, policy coordination seems unlikely to go beyond this rather minimal level. This reflects both genuine differences in national perspectives and a common desire not to be seen by the islands as conducting a coordinated policy on island issues. The combination of broad common interests with distinctive individual perspectives and (frequently) differing positions on specific issues seems most likely to continue to characterize the three countries' policies in the islands region.

SECTION III

Regional Economic Policies

In this section we turn from security-related issues to economics, looking at the economic policies of each of the ANZUS states toward the Asia-Pacific region. The chapters in this section consider the approach each government has taken with respect to efforts to create a more cohesive set of economic consultative arrangements and institutions in the region. We specifically consider the respective roles and attitudes toward the Asia Pacific Economic Cooperation (APEC) process launched through an Australian initiative in 1989. We want to know what benefits each expects from explicitly regional economic cooperation as distinct from more global institutions, subregional arrangements, or individual national efforts. We ask what role each sees for bilateral or trilateral cooperation on economic policy issues.

The term "regional economic policy" is, in a sense, a misnomer. Very few governments, certainly none of the three we are considering, have one set of economic policies that they apply in their own region and another for the rest of the world. Rather, what is meant here by regional economic policy is how each of the three ANZUS states has dealt with the emergence of the Asia-Pacific region as a dynamic growth center and a major economic force in its own right.

This development is a very recent phenomenon, one that has come to be widely recognized and responded to by the region's governments only since 1980. Thus it is one of the truly new developments of the era of the ANZUS alliance, and how the three ANZUS countries have responded to this dramatic change in the regional environment should tell us something about the habits of cooperation and the broader commonalities of outlook that have developed over the period of the alliance.

THE EMERGENCE OF A REGION

The dramatic economic growth of the Asia-Pacific region is widely known and well documented. Per capita real income growth among the developing countries of the region averaged over 5 percent per year during the decade of the 1980s, the highest rate recorded by any group of countries in any decade since the end of the Second World War. Among the developed countries of the region, Japan continued to lead the entire industrial world in income growth, with inflation-adjusted per capita incomes rising almost 4 percent per year during the 1980–90 period.

Equally impressive, but less widely recognized, is the fact that the 1980s also witnessed a significant binding together of the Asia-Pacific economies, as both trade and investment flows between countries in the region accelerated. [1]

Between 1978 and 1985, exports within the Asia-Pacific region more than doubled, reaching $164 billion and accounting for over two-fifths of the region's total exports. However, by 1991 intraregional trade had grown by another two and one-half times to reach $409 billion, and the share of total exports staying within the region increased to 47 percent. During the 14-year period, trade between the developing countries of the region expanded by an average of 17 percent per year. Although the United States and Japan continued to be major markets for all these countries throughout the 1980s, the rapid growth in intraregional trade benefited from efforts by many Asian countries to reduce import tariffs and liberalize their domestic trade regimes, particularly during the latter half of the decade.

Moreover, rising real incomes and stronger currencies in the so-called four tigers or newly industrialized economies (NIEs)—the Republic of Korea, Taiwan, Hong Kong, and Singapore—stimulated import demand within these economies, demand satisfied by rising purchases not only from the industrial countries but also from the developing countries of the region. Even Japanese consumers, with their historically strong "cultural" preference for locally produced goods, began purchasing more imported products. [2] Although raw materials and semiprocessed goods still dominate Japan's imports, with imports of manufactured goods accounting for only 2 percent of Japan's GNP, between 1985 and 1989 manufactured imports jumped 80 percent. A large part of this growth came from within the region, particularly the NIEs, Malaysia, and Thailand.

The 1980s also saw the emergence of truly regional financial and investment markets. Japan became the acknowledged financial center of the Asia-Pacific regional economy. Direct Japanese investments in the Asia-Pacific region skyrocketed. The United States had long accounted for the majority of direct foreign investment in developing Asia, but by the end of 1983, total Japanese investment in these countries amounted to $14.6 billion, surpassing that from the United States by over $1 billion. By 1991, Japanese direct investment in developing Asia exceeded $53.4 billion, against $25 billion for the United States. While the depreciation of the U.S. dollar after 1985 accounted for much of the relative change, the increase in Japanese investment in Asia is impressive even when calculated in yen. A further sign of economic regionalization was that, while earlier Japanese investment was largely in plants producing for the U.S. market, more recent investments have been directed increasingly to production for other markets including Japan itself.

Sources of investment within the region have also become more diversified, especially with the growth of investment from the Asian NIEs. In the case of Thailand, for example, investors from Japan and the United States dominated between 1986 and 1988, but combined investments from Hong Kong and Taiwan rose from 13 percent of total inflows in 1986 to almost 24 percent in 1988. A similar trend could be identified in Indonesia and Malaysia. Beginning in 1990, direct inflows of equity investment into Thailand, Malaysia, and Indonesia began to taper off, partly due to the slowdown in world economic growth and partly because these economies could not continue to absorb the large inflows of the previous five years. By comparison, investment flows into China from Hong Kong, Taiwan, and South Korea grew at an explosive rate during the first years of the 1990s. For example, government approvals of foreign investment projects in China during the first six months of 1992 more than exceeded the value of investment approvals for all of 1991. Thus, a genuine, multidimensional regional economy appears to be emerging for the first time in the Asia-Pacific region.

REGIONAL ECONOMIC COOPERATION

Because this subject has a rather complex history of its own, a brief review of the history of regional cooperation efforts can help provide a common background to the discussions that follow.[3]

Origins

The growth of economic interaction and interdependence within the Asia-Pacific region served to focus attention on the absence of a regional institutional structure comparable to those in Europe (or even Latin America or Africa). The first specific conceptions of such a structure for the region were put forward in the 1960s, principally from Japan. A prime mover was Professor Kiyoshi Kojima of Hitotsubashi University, who in 1965 proposed the establishment of a Pacific Free Trade Area (PAFTA). PAFTA was inspired by the European Economic Community and the European Free Trade Association, and it was to include Japan, the United States, Canada, Australia, and New Zealand. Yet Kojima realistically recognized that the proposed members lacked the necessary degree of integration at that stage for such an idea to work (Kojima 1971).

There was little government interest in Kojima's idea, but it was taken up by the academic and business communities. This led first to the formation in 1967 of the Pacific Basin Economic Council (PBEC), a private organization of business interests that grew out of an Australian-Japanese grouping, and then in 1968 to the first Pacific Trade and Development Conference (PAFTAD), designed for policy-oriented economists of the five PAFTA countries (and subsequently expanded to a far broader Asia-Pacific membership).

Kojima continued to develop options for regional cooperative institutions, including an Organization for Pacific Trade, Aid and Development (OPTAD) that was also to involve developing countries (Kojima 1976). This idea found resonance in Australia, Japan, and the United States. An Australian-Japanese team recommended, in 1976 and again in 1978, that their governments sponsor the establishment of an intergovernmental forum (Crawford and Okita 1976, 1978). An Australian-American academic team further elaborated the concept in a study for the U.S. Congress on the potential for an Organization for Pacific Trade and Development (Drysdale and Patrick 1979). This proposal (also using the acronym OPTAD) was modeled on the Organization for Economic Cooperation and Development (OECD).

By 1980 the process of Asia-Pacific economic regionalization had progressed to the point where governments began to take a more serious interest in the subject. In 1980, a visit by Japanese Prime Minister Ohira to Australia produced a joint agreement with Australian Prime Minister Fraser to explore the idea of a "Pacific Community," and a seminar on this subject was held at the Australian National University later the same year. The seminar in turn led to the establishment of the Pacific Economic Cooperation Conference (PECC, now changed to Council), a tripartite organization that brought together academics, business leaders, and government officials (putatively in their private capacities) for study and discussion of regional economic and trade issues.

The establishment of PECC was a significant milestone. Operating through task forces and general meetings (at 18-month intervals), PECC helped form an Asia-Pacific perspective on trade and development (Harris 1989), sustained the momentum of the concept of regional cooperation, and involved government officials in these deliberations on a regular basis. However, this still fell short of creating a regional intergovernmental forum. A number of factors, including heterogeneity in culture, ethnic composition, ideology, and security interests, as well as differences in levels of economic development throughout the Asia-Pacific region, inhibited the establishment of an official organization on a regionwide basis.

In the meantime, more success in intergovernmental cooperation was being achieved at the subregional level. Most significant was the formation of ASEAN in 1967 comprising Indonesia, Malaysia, the Philippines, Singapore, Thailand, and later Brunei. ASEAN's objectives included closer economic integration, but very limited progress was made in this area until the 1992 agreement to form an ASEAN Free Trade Area (AFTA) over a 15-year period. The only other subregional free trade area is that between Australia and New Zealand, launched by their Closer Economic Relations (CER) agreement in 1983 and subsequently accelerated so that virtually all barriers to trade between the two countries were removed by July 1990.

Establishment and Evolution of APEC

Over the course of the 1980s, several significant changes occurred in the environment for regional cooperation. The explosive economic growth in the region, coupled with the growing regional economic interdependence already noted, made the economic logic of cooperation increasingly persuasive (see Drysdale 1988). PECC membership expanded to include the "three Chinas" — paving the way for the formula later used in APEC — and several Latin American states (Russia joined in 1992). PECC meetings helped establish a process and style for regional economic dialogue that participants from the wide variety of cultures represented in the organization were comfortable with.

By the end of the decade, with the end of the Cold War and economic reform processes underway in most of the communist states, a more congenial political atmosphere had developed for regionwide cooperative undertakings (Bonnor 1990). PECC itself was pushing for the establishment of a council of ministers to which it could make policy recommendations, and the Australian national committee of PECC was actively lobbying its government to promote such an initiative.

Australian Prime Minister Bob Hawke seized this opportunity on a visit to Korea in January 1989. Hawke proposed the establishment of a "more formal intergovernmental vehicle of regional cooperation" with the capacity for analysis and consultation to help inform economic policy-making (Hawke 1989: 4). Initial hesitation on the part of the ASEAN states, who were concerned that a new organization might detract from the role and standing of ASEAN, and the United States, which was not included in Hawke's original suggested membership of APEC although it was quickly added, was overcome in an extensive consultative process over the course of the year. Ultimately, in November, ministers from the six ASEAN nations, Australia, New Zealand, South Korea, Japan, Canada, and the United States gathered in Canberra for the first intergovernmental meeting on Asia Pacific Economic Cooperation.

The first APEC meeting resulted mainly in a statement of general principles on trade, including support for the multilateral GATT negotiations and disavowal of any interest in forming an exclusive trading bloc. Perhaps a more important achievement was an agreement to meet again, in Singapore in July 1990. The Singapore meeting reiterated the participants' agreement on principles (and expressed concern over the lack of progress in the Uruguay Round), but also agreed that annual APEC meetings would continue at least through 1993. At the third ministerial, in Seoul in November 1991, China, Taiwan, and Hong Kong joined the group and a formal declaration of objectives and operating procedures was adopted (Joint Statement 1991). A fourth meeting, in Bangkok in September 1992, agreed to the formation of a small secretariat (to be located in Singapore), effectively institutionalizing the new forum.

The full membership scope and criteria of APEC are still not settled. A number of additional countries (e.g., Mexico, Papua New Guinea) have expressed interest, and other applications are likely. The Bangkok ministerial in 1992 commissioned a study of the question of admission of further members.

The institutional structure of APEC is also still an open issue, and the evolution of the role of the newly established secretariat will be critical in this regard. The secretariat is authorized to draw on work being done elsewhere, or commission additional work as needed. It will act as APEC's institutional link with other regional organizations such as ASEAN, PECC (as a conduit for contributions from the private sector), and the Asian Development Bank (ADB), as well as global economic institutions including the General Agreement on Tariffs and Trade (GATT), the Organization for Economic Cooperation and Development (OECD), and the International Monetary Fund (IMF). However, the ultimate size of the secretariat and the degree to which it will become an active generator of proposals and initiatives, in addition to coordinating implementation, remain to be seen.

APEC Priorities and Activities

One subject whose importance to APEC's members was agreed from the start was trade, specifically, the ongoing but beleaguered Uruguay Round of international trade negotiations under the GATT. In Canberra, and again in Singapore, this subject was at the top of the APEC ministers' agenda:

> Ministers agreed that the primary objective of APEC this year was to ensure a successful conclusion of the Uruguay Round. This was essential to preserve and enhance the open multilateral trading system on which their economies all depended. (Joint Statement 1990)

Other than declarations of solidarity and exhortations, however, there was relatively little of an operational nature that APEC as a grouping could do to advance the GATT negotiations. The agenda and negotiating positions were by that time firmly established. APEC's continuing program had to focus on explicitly regional issues.

Over the period leading up to APEC's formalization at the 1991 Seoul meeting, the participants worked to define the substance as well as the procedures of the APEC dialogue. The most tangible outcome of this process was the formation of 10 working groups to deal with various practical aspects of regional economic relations on which there appeared to be a need for better information or analysis. These groups deal with trade and investment data, trade promotion, investment and technology transfer, human resources, energy, marine conservation, telecommunications, fisheries, transportation, and tourism. The process is open for the inclusion of other projects.

Although it was implicit in the basic concept of regional economic cooperation, regional trade liberalization was first explicitly put on APEC's agenda as an area for further study at an APEC senior officials meeting in Cheju, South Korea, in March 1991. At the ministerial meeting in Seoul in November 1991, the ministers instructed the senior officials to identify options and make recommendations on approaches to regional trade liberalization. This led to the establishment of the APEC Informal Group on Trade Liberalization that first met in Bangkok in June 1992.

The fourth APEC ministerial meeting, in Bangkok in September 1992, agreed to implement a limited number of practical measures to work toward regional trade liberalization. It also endorsed a proposal by Australian Foreign Minister Gareth Evans to establish an Eminent Persons Group "to enunciate a vision for trade in the Asia Pacific to the year 2000" (Joint Statement 1992: 3).

By the end of 1992, APEC had evolved, remarkably quickly for an international organization, to the point where it had an agreed structure, a critical mass of membership, and at least the beginnings of an agenda. It had not, however, yet posted any concrete achievements in facilitating regional economic interchange and growth. Those accomplishments, if they were to come, lay in the future.

THE COUNTRY STUDIES

In the first chapter of this section, Jenelle Bonnor documents the very high priority that Australia places on regional economic cooperation and the leading roles individual Australians and the Australian government have played in the establishment first of nongovernmental cooperative institutions and then of APEC. Bonnor explains that Australia sees these efforts as advancing Australia's national economic objectives, including the achievement of closer economic integration with the countries of the region and mobilizing the widest possible support for the maintenance of an open international trading regime. She also notes, however, that should the global trade liberalization effort fail, regional approaches could provide an alternative approach. In addition, regional cooperation has offered opportunities for Australia to exert leadership and define a political role for itself in the region of which it increasingly regards itself as a part.

Bonnor sees scope for future cooperation among the three ANZUS governments on regional economic issues. But she points out that the Australia–New Zealand relationship (increasingly integrated within a bilateral free trade area) is likely to be easier than Australian-American relations, which will continue to be punctuated by further unilateral U.S. actions that harm Australian trade interests.

Alastair Bisley traces New Zealand's growing interest and involvement, after a period of initial skepticism, in the movement for Asia-Pacific economic cooperation. Among the reasons for this interest he cites New Zealand's desire to gain better entrée into the dynamic Asian economies, and the utility of APEC, in particular, as a forum for dialogue with important economic actors (including the United States) as well as an opportunity for New Zealand to be "in the room" when larger players are debating issues that impact New Zealand.

However, Bisley emphasizes New Zealand's strong preference for trade liberalization on a global basis as the approach that offers the greatest benefit to a small country with global trading interests. Another attraction of APEC for New Zealand has been the fact that to date it has assisted multilateralism by lobbying strenuously for the success of the GATT global negotiations. However, he also acknowledges that should GATT fail, regional arrangements such as APEC could help limit the fragmentation of the international system.

With respect to bilateral and subregional cooperation, Bisley focuses on New Zealand's experience with its Closer Economic Relations agreement with Australia, the success of which he attributes in large part to the fact that its implementation coincided with and supported a general reduction of protection in both markets. He canvasses the major options that have been suggested for expanding CER—to include Canada and/or the United States—and suggests that any expansion would be more advantageous if it were as broad as possible, in keeping with the overall objectives of maximal multilateral liberalization and trade creation.

Thomas Layman and the editor argue that the United States has pursued an essentially eclectic course in its economic policies in the Asia-Pacific region. The impressive growth of American trade with the region has brought with it a highly visible trade deficit. Although formulated on a global basis, U.S. efforts to deal with the deficit have had a disproportionately heavy impact in this region. An increasingly aggressive and unilateral U.S approach has exacerbated problems in U.S. relations with many regional countries including Japan and China.

However, Layman and Baker point out that the United States has also continued to seek international trade liberalization. Although preferring the global approach, in the face of the urgency of its own trade problems and the difficulties of the GATT negotiations, the United States has increasingly tried regional and bilateral options as well. On Asia-Pacific regionalism, the authors see a mixed U.S. record. An initially guarded attitude toward regional initiatives has given way to progressive acceptance, and in the case of APEC, genuine support. But overall the U.S. role has been reactive, with no significant initiatives or real leadership.

Consistent with the general pattern of U.S. economic policy in the region, Layman and Baker describe U.S. dealings with Australia and New Zealand on these matters as essentially pragmatic and ad hoc. The United States sees common objectives and seeks cooperation but gives no special priority to their views or to cooperation among the three.

Finally, in the concluding comment, the editor and Gary Hawke note that, within the context of broad agreement on the objective of a liberal international economic order, there are striking differences in the specific approaches and emphases of the three countries. They attribute these differences principally to the differing power positions and ranges of interests of the three. Australia can aspire to an active leadership role in the Asia-Pacific region and so accords a particularly high priority to regional cooperation. As a smaller player, New Zealand sees important opportunities in the regional economy, but only as one element in an overall strategy to develop and exploit market openings on a global basis. For the United States, even as the relative importance of its economic links with the region grows, global interests and other (including domestic) considerations detract from its willingness and ability to give priority to specifically regional undertakings.

NOTES

1. The material in this section was provided by Thomas Layman, co-author of Chapter 9. The statistics are drawn from the International Monetary Fund's *Direction of Trade Statistics* and other publications, as well as national statistical sources.

2. For a good survey of the cost differentials over a wide range of products produced in Japan versus those in other Asian countries, see Darlin 1988.

3. Most of the material in this section was provided by the authors of the country chapters, particularly Jenelle Bonnor. The editor gratefully acknowledges these contributions. More detailed treatment of this subject can be found, inter alia, in Japan Center for International Exchange 1980 and 1982, Hooper 1982, Soesastro and Han 1983, and Scalapino, Sato, Wanandi, and Han 1988.

7

Regional Economic Cooperation in the Asia-Pacific: An Australian Priority

JENELLE BONNOR

The examination of the regional economic roles and relationships of Australia, New Zealand, and the United States in the Asia-Pacific is especially pertinent in a decade when there is likely to be substantial change in traditional methods of managing the global economy.

This chapter focuses on Australia's response to these changes. It examines the increasing emphasis Australia is placing on economic integration with the Asia-Pacific region in the pursuit of national economic well-being. However, it argues that this priority needs to be seen in the context of Australia's long-term commitment to an open, international trading order. Australia's bilateral economic relations with New Zealand and the United States continue to provide an important focus of Australia's international economic policies, and there is also scope to strengthen these relationships in both a bilateral and regional context.

To date, Australia has invested most of its diplomatic trade effort in promoting the success of the General Agreement on Tariffs and Trade (GATT). For the Australian government, the rationale for such an approach has been the belief that participation in multilateral bodies has generally resulted in greater trade and economic gains than unilateral or bilateral action. However, the parameters of global economic interaction are changing. As the trend toward regional arrangements strengthens, Australia, as a small player, has been compelled to focus on alternatives in addition to multilateralism. The extent to which these alternatives are pursued will very much depend on the outcome of the Uruguay Round of the GATT.

Although the achievement of a liberal, international trading order is still the first priority of Australian trade policymakers, the increasing importance of trade with Asia means that Asia is the logical place for Australia to focus its pursuit of trade opportunities. Asia has become the main subject of Australia's evolving, and increasingly interlinked, foreign and economic policy objectives. Participation in regional economic cooperation is one means by which Australia can achieve greater integration with the economies of the Asia-Pacific.

AUSTRALIA AND APEC

Precursors

Australia's attention to regional economic cooperation is not new. Australia has participated in the exploration and refinement of the idea since the 1960s. The major reason for this has been the changing nature of Australia's trade relations. In 1964–66 for instance, the Asia-Pacific (Japan, China, ASEAN, and North America) was the market for 49.9 percent of Australia's exports and the source of 44.8 percent of its imports. By 1979–81, 61.8 percent of exports were directed to, and 60.1 percent of Australian imports were received from, the Asia-Pacific (Drysdale 1988). These shares continue to grow. Over the five year period between 1987–88 and 1991–92, average annual growth of Australian exports to the economies now represented in APEC was 10.3 percent, with imports from APEC members growing by 4.9 percent; by 1991–92, trade with APEC members accounted for 73.1 percent of Australia's total exports and 63.3 percent of Australia's imports, respectively (DFAT 1992).

A brief outline of Australia's historical involvement in Asia-Pacific regional economic cooperation is useful as a context in which to place Australia's current efforts (Bonnor 1990). Virtually from the start, Australia was involved in the development of this concept as one of the projected members of Kiyoshi Kojima's original PAFTA free trade area proposal. Australian economists have participated in the related PAFTAD meetings of economists from the PAFTA countries (and others) begun in 1968. As indicated in the introduction, Australian-Japanese business activity formed the basis from which the Pacific Basin Economic Council evolved.

Australian academics, particularly Australia National University Chancellor Sir John Crawford and ANU economist Peter Drysdale, played key roles in the development of the OPTAD proposal. Crawford chaired the 1980 seminar at ANU that led to the establishment of PECC. These informal efforts to advance the process of regional economic cooperation also had Australian government support, most visibly illustrated in Prime Minister Malcolm Fraser's role in initiating the 1980 ANU seminar.

The Launch

The Australian government took the lead in the launching of APEC in 1989. In a hastily put together initiative during a visit to Seoul in January

1989, Prime Minister Bob Hawke (1989: 4) proposed the establishment of a "more formal intergovernmental vehicle of regional cooperation" with the capacity for analysis and consultation to help inform economic policy-making.

Hawke sketched his idea in the explicit context of trade pressures throughout the world, tension in the GATT Round, and a trend toward trading arrangements that might undermine the multilateral system. These issues reflected Australian concerns. He suggested that cooperation could make the Uruguay Round more constructive, and that obstacles to regional trade could be discussed and common economic interests identified.

The most immediately controversial element of the original Hawke proposal was the initial exclusion of North America. The government responded to this criticism, and in March 1989, Minister for Foreign Affairs and Trade Gareth Evans indicated that Australia had no problems with a Pacific-wide concept. Although it was envisaged that China and Hong Kong would participate, the events of Tiananmen Square in June 1989 and China's sensitivities meant that the participation of China, Hong Kong, and Taiwan (as Chinese Taipei) did not occur until the Seoul ministerial meeting in 1991. There was strong bipartisan political support in Australia from the beginning for the inclusion of the "three Chinas."

In order to promote and elaborate Hawke's idea, immediately following Hawke's Korean trip, the head of the Department of Foreign Affairs and Trade, Richard Woolcott, and a delegation of DFAT officials, visited eight regional countries and both Evans and Hawke visited the United States. They eventually gained the agreement of all nominated countries to participate in the first APEC meeting in Canberra in November 1989.

Motivations

Australia's role in the creation of APEC in 1989 was motivated by a number of factors that are still relevant today. Among these was an important domestic political impetus. The Hawke Labor government used the APEC initiative as a means of gaining "some respite from criticisms of its inability to manage the domestic economy at a time of increasing inflation, mounting interest rates, and record current account deficits" (Higgott, Cooper, and Bonnor 1990: 850).

At the time, the Australian federal opposition (a coalition of the Liberal and National Parties) criticized the vagueness and haste of Hawke's proposal, as well as the lack of regional consultation before its announcement (Hill 1989b). Shadow (opposition) Minister for Foreign Affairs Robert Hill (1989a) initiated a parliamentary enquiry into APEC which heard comprehensive submissions from a wide range of Australian interest groups and government departments (see Australian Parliament 1989b). The debate in Australia on APEC became quite lively.

Domestic factors, however, are not a sufficient explanation for the interest aroused by the idea in Australia. APEC also needs to be seen in the context of Australia's attempts to respond to changing international economic circumstances. Australia's relative economic position, in terms of its share of world trade, is declining. That its position has not deteriorated further is largely due to Australia's increasing dependence on dynamic Asian markets noted at the start of this section. The proposal for the APEC forum was directly related to the perception that Australia could improve its domestic economic position by increasing its integration with the region.

Nevertheless, it should also be noted in this context that it was argued at the time — and is still argued today — that merely increasing Australia's interdependence with Asian economies would not set Australia on the path to economic growth (Hughes 1988). It is widely recognized that for Australia to be attractive as a trade partner for regional countries, Australia must improve its domestic economic position and improve its competitiveness (see, for instance, Garnaut 1989). This means addressing labor market reform, adjusting wage and productivity policies, removing industry protection, and addressing structural inefficiencies. Domestic economic reform must accompany a regional economic role.

A third factor behind Australia's interest in APEC was that a cornerstone of Australian foreign policy has long been the support for the GATT. Since the launching of the Uruguay Round of negotiations in 1986, this support has been focused on gaining a successful outcome for the round, especially in agriculture and services. At the time of APEC's inception, it was hoped by Australian officials that a coordinated APEC position on the Uruguay Round might provide the impetus the round needed for a successful conclusion.

A fourth factor in the priority Australia attached, and still attaches, to APEC was Australia's desire to define a regional political role for itself. Not only was establishing regional dialogue, in which Australia could participate, seen as an important end in itself — especially in the light of U.S.-Japan trade tensions — but Australia saw the opportunity to improve its own regional credentials. Leadership of the Cairns Group of nonsubsidizing agricultural exporting nations in pressing for global agricultural reform in the GATT had already shown its advantages for a middle power such as Australia (see Cooper and Higgott 1990); this experience may have helped give Australia the confidence — and credibility — to play such a role in Asia-Pacific regional cooperation.

This effort has been described as "part of a signalling process that . . . is meant to inform the region of the break with Australia's regionally insular and protectionist past and express its desire for a greater regional role" (Higgott, Cooper, and Bonnor 1990: 848). Australia's foreign minister explicitly stated that "our whole approach to the conduct of foreign policy in recent times has been to play the role not of an outsider looking into the region, but of an active participant in the region's affairs, a cooperative partner in the resolution of regional problems" (Evans 1991b).

With Evans as foreign minister, Australia's approach to foreign policy has been characterized by a series of initiatives covering a broad range of areas, including economics. APEC fitted well into this approach. Indeed, Evans (1991c) has said that "the most important regional economic initiative we have undertaken has been unquestionably the inauguration of the Asia Pacific Economic Cooperation (APEC) process."

AUSTRALIA AND APEC'S AGENDA

The Australian government's priorities for regional economic cooperation remain focused on APEC, but Australia's emphasis on areas of importance within APEC has shifted since 1989.

The successful conclusion to the Uruguay Round has remained an important focus of Australia's efforts within APEC. The joint statements from all four of APEC's ministerial meetings to date—Canberra 1989, Singapore 1990, Seoul 1991, and Bangkok 1992—have given major attention to the round.

The GATT Round was perhaps the easiest and most obvious subject to take up in the earlier APEC meetings. The round's importance to the world trading system and the commonality of interests within the region in seeing a successful conclusion made it the natural focus of discussion. The idea of a collective bargaining position in international forums remains an attractive one, especially given that a coordinated Asia-Pacific regional voice is too often lacking in major world organizations.

However, APEC came too late to develop any real consensus on the Uruguay Round, and so its practical role in this respect has been limited. The GATT Round was the focus of the 1990 Singapore meeting and the subsequent meeting of APEC trade ministers in Vancouver in September of that year. Nevertheless, as an Australian analyst of APEC, Andrew Elek, has pointed out (1991), insufficient agreement was reached on the crucial issues—especially agriculture—to make an effective negotiating approach.

Nevertheless, a successful outcome of the GATT Round will remain one of Australia's highest priorities. As a small, open, and vulnerable economy, Australia has relied heavily on the multilateral trading system for its welfare. It will continue its commitment to such a system but will need to do so at a number of levels.

Beyond any influence on the negotiations themselves, APEC also has potential as a vehicle through which the region's response to the GATT Round can be managed. There has been a growing concern that resort to discriminatory and protectionist policies might be seen by some as the most effective way to enhance national well-being in the event of the expected less-than-optimal result of the round. The United States Export Enhancement Program (EEP), which provides subsidies to American wheat exports and has been such a serious issue in U.S.–Australian relations, is seen as a prime example of such measures; reassurances that Australia was not a target of this program did not negate the reality of its impact on Australian producers.

In APEC, therefore, Australian attention has shifted from efforts to develop a consensus negotiating approach in the GATT, to an exploration of ways to achieve some of the practical benefits of trade liberalization for the region. The establishment of a small APEC secretariat in Singapore, agreed on at the 1992 ministerial and supported by Australia, can assist APEC in moving in this direction.

It could be argued that work toward reducing regional trade barriers has already commenced through the formation of the 10 APEC working groups. However, there is a perception in Australia that a qualitative shift is needed in APEC from efforts to exchange information and build communication networks on economic and trade issues, with which the working groups have been mainly concerned, to actual efforts to reduce barriers to trade.

Such an approach offers two potential benefits for Australia. First, it is another step toward the general aim of multilateral trade liberalization. Second, it is an insurance policy—in case the GATT does not fulfill expectations. Then the benefits of trade liberalization for regional countries can still be pursued. Thus, Australia was actively involved in the efforts that led to the establishment of the APEC Informal Group on Trade Liberalization in 1992.

The Labor government is pursuing a step-by-step or, as Evans describes it, an "incremental" approach to regional trade liberalization (Evans 1992a). The government believes that a gradualist approach is necessitated by the difficulty of achieving regional agreement on practical areas for reducing trade barriers. There is debate on this point in Australia, however. The opposition has been critical of APEC for having moved too slowly in putting regional trade liberalization explicitly on its agenda (Hill 1991b, 1992; Downer 1991). Opposition spokesmen argue that more must be done to make the APEC working groups relevant to the aim of trade liberalization. To this end, Shadow Foreign Minister Hill (1990, 1991b, 1992) has advocated a more explicit role for business groups and existing regional groups such as the PECC and PBEC in APEC meetings and in its working groups.

Although Australian officials had previously referred to the importance of regional trade liberalization (see Woolcott 1991; Berry 1991), the first major public government exploration of APEC's potential in this regard was by Foreign Minister Evans in August 1992 (Evans 1992a). Evans identified potential action in four areas: reducing uncertainties in the regional trading environment, addressing physical impediments to trade, harmonization of regional regulations and standards, and improvement of market access. He also continued to promote the establishment of an Eminent Persons Group to examine regional trade liberalization, an Australian idea first proposed in 1991. Some practical measures to work toward regional trade liberalization were agreed to at the 1992 Bangkok ministerial meeting. That meeting also endorsed Evans's Eminent Persons Group.

The Australian government greeted these steps with enthusiasm. Evans (1992b) even went so far as to say that APEC might lead to "a European Community-type concept down the track," a thought he repeated on a subsequent visit to the United States (Evans 1992d). This rhetoric appeared to go well beyond the incremental approach previously advocated by Evans, and reactions to these statements, including a negative response from Japan (Byrne 1992), indicated that the regional preference is indeed for a step-by-step approach.

For the longer term, the Australian government also sees APEC as playing a useful general political role. It does not necessarily see the benefits of APEC as limited to economic issues, but as part of a broader process of building regional linkages (Woolcott 1991). As one example of the potential wider utility of the APEC process, Evans used the opportunity of the 1992 Bangkok meeting to pursue negotiations about the troubled Cambodian peace process (Evans 1992b).

Prime Minister Paul Keating's proposal for a regional heads of government meeting based on APEC indicates that the Australian government regards APEC as a useful venue for further regional leadership efforts and initiatives. However, coming as it did from one of the newest heads of government in the region, the regional summit proposal did not carry great weight, and the initial response, especially from the United States and Indonesia, was cautious. However, U.S. President Bill Clinton took up the idea in mid-1993, inviting APEC leaders to an "informal conference" following the 1993 APEC ministerial meeting in Seattle.

There is ongoing debate in Australia as to the merits of APEC and its appropriate emphases. In the future it can certainly be expected that regional trade liberalization will be pursued by whichever party is in government. While the Labor government's efforts in this regard have focused on APEC, the Liberal and National Parties have committed a Coalition government to action over a much broader spectrum (Hewson 1992b).

GLOBAL INSTITUTIONS

In accordance with the priority placed by the Australian government on a successful conclusion to the GATT Round, the Department of Foreign Affairs and Trade has devoted a substantial proportion of its resources over recent years to the round. Almost regardless of the outcome of the round, on which there are numerous alternative scenarios and a great deal of debate in Australia, and because of its dependence on world markets for its exports, Australia will continue to give high priority to such multilateral efforts to preserve and further liberalize the international economic and trade system.

Although GATT ranks as the most important of the global economic institutions to Australia, it is not the only one to which Australian efforts have been directed. For example, Australia is an active supporter of and participant in the International Monetary Fund and various UN bodies dealing with economic issues.

The OECD, of which Australia has been a member since 1971, has been useful as a forum for regular consultations on a range of economic issues with the other advanced countries, especially the United States, the European Community states, and Japan. Australia values the capacity of the OECD for quality analysis of economic trends and developments in member countries and nonmembers of interest, and of international trade issues (Willis 1992).

However, the lingering impression of a European focus within the OECD detracts from its usefulness as a global institution. In light of Australia's own increasing focus on the Asia-Pacific region, and the lack of representation of Asian countries in the OECD, Australia is unlikely to turn to the OECD to compensate for any shortcomings in the multilateral trade system.

REGIONALISM AND TRADE BLOCS

The uncertainties in the multilateral trading environment, and the fear of a trend toward powerful trading blocs, require that countries such as Australia consider what their best options are in such circumstances.

Signs of a trend toward trading blocs are readily apparent in the Asia-Pacific region. There has been the agreement between the ASEAN nations on a Free Trade Area (AFTA). From 1993, AFTA will use a Common Effective Preferential Tariff (CEPT) scheme that will be applied to 15 categories of products. The aim is the reduction of tariff levels on these products to between zero and 5 percent by 2008 (ASEAN Heads of Government 1992). There is also Malaysia's proposal for an East Asia Economic Caucus (EAEC) excluding Australia, New Zealand, the United States, and Canada. At this stage, the EAEC is supposed to be an East Asian consultative group, but it may provide the option for a more formal trade bloc in the future.

The development that has attracted the most attention and stimulated the most debate in Australia is the conclusion in August 1992 of the North American Free Trade Agreement (NAFTA), encompassing the United States, Canada, and Mexico. Shortly thereafter, in a campaign speech in September, President George Bush expressed the willingness to negotiate free trade arrangements with a variety of other countries including several in the Asia-Pacific, among them Australia and New Zealand.

The debate in Australia has centered on NAFTA's implications for Australia, and on how Australia should respond to the Bush offer. Even before the Bush speech, opposition leader John Hewson proposed that Australia apply to join NAFTA. This position was based on the coalition parties' policy of pursuing trade opportunities wherever they exist, using multilateral, regional and bilateral negotiations (Hewson 1992a). Although commonly portrayed in the Australian media as indicating a preference for North America over Asia, Hewson in fact argued that Australia could maximize trade benefits in both regions.

Despite an initially positive reaction, Prime Minister Keating rejected the idea of negotiating a bilateral trade arrangement with the United States. He argued that a hub-and-spokes model, along the lines of the U.S. security arrangements throughout the Asia-Pacific, was an inappropriate system for organizing regional trade relations (Kitney 1992; Grattan 1992). Keating also indicated that he believed Australia would not have much to gain in terms of increased access to agricultural markets by attempting to join NAFTA (Keating 1992a).

In a statement to the Australian Parliament in October 1992, Keating (1992b) elaborated and slightly modified his position. He indicated that in an uncertain trading environment Australia would not rule out bilateral or "plurilateral" agreements, but said that he had reservations about a network of bilateral preferential agreements centered on the United States. In the case of an Australia–U.S. agreement, he was also concerned over the possible perception in Asia that Australia would be turning its back on the region.

This latter concern was echoed by two Australian academics, Peter Drysdale and Ross Garnaut, in a joint paper on the implications of NAFTA for Australia and New Zealand (Drysdale and Garnaut 1992). They argued that if Australia joined a preferential trade arrangement with the United States, the interpretation in the region would be that Australia was avoiding East Asia and choosing its old cultural and political affinities, which would exacerbate wider Pacific trade tensions. However, Drysdale and Garnaut concluded that the extension of NAFTA-type arrangements to all APEC members would not have the same negative implications.

The debate about how Australia should best respond to NAFTA and other potential regional blocs is predicated on the uncertainties of the outcome of the GATT Round. A major study commissioned by the Australian government (Snape, Adams, and Morgan 1992a, 1992b) on the implications of regional trade agreements and Australia's response, outlined a number of options for Australia linked with different scenarios for the GATT.

This study, commonly referred to as the Snape report after its primary author, concluded that unilateral action aimed at gaining access to markets is probably beyond Australia's means. It determined that action of this nature would be unlikely to change trade policies that discriminate against Australian products. It did not, however, completely dismiss unilateral action. It pointed to some actions Australia could take completely on its own such as further liberalizing its own markets, and some toward other countries that might have some impact such as publishing lists of restrictions on Australian exports imposed by other countries that are inconsistent with the GATT (Snape 1992).

The Snape report also examined the option of pursuing bilateral free trade agreements in the event of an unsuccessful or less than optimal Uruguay Round. The conclusion was that such arrangements might be worth considering with Japan, South Korea, Taiwan, or in the long term, China.

Regarding "plurilateral" options, the Snape team believed that there was limited attraction for Australia in joining AFTA, largely due to its restricted product coverage. They saw greater merit in an APEC-based free trade arrangement in the absence of a "healthy multilateral system." The practical difficulties of gaining agreement on a free trade area acceptable to all APEC members, however, would be considerable, and the report concluded that it would be unlikely that APEC could resolve the factors that had contributed to the failure of the Uruguay Round.

Partly in recognition of these difficulties, Drysdale and Garnaut (1992) believe that APEC should give priority to sectoral trade liberalization. A failure of the GATT Round would make this even more advisable, given that the dynamic growth of Asian economies has been dependent on an open trading system.

It is generally agreed in Australia that subregional arrangements that discriminated against nonmembers would not be in Australia's best interests. However, in an uncertain post–GATT Round environment, Australia would need to explore opportunities that enhanced Australia's trade in a way that would not be detrimental to third parties.

BILATERAL COOPERATION–NEW ZEALAND

Australia has worked with the United States and New Zealand actively and constructively in APEC and in the GATT process. Australia has also worked with both countries on a bilateral basis.

Economic cooperation between Australia and New Zealand has a long history, aimed (to differing degrees at different times) at enhancing the efficiency of and opportunities for bilateral trade, and at improving the competitiveness of both countries in the world trading system.

A major milestone was the 1966 New Zealand–Australia Free Trade Agreement (Burnett 1988). While this agreement succeeded in removing tariffs and quantitative restrictions on 80 percent of trade, it involved a cumbersome item-by-item negotiating process. When both countries embarked on a course of overall liberalization of trade in the 1980s, the existing mechanism was not considered an effective way to proceed (DFAT 1991). The result was the Closer Economic Relations (CER) agreement, providing for a more automatic process of across-the-board removal of trade restrictions, which came into effect on 1 January 1983.

Both Australia and New Zealand have benefited substantially from CER. Total bilateral trade has expanded and by 1992 stood at A$5 billion, up from A\$2 billion in 1983. Although the Australian share of New Zealand imports has remained relatively constant, New Zealand's share of Australian imports has increased substantially. Free trade in goods was achieved in July 1990, ahead of the original schedule, and significant liberalization of services was undertaken as a result of an overall review of the arrangement in 1988. A second review in 1992 addressed further areas of liberalization such as business law and customs procedures harmonization, regulatory standards for goods and occupations, taxation, and the creation of a single aviation market (Kerin and Burdon 1992).

Liberalization of trade between Australia and New Zealand has always been placed in a wider context. This was again reiterated in the joint statement following the 1992 review: "CER is an outward-looking agreement and an important part of our wider effort to encourage export awareness and make our economies more internationally competitive. It is evidence of our commitment to a more open, liberal multilateral trading system" (Kerin and Burdon 1992: 1). Of particular significance is that CER has not raised barriers to third countries, and that it has been implemented at a time when the economies of both countries have been progressively liberalizing.

Thus, in addition to its obvious bilateral advantages, CER has been consistent with Australia's aims in the multilateral GATT system; both Australia and New Zealand have had similar aims in this respect. Further, as the first genuine free trade agreement in the Asia-Pacific region, CER is now also seen as supporting a push for greater trade liberalization throughout the region.

Both sides of Australian politics are committed to the continuation and further development of CER. The Labor government has indicated that it will continue a "practical and pragmatic approach" in CER toward the benefits of closer integration (Kerin 1992). The stated goal of the Liberal-National coalition is economic integration with New Zealand through the establishment of a single domestic market in all areas of trade (Peacock 1992). Shadow Trade Minister Andrew Peacock has gone further, saying there may be scope for the development of a coordinated trade strategy with New Zealand, and for cooperation in the promotion of trade, investment, and tourism in the Asia-Pacific region (Peacock 1992).

It is clear that Australia intends to continue to work closely with New Zealand on bilateral trade issues, but also sees New Zealand as a partner in wider regional and multilateral forums. For instance, in the creation of APEC, Australia believed it was important to have New Zealand's support early. In the Cairns Group, Australia has worked closely with New Zealand as another efficient agricultural producer in the promotion of agricultural interests in the GATT Round. The perception of similarity in economic interests indicates that Australia will continue to regard New Zealand as a partner in these cooperative efforts.

BILATERAL COOPERATION – THE UNITED STATES

Notwithstanding the debate over Australia's response to NAFTA discussed above, a number of mechanisms are already in place for the management and promotion of the U.S.–Australia economic relationship.

The United States is Australia's largest supplier of imports and Australia's largest international investor. The United States has a large surplus across virtually every category of transaction with Australia, and the deficit in trade with the United States was the largest Australia had with any country in 1990–91 (Taylor 1992). Nevertheless, the United States is also a significant export market for Australia, accounting for 10 percent of Australian exports in 1991–92.

The annual Australia–United States Ministerial Talks provide the most regular opportunity for high-level discussions on a range of issues, including economic and trade questions, although the effectiveness of this mechanism in the economic field is somewhat limited because it does not always involve economic ministers. The 1992 discussions, for example, provided an opportunity for both countries to reiterate the importance they attach to a successful conclusion to the Uruguay Round as well as the urgent need for a breakthrough on agriculture.

In order to facilitate and expand the dialogue on economic issues, in 1992, the two countries concluded a bilateral Trade and Investment Framework Agreement (TIFA) that provides for regular high-level economic consultations (Keating 1992c). Australia's foreign minister has described the TIFA as "improving, formalising and regularising consultative arrangements on a whole range of trade and investment issues" (Evans 1992c: B331). The TIFA is not, at this stage, designed as a mechanism for reducing tariff or nontariff barriers. It will, however, be useful in the overall management of the economic relationship.

The U.S. response to the difficulties in the GATT and its own economic circumstances has in many instances taken the form of unilateral actions. These include the use of the EEP, "Section 301" provisions in trade legislation requiring progressively stronger action against foreign restrictions on U.S. exports, and the initiation of bilateral negotiations such as the Structural Impediments Initiative with Japan. Australia has both benefited and suffered from these U.S. actions. Australia has in some cases gained improved access to markets as a result of U.S. negotiations, for example, beef exports to South Korea and Japan. However, as discussed previously, the use of the EEP has significantly reduced earnings from some Australian agricultural exports, and has led to strong Australian protests to the United States.

Despite differences on some questions, Australia has enjoyed the support of the United States in the APEC process, particularly in the elaboration of the APEC working groups. As host of the 1993 APEC ministerial meeting, the United States has a significant opportunity to contribute to the further evolution of APEC, including the development of pragmatic proposals for the reduction of trade barriers in the region. Australia would undoubtedly work with the United States to gain regional agreement on further steps toward this end.

FUTURE COOPERATION BETWEEN
ANZUS GOVERNMENTS

There is scope for future cooperation on trade and broader economic policy questions between Australia, New Zealand, and the United States.

Australia will continue to work with both countries in the development of the bilateral economic relationships. Australia's trade relationship with New Zealand is likely to be easier than that with the United States. The development of CER will continue and there is sufficient commitment on both sides of the Tasman to address the more difficult areas necessary to achieve truly free trade between them.

The economic relationship with the United States will be more difficult, especially given the likelihood of further unilateral U.S. trade actions that will be detrimental to Australian (and New Zealand) access to markets. The relationship may also be complicated by the evolution of NAFTA, depending importantly on the outcome of the Uruguay Round and its impact on the world trading system as a whole. In any event, however, there are likely to be opportunities for Australia and the United States to work together to secure market access for primary products, one example being rice markets in South Korea and Japan.

Opportunities for trilateral cooperation between the three ANZUS governments will probably be confined to working together in regional and international forums, such as APEC and the GATT. However, regional sensitivities will need to be taken into account. Given the continuing discussion of an East Asia Economic Caucus that appears motivated by a perception that Asian interests are not being adequately represented in other forums, cooperation between the three ANZUS countries will have to be conducted sensibly to avoid the perception of a "Western" viewpoint at odds with Asia's interests. Nevertheless, there could well be scope for the ANZUS governments to use their collective influence and national examples of trade liberalization to encourage the reduction of trade barriers throughout the region.

In the current climate of global economic uncertainty it is particularly important that the conditions be preserved that have enabled the phenomenal economic growth throughout the Asia-Pacific region in the postwar period. Further opportunities for trade must also be enhanced. New ways of managing trade and economic relationships are likely to develop during the 1990s as new pressures for change and new priorities arise. As an economy dependent on a liberal international trade order, Australia needs to clearly identify its own national trading interests, but it also needs to pursue those interests in a manner that will not only achieve maximum benefit for Australia, but at the same time contribute to the preservation of an open world trading system.

NOTE

The views expressed in this paper are entirely those of the author and do not necessarily represent the views of the Australian opposition or the shadow minister for foreign affairs.

8

Regionalism, Bilateralism, and Multilateralism: A New Zealand View

ALASTAIR BISLEY

NEW ZEALAND AND REGIONAL ECONOMIC CONSULTATION

New Zealand has been closely associated with the efforts (increasingly successful over the last 10 years or so) to create a more cohesive set of economic consultative arrangements and institutions in the Asia-Pacific region. Perhaps at first, it was more interested than active. Successive political leaders, reflecting an awareness which existed also in the academic and business communities, have been struck by the dynamism of the countries in the Asia-Pacific region—countries with which New Zealand, especially in the period after the Second World War, established important links through trade, development assistance, and security arrangements.

There was some skepticism about the quick realization of some of the more evolved forms of economic cooperation. Sir Robert Muldoon said in a speech in Sydney in 1982, that he could not see a Pacific economic community being established within the next 20 years (Muldoon 1982). There was also anxiety that Pacific forms of cooperation should not damage other important economic relationships outside the region. However, politicians were open to the idea that new arrangements for regional economic cooperation might be useful, and were prepared to speculate about the principles that might underlie them (Cooper 1983).

New Zealand leaders welcomed the 1985 initiative of Australian Prime Minister Bob Hawke to hold regional consultations on the upcoming round of trade negotiations under the General Agreement on Tariffs and Trade (GATT). The consultations were aimed, according to Minister for External Relations and Trade Mike Moore, "to ensure the region's negotiating priorities are not totally overshadowed by the priorities of nations bordering on the Atlantic" (Moore 1985). Neither the United States nor Canada were participants in the regional consultations. Mr. Moore also had a lively eye for possible future developments of this idea: "We want to look beyond CER and the GATT and see what opportunities we can develop for ourselves" (Moore 1985). New Zealand has participated vigorously in the Pacific Group (an informal gathering of South Pacific governments discussing issues on an ad hoc basis) and hosted one of its meetings in Wellington in September 1988.

Following the establishment of the Pacific Economic Cooperation Conference in 1980, New Zealand set up its own New Zealand National Committee for Pacific Economic Cooperation (NZCPEC) under the chairmanship of Rt. Hon. Brian Talboys in 1982. The New Zealand committee took a leadership role in the Agriculture Task Force, and hosted the seventh conference (PECC VII) in 1989. Through the support it gave to PECC VII and in its active participation in PECC affairs, the New Zealand government demonstrated its interest in regional consultative arrangements in what was, and in some respects still remains, their most comprehensive version.

Finally, New Zealand was heavily involved in the discussions that were going on in the region before Mr. Hawke's proposal in Seoul in January 1989, but which his speech and Australia's diplomatic initiative crystallized and intensified, leading to the Canberra ministerial meeting on Asia Pacific Economic Cooperation in November of that year. These discussions obliquely involved PECC (which was also considering the possibility of a ministerial meeting). They were conducted mainly by Australia and its various regional partners, and they reached a preliminary resolution at the ASEAN PMC in Brunei in July. It was the debate of the ASEAN PMC that cleared the way for the Canberra meeting.

The New Zealand government supported the notion of intensified consultative arrangements involving Japan and Korea, the United States and Canada, the ASEAN six, and Australia and New Zealand. It was anxious that China, Hong Kong, and Taiwan should also be involved if possible, and emphatic that the United States and Canada should be there from the start. It wanted the ASEAN secretariat to be associated in some manner, and PECC as well, to bring to bear the contribution of its nongovernmental interests. It was anxious that South Pacific Island countries should not be forgotten in the process. Finally, it wanted the process to be handled in such a way as to avoid any diversion of effort from the GATT Uruguay Round. But all these reservations were within an overall attitude of support for the development of Pacific economic cooperation.

New Zealand has participated at both ministerial and officials levels in the APEC process, and APEC activities have involved several government departments, the private sector, and academics. These last two groups have been involved both through NZCPEC and directly. APEC and its affairs have occupied a significant share of the time of New Zealand missions in the capitals of APEC participants. At a time of considerable constraint in its diplomatic resources, New Zealand has placed a high priority on economic consultative arrangements in the region, and especially on APEC.

BENEFITS OF APEC

The reasons for New Zealand's interest in APEC are largely shared with the other APEC participants. APEC is, after all, the result of a coalescence of views about economic developments in the region and how they should be regarded. But to some extent New Zealand also has particular interests.

One classic and comprehensive statement of the reasons for enhancing Asia-Pacific regional economic cooperation is a 1988 paper by Japan's Ministry of International Trade and Industry (MITI), *Toward New Asia Pacific Cooperation: Promotion of Multilevel Gradually Advancing Cooperation on a Consensus Basis.* The MITI paper describes the region's dynamism, the imbalances that threaten its equilibrium, and their possible consequences, both global and regional. It notes the fragility of some of the Asian economies in spite of the rapidity of their economic growth. It seeks, in enhanced regional economic cooperation, a recipe for dealing gradually but systematically with these related problems of developed and developing players, in an atmosphere of increased understanding, and in such a way as to strengthen, not weaken, global systems.

This analysis was well noted in New Zealand, and drawn on by Sir Frank Holmes, whose influence in discussions of regional relationships has been significant. But although New Zealanders were aware of this kind of thinking, that is probably not exactly the way they thought. So it may be useful to give an account of New Zealand motives, or of the New Zealand angle on the general case. What follows is not an attempt to establish an authoritative New Zealand philosophy on Asia-Pacific regionalism, and it is not an authoritative history of the views of the New Zealand government either. It is an impressionistic account of some views that seemed to be shared by various people, in government and outside it, who were working in the area at the time.

First, New Zealand shares, of course, the wide perception of the region's dynamism, of its increasing wealth, its growing share of world exports, and of the way in which intra-regional trade is growing more rapidly than the region's trade with the rest of the world. As Stuart Harris has remarked, the significance of the emergence of the Asia-Pacific region "is that there is now a multipolar system replacing a unitary or bipolar system" (Harris 1989: 12–13).

To a point, New Zealand can see its own experience in these changes. The pattern of its trade has moved quite heavily toward the region. New Zealand's exports to other PECC countries grew from 43.1 percent of its total exports in 1970 to 67.2 percent in 1988; imports from other PECC countries grew from 51.8 percent to 69.2 percent of the total over the same period. Its aviation links in the region, vital for tourist flows and important for trade and commerce, have expanded dramatically.[1]

But New Zealand has not been one of the high-growth countries of Asia-Pacific; the rapid and pervasive economic reform that it has undergone since 1984 is only now beginning to be rewarded by higher growth. Further, while direct investment in New Zealand from the region has increased, the increase has been slow by comparison with flows within the region in general. Indeed, a 1990 study suggested that direct investment in New Zealand from Japan, the region's primary source of capital, actually decreased between 1987 and 1989.[2]

The causes of New Zealand's recent low rates of growth are complex and disputed; but what is entirely clear is that the expanding markets that other Asia-Pacific countries provide, the capital flows, the technology, the cheap and high-quality imports, are vital for New Zealand's improved economic performance. Regional economic cooperation and APEC provide one means for tying ourselves better into the region, understanding it better and influencing, in conjunction with others, the way in which it evolves. New Zealand and Australia, while not the same as each other, are still different from most of the other categories of APEC members. For them (and perhaps also for Canada), APEC is a means of improving their entrée to a region with which they increasingly identify their futures. The basis of New Zealand's economic strategy is to develop links between New Zealand and the most dynamic parts of the world economy; APEC provides a range of contacts with the principal target areas.

So, as a small country that had made dramatic changes in the way in which it managed its economy, and thus in the way in which it related to the rest of the world, New Zealand welcomed the chance for an intensified economic dialogue that could be carried on at government level with other APEC participants. This was valuable not only in relation to Japan and the United States (with the United States, APEC provided some valuable common and neutral ground as the disagreement over nuclear ships lost some of its emotional intensity) but also in relation to the ASEAN countries. New Zealand values its participation in the annual ASEAN PMC, but bilateral economic consultation with its ASEAN opposite numbers did not seem to have kept up with the increasing importance of the trade and economic relationship. APEC promised a dialogue, supplementing the one in the PMC, with a rather broader agenda. With Korea, too, a country that had become New Zealand's sixth largest trading partner, APEC seemed to offer new and wider perspectives for a dialogue that had recently focused on problems in trade.

New Zealand was also vitally interested in what happened to the multilateral trading system. It was aware of the threats to that system both from the imbalances that existed within the region, from bilateralism, from the rise in protectionism, and from the proliferation of regional trading arrangements. Though some in New Zealand shared a more general anxiety that the formation of an Asia-Pacific grouping might add to centrifugal forces, or at least divert attention from the Uruguay Round, APEC seemed, on balance to offer a means of enlisting a unique coalition consisting of three of the majors, plus developed and developing countries, all of whom owed economic success to an open system, for pushing the round to a successful conclusion. It suggested to some the possibility of putting a little pressure on negotiating partners in the round that were holding up the negotiations. For New Zealand, APEC meant that if there was some falling away from the multilateral system, it would not find itself on its own.

Another consideration had to do with the relations between the economic superpowers. The Structural Impediments Initiative, which followed the U.S. 301 action against Japan, like U.S. Secretary of State Baker's acknowledgment of the global partnership between the United States and Japan, demonstrated the significance that a massive, but by no means straightforward relationship could have for the Asia-Pacific region (and globally, too, no doubt). There seemed to be great benefits for New Zealand in being involved in a grouping — one that included other important partners of Japan and the United States — that could provide an important theater for the working out of their relationship. It seemed better to be in the room where the decisions were taken, even as a small player, than outside it.

Finally, though this catalog of motives is not exhaustive, there were subregional considerations. In thinking about APEC, New Zealand could not, of course, fail to reflect on its relations with the Pacific Island states. It wanted to try to ensure that their interests were not left out of account. Nor, of course, could it divorce the question of Asia-Pacific regionalism from the question of its relations with Australia. The initiative for a ministerial meeting in November 1989 was, like many earlier suggestions for regional economic cooperation, an Australian initiative. The Australian team came to New Zealand first to explain their approach, both because they recognized the commonality of interests in this area and because a marked lack of enthusiasm from their CER partner would not have helped their initiative. Then New Zealand prime minister, David Lange, was quick to write to Bob Hawke, offering his support. If there were differences of emphasis over timing, for example, the broader objectives were very much the same.

A PACIFIC OECD?

The notion of a Pacific Basin OECD, parenthetical in Mr. Hawke's January 1989 speech in Seoul, has been around since Professors Patrick and Drysdale put forward their conception for an OPTAD at the 1977 PAFTAD conference. The essential notion, then as 10 years later, was that the emphasis of cooperation should lie in information and analysis, rather than negotiation. The idea of a Pacific OECD, however, seemed to contain within it the notion of a duplication. If you belong to the Pacific one, to put it crudely, would you want to belong to the Atlantic one as well? But how could you want to withdraw from the Atlantic one, in view of the links and analysis it provides?

Briefly, through a powerful secretariat and a highly developed committee system, the OECD provides for the exchange of information and analysis on the economies of its members, on the global economy, and on a range of macro- and microeconomic questions. It does not depend only on the inter-mediation of diplomats, because it brings together representatives from the full range of interested departments of its member governments to exchange ideas. It also establishes standards of economic behavior through a variety of methods including peer reviews of economic management and its negotiated codes. All this, and the oblique access OECD provides to other important discussions (for example, the G-7 Summit), New Zealand values highly. OECD membership is an important link with Europe and an institutional means of tapping into and contributing to the economic thinking of the industrialized world.

At the same time, especially in the aftermath of the changes in Central and Eastern Europe, the OECD's principal preoccupation does seem to be with Europe. That is not to say that it is not reaching out toward the Pacific where five of its current members are located. Dialogue with the developing Asian economies (DAEs), a series of seminars on economic topics arranged for OECD members together with participants (academics, business people, and public servants) from Korea, Hong Kong, Singapore, Malaysia, Taiwan, and Thailand, has been a useful initiative — if rather tentative in comparison with the OECD's approach to the Eastern Europeans. It should broaden the OECD's view of what matters in the global economy. However, it does not seem likely to lead quickly to OECD membership for more than one of the DAEs — for a start, the other five do not want to join. The dialogue does not include a number of important members of the Asia-Pacific community. The OECD, in short, does not really cater to a range of countries, increasingly significant to New Zealand, whose economies are of growing (local) and (collectively) even global importance.

A fundamental reason for this is the stage of economic development of the countries concerned. Current members are quite understandably anxious not to change the focus of the OECD. At the same time, existing and potential DAEs are anxious that their developing status should be recognized. In short, they do not accept that they should necessarily be subject to all the same disciplines as the developed countries. Therefore, any institution designed to enhance economic cooperation in Asia and the Pacific must deal with a more heterogeneous grouping than the OECD wishes to do. It must make sense for a range of economies, including at one end of the spectrum three members of the G-7, and at the other economies that have significant fragilities underlying their spectacular rates of growth.

THE EVOLUTION OF APEC

APEC was only established on a provisional basis until the third ministerial meeting in Seoul in 1991. As noted in the introduction to this section of the book, APEC's evolution has been rapid on a number of dimensions but is not yet complete. The coverage of its work program and the focus of the results as these begin to emerge, will be important indicators of the kind of process APEC members want.

The experience to date suggests that Ernest Preeg was right when he said, "What is distinctive about Asia-Pacific growth is that it is based on a shared economic strategy of open trade, driven by private-sector investment and rapid technological advance" (Grant, Jordan, Preeg, and Wanandi 1990: 16). The question, really, is what governments can do to promote this strategy, which has developed without their collective intervention. It is here that recipes may differ. Jusuf Wanandi has offered some valuable suggestions about dealing with issues that APEC members regard as important, but where a satisfactory methodology has been elusive. His suggestion of a study of the pattern of investment sourcing and interfirm trade resulting from the restructuring of the economies of Japan and the Asian newly industrialized economies is a case in point. We need to know causes before we can prescribe remedies (Grant, Jordan, Preeg, and Wanandi 1990: 5ff).

APEC can certainly perform the service of producing and drawing together information and analysis on regional economic questions. In addition, centered on its ministerial meetings, APEC will be able to act as a catalyst for action. This could be taken through its members individually, or through some other regional organizations, or in the context of global institutions — be they the GATT, the IMF, or the OECD — where it would reflect a regional consensus. APEC must respect the ways in which Asia differs from Europe, the Pacific from the Atlantic, and accommodate existing important relationships within the region (e.g., ASEAN). It has to provide additional value to all members. This is not an easy set of criteria to satisfy, and the evolution of APEC's structure will be important to its success in this regard. So far, all the omens are good.

NEW ZEALAND AND MULTILATERALISM

The first area in which APEC sought to take joint action was trade. Indeed, anxieties about trade were a powerful reason for establishing a regional process. Was the multilateral system breaking down? Was there an irreversible trend toward trade blocs? Would trading rivalries, or a trade pact, between

Japan and the United States damage the interests of other regional economies? Could an Asia-Pacific grouping bring a constructive influence to bear on the Uruguay Round, or would it constitute a distraction? Would it provide the basis for a defensive strategy if the round fell significantly short of the expectations?

New Zealand's trade policy in the postwar period has had both a multilateral and a bilateral focus. As a founder-member of the GATT, New Zealand has traditionally sought multilateral trade liberalization, particularly for agricultural products. However, it has also negotiated bilateral trade arrangements where these have served its interests, and it has done so for historical, political, trade, and industry policy reasons.

New Zealand was part of the British preferential tariff system, which it eventually allowed to wither. But from that base, it negotiated a preferential trading arrangement of a rather limited scope with Canada, and more important, a free trade agreement with Australia in 1965 (NAFTA) that was broadened and deepened in 1983 to become CER. Earlier, in 1973, when the United Kingdom joined the European Community (EC), New Zealand concluded a bilateral arrangement with the community to safeguard, to the extent possible, its major trade in dairy products and lamb. A great deal of its trade diplomacy since has been devoted to renewing and extending that arrangement, as the level of agricultural protectionism in Europe has increased. Until the middle of the 1980s its own level of border protection remained relatively high partly, it claimed, because the multilateral system was unable to devise satisfactory trading rules for those products in which New Zealand had a competitive advantage, but more fundamentally for industry policy and balance of payments reasons.

Since the launch of the Uruguay Round in 1986, with a mandate to bring trade in agricultural products under GATT rules and disciplines, New Zealand has put primary emphasis on multilateral solutions. This has not stopped continued work to examine the scope for regional cooperation, consistent with the GATT, or to broaden and deepen bilateral relationships, most notably CER. The conclusion in September 1992 of a trade and investment framework agreement with the United States was consistent with this strategy, though that development is too recent to have been fully considered in this chapter. APEC itself is seen as a key part of the regional strategy outlined above, and also as providing a potential fall-back to an unsuccessful Uruguay Round. But that should not disguise the preference New Zealand has had for the multilateral approach.

For New Zealand there are both general and particular reasons for preferring the multilateral approach. Discriminatory trade policies are undesirable on several counts. First, they lead to global resource misallocation. Preferential trade arrangements encourage countries to purchase products from sources other than the least-cost producers (trade diversion), with consequences for their own economic efficiency. Second, they can involve higher transaction costs, among them the costs of devising and enforcing rules to prevent evasion of the preferential system (Pomfret 1988).

Finally, history underlines the serious consequences of discriminatory trade arrangements, whereby hard negotiations generate grievances between bilateral partners at the same time as resentment builds among countries excluded from the negotiations. Discriminatory policies designed to protect domestic industries against subsidized competitors, or as reprisal for "unfair" trading practices (as provided for in Section 301 of the U.S. Trade Act of 1974 and its successors) are likely to be seen in a different light by the country imposing the restriction and the country affected by it. Moreover, discriminatory measures affect geographical trade patterns and hence, can be used as a political tool to create or cement spheres of influence.

These are the general grounds. For New Zealand, as a small country with global trading interests, there are also specific ones, three in particular. First, New Zealand, even when combined with Australia under CER, is a small market in global or regional terms, and holds only limited attractiveness to other larger economies seeking new trade access.

Second, the major barriers facing New Zealand's exports lie in the agricultural area. Agriculture remains a sensitive sector for many of our trading partners. It is unlikely that they would readily reduce these barriers for New Zealand, on a bilateral basis, in the absence of the wider benefits of a multilateral tariff reduction or liberalization of sectors such as services, or without the added attraction of gaining significant new access opportunities. In this respect, the small size of the New Zealand domestic market can be a disadvantage.

Third, New Zealand's trading interests are not confined to any single area. East Asia, Europe, Oceania, and North America are all of major importance, and it has significant markets in other regions also, for example, the Middle East.

The broad Asia-Pacific region, including Australia and North America as well as East Asia, is of increasing and crucial importance to New Zealand in trade terms. While exports to the region accounted for about 40 percent of total exports in 1970, in 1990 they accounted for nearly 65 percent. New Zealand exports to Australia, Japan, the NIEs, and ASEAN all increased markedly between 1970 and 1992, and the United States continues to be a major trading partner. New Zealand's imports from the region have also increased markedly, both as a percentage of the total and in absolute terms. Imports from the region rose from 50 percent in 1970 to over 65 percent in 1990. More and more, New Zealand's trading future depends on the vitality and outward orientation of the Asia-Pacific region.

Within this region, as of 1990, the countries of East Asia — Japan, Korea, China, Taiwan, Hong Kong, and the six ASEAN nations — were taking nearly one-third of New Zealand's exports and providing over one-fourth of New Zealand's imports. East Asia's share of New Zealand's total trade rose steadily through the 1980s.

Oceania (Australia and the Pacific Islands) took 22 percent of New Zealand's exports and supplied 21 percent of imports in 1990. Oceania's share of New Zealand's total trade grew during the 1980s. North America (Canada and the United States) took just under 15 percent of New Zealand's exports and supplied 20 percent of imports in 1990, but its share of New Zealand's total trade remained constant during the 1980s.

Europe remains an important trading partner, but its share of New Zealand's total trade has declined as that of Asia and the Pacific has been growing. Europe as a whole—the European Community, the other Western European countries, Eastern Europe, and the former Soviet Union—took over 20 percent of New Zealand's exports and supplied one-fourth of our imports in 1990. However, exports to the present members of the European Community declined from nearly one-half to less than 20 percent of New Zealand's total exports between 1970 and 1990, and imports from the EC countries declined substantially also.

New Zealand's other significant regional markets are the Middle East, which took 3 percent of exports and supplied 5 percent of imports in 1990, and Latin America which took 3 percent of exports and supplied 1 percent of imports. During the 1980s, these shares did not change significantly.

THE MULTILATERAL SYSTEM: ACHIEVEMENTS AND THREATS

In practice, the achievements of the multilateral system have been great. The eight rounds of multilateral trade negotiations held since the GATT was formed have reduced the average tariff on manufactured goods from 40 percent in 1947 to around 5 percent. These cuts, together with wide acceptance of the most-favored-nation (MFN) principle and the Bretton Woods international exchange and payments system, have encouraged rapid trade growth in the postwar period. Between 1950 and 1975, for example, the volume of world trade expanded some 500 percent, compared with an increase in global output of 220 percent.

However, against this progress toward free trade there has been a proliferation of preferential trading arrangements since the inception of the GATT. The 1950s and 1960s saw the establishment of the European Economic Community, the European Free Trade Agreement (EFTA), the New Zealand–Australia NAFTA, the UK–Ireland FTA, the Latin America Free Trade Agreement, and the Central American Common Market. A second wave, in the mid-1970s and 1980s, included CER and a range of FTAs negotiated by the United States, including its FTA with Canada (subsequently expanded to include Mexico in a North American FTA — another NAFTA). The European Community agreed to complete the creation of a single European market in 1992.

These arrangements, including in particular the American and European ones, have suggested to a number of commentators the danger that the multilateral trading system could break down into a series of rival trading blocs, especially when they are taken together with the other great exception to the MFN principle, the nontariff or so-called "grey area" measures, which have also multiplied since the 1970s. There are now almost 300 so-called voluntary export restraint and similar agreements, covering textiles, clothing, steel, cars, shoes, machinery, consumer electronics, and agricultural products (*The Economist,* September 1989). Most protect U.S. and European markets. Fifty affect exports to Japan and another 35 affect exports to Korea. There are also other weapons in the armory of the new protectionism, including process protection — the use of administrative procedures for protective ends.

The Uruguay Round, launched in 1986 to strengthen the multilateral trading system and extend its coverage, encountered serious difficulties and missed its original 1990 completion target. Although it remains unclear whether the round will ultimately produce an agreement, it is generally accepted that even a nominally successful conclusion will be well short of the original ambitious goals in many areas. If the outcome is widely regarded as unsatisfactory, the pressures on the system may well intensify, through increasing use of bilateral pressures (including the U.S. Super 301) and preferential arrangements. Either way, the MFN principle is likely to come under further pressure. Under these circumstances, New Zealand will need to reassess its options. But in any case, the end of the Uruguay Round, in success or failure, will mark an important watershed, and will require a new trade agenda. Australian views and those of other regional partners will, for different reasons, be important to New Zealand in determining its new priorities.

BILATERAL AND SUBREGIONAL ARRANGEMENTS

As already indicated, New Zealand has experience with bilateral trade arrangements. There is, of course, provision for these under Article XXIV of GATT, provided that restrictions are eliminated on "substantially all of the trade" among members and that the level of protection against nonmember country exports is no higher than before. The questions to be asked of bilateral, and indeed regional, arrangements are: whether they will create trade or merely divert it from other, more efficient suppliers; and whether they will contribute to a wider liberalization, as the Article XXIV exception assumes.

The New Zealand–Australia CER agreement, New Zealand's most important bilateral trading arrangement, can be developed further. Suggestions have been made about expanding it. At various times, the question has been raised if Canada should be brought in, or if an FTA could be negotiated with the United States. Now the issue is whether CER provides guidance on how the Asia-Pacific region can form a positive and constructive relationship with the North American Free Trade Agreement.

CER covers all trade in goods, and during the period of the agreement, the level of protection against nonmember countries has declined. Trade in goods with Australia is already free; Australia is now New Zealand's largest market for exports and source of imports (18 and 20 percent, respectively, of the total as of 1990). Trade with Australia has expanded more rapidly than New Zealand's trade has expanded on average. Analysis done on the Australian side has suggested that CER has been trade-creating rather than trade-diverting (Bureau of Industry Economics 1990). Trade grew most strongly during the 1980s in the sectors that, at the time the studies were carried out, had already been affected by CER. This effect is likely to have continued as barriers continued to be reduced.

CER has a historical importance in New Zealand because it led a significant change in New Zealand industry policy. It has been successful (i.e., it has created rather than diverted trade) in large part because it coincided with and helped to create the climate for a general reduction in protection in both markets, especially in New Zealand's case.

Because relations with Australia are of fundamental importance to New Zealand, it is interesting to reflect on the remarks of Kerrin Vautier, Chairperson of the NZCPEC, to the Australia–New Zealand Business Council in November 1990. She pointed out that economic integration between Australia and New Zealand was relatively limited compared with economic integration in Western Europe and in North America. In considering where to take the trans-Tasman partnership—not, she suggested, an end in itself— she believed that the two governments should look at the relationship in its wider context. Cooperation between the two countries should start with:

> the common interest . . . in liberalising trade policies in what is a trade intensive region with a relatively high level of intra-regional trade. . . . What all this suggests for the CER agenda is that we focus on those aspects of the relationship which clearly and positively support this outward-looking strategic thrust. (Vautier 1990)

One expansion that was earlier envisaged is a Canada–Australia–New Zealand (CANZ) free trade area, the subject of a 1988 study led by Sir Frank Holmes (Holmes, Lattimore, and Haas 1988). Sir Frank suggested that free trade between the three countries might be a stepping stone to more general liberalization, especially if the Uruguay Round had a disappointing result.

He further suggested that the South Pacific Regional Trade and Economic Cooperation Agreement could be associated with these arrangements and "some form of special relationship" might be negotiated with ASEAN. More recently this thinking has been updated in the light of developments including APEC, NAFTA and the ASEAN Free Trade Area, but the notion of "stepping stones" continues to have currency in thinking about relations between the Pacific and NAFTA.

Ernest Preeg has suggested that two basic characteristics normally underlie the rationale for establishing a regional economic grouping: a common or closely aligned economic policy strategy and a high degree of economic interdependence (Grant, Jordan, Preeg, and Wanandi 1990: 16). Between Australia, Canada, and New Zealand there is a particularly low degree of economic interdependence, as Canada is a very minor trading partner—for both of the Oceania countries and they for it. In the economic policy area, agricultural strategies are not wholly compatible, and there could well be difficulties in negotiating satisfactory outcomes in areas of central interest to New Zealand. The dairy sector, for example, is very sensitive in Canada, which has distinguished its position from other members of the Cairns Group (of nonsubsidizing agricultural exporting countries) in order to preserve its supply management programs. Finally, there is the question of the agreement's overall economic effect. Would it be trade-creating or trade-diverting? This question is difficult to answer without knowing the extent of participation by other countries; there are fears that a "CANZ" agreement might divert trade away from more efficient third-country suppliers.

From the point of view of New Zealand, a free trade agreement with the United States might seem to make greater sense. A far higher proportion of New Zealand trade is with the United States than with Canada (13 percent of exports and 18 percent of imports in 1990 as opposed to 2 percent in each case with Canada) although it is also true that U.S.–New Zealand trade hardly figures in American statistics. The United States is also a major trading partner of Australia. There is a disposition, moreover, from the New Zealand side to look for an improvement in the overall relationship with the United States. Former U.S. Secretary of Agriculture Clayton Yeutter is reported to have remarked on the possibility of some trading arrangement when talking of the consequences of a failure of the GATT negotiations on agriculture.

There is no detailed New Zealand analysis of the effects a trade arrangement with the United States would have, but a study by Richard Snape for the Economic Planning Advisory Council in Australia entitled *Should Australia Seek a Trade Agreement with the United States?* (1986) is germane to New Zealand as well. With the United States, as with Canada, there could be problems in negotiating a satisfactory arrangement. For New Zealand, and for Australia, trade gains would derive from the removal of United

States nontariff barriers on a few agricultural commodities. The question is whether the offer of enhanced access even to the combined market of the two countries would be a sufficient inducement for the United States to remove these barriers, or whether this could only be achieved in the context of some more general liberalization. It is fair to add that the conditions for tackling this question might be optimal in the aftermath of a GATT Round that stalled on agriculture.

Would a trade agreement between Australia and New Zealand and the United States be trade-creating or trade-diverting? Snape was pessimistic about the trade-diversion costs in his study of a U.S.–Australia agreement. The issue would need careful study from New Zealand's standpoint, especially given the way its patterns of trade have been developing.

As New Zealand liberalized its border regime during the 1980s, imports grew most strongly from Northeast Asia (Japan, Korea, Taiwan, Hong Kong, China). In the latter three years of the 1980s, imports from the ASEAN countries also grew very strongly as a consequence of the heavy investment from Northeast Asia in their manufacturing industries. The East Asian region has emerged clearly as the lowest cost source of New Zealand's imports. In formulating trade policy for the 1990s, New Zealand needs to ensure that it can continue to tap this highly competitive source of imports.

Looking at New Zealand's export markets, the strongest growth area in the past decade has been exports of agricultural goods and semi-processed raw materials to the markets of Northeast Asia: Korea, Japan, Taiwan, Hong Kong, and China. Australia has been New Zealand's other major growth market, especially for manufactured items. Toward the end of the 1980s, New Zealand's exports to Southeast Asia also started to grow strongly.

In this context it is particularly interesting that Richard Snape, in responding to the Holmes study on CANZ, suggested a broader focus for intermediate attempts at trade liberalization. "If major aims of the CANZ proposal are to push along the multilateral negotiations and to provide a safety net of trade agreements should the world close up into discriminatory blocs, why not enter into negotiations with some of the big players?" (Holmes 1989: 30). Snape proposed Japan, or better still, Japan and the United States and perhaps other regional traders as well. His approach implies a conditional MFN arrangement to put pressure on nonregional countries, for example the EC, to liberalize their own policies. Snape's suggestions carry us out into the area of regional cooperation in a broader sense.

REGIONALISM AND MULTILATERALISM

Regionalism is a force that can be used either to substitute for multilateralism or to assist it. So far, within APEC there has been a determined intention to take the second of those options. This has been manifested in the repeated reaffirmations by APEC ministers that APEC should be outward looking. In spite of the importance of the trade flows between its members, the Asia-Pacific region is not a closed system, and all the economies in it — New Zealand is not alone in this — have vitally important trade relations with the rest of the world.

Thus far APEC has seen its principal role as a lobby for improving the multilateral trading system in the context of the Uruguay Round, and has made the success of the round a principal objective. Its interests do not stop there, however. Ministers have also asked that thought be given to trade liberalization in the region after the round is over.

It is hard to speculate on the way in which this topic will be developed before knowing the outcome of the Uruguay Round. If the round stalls, it may be necessary to look at ways in which the region's aspiration to free trade can move the multilateral system forward. Snape and Drysdale and Garnaut (in Holmes 1989) have made similar but not identical suggestions in this respect.

Snape's approach is based on a liberalization process in which outsiders could also participate provided they were prepared to contribute — in effect, conditional MFN (Holmes 1989: 30–31). Drysdale and Garnaut suggest that the regional countries could so frame the agenda of a "Pacific Round" as to make the Europeans feel obliged to participate in order to influence the agenda though they acknowledge that the problem of European free-riding might require joint action against agricultural subsidies (Holmes 1989: 68, 70; see also Holmes and Falconer 1992). What is important about both these suggestions, which represent two different modes of persuading the Europeans to reengage in a multilateral process, is that both are joint ventures involving East Asia and North America, along with Australia and New Zealand. Regionalism would limit the fragmentation of the multilateral system and help review it.

PROSPECTS

Asia-Pacific regionalism has not been easy to organize, and it is still in the process of defining its form (or forms). A fundamental characteristic is that it is outward-looking, and represents an increasingly important part of the global community. It will need to address the specific and local concerns of its members. By doing so, it will accustom them to working together. At the same time, if it is to reflect their wider interests it will have to engage in global issues and promote multilateral solutions.

Despite the achievements to date in terms of institutionalizing the APEC process, the concrete benefits of APEC are largely in prospect. A principal criterion for APEC's success will be that members find no contradiction between their participation in APEC and their participation in the global institutions. They will then also find that regional economic cooperation enhances the cooperation that they have, both bilaterally and also in multilateral institutions.

ACKNOWLEDGMENTS

The author is grateful for the assistance of several colleagues, often contributed in their own time, with this paper. The views it expresses are, however, entirely his own, and not those of the New Zealand government or the Ministry of External Relations and Trade.

NOTES

1. In November 1985, New Zealand had air service agreements with 11 countries; there are now 20. Most of the new countries are in the Asia-Pacific region: Indonesia, Malaysia, Thailand, Cook Islands, Solomon Islands, Niue, and Vanuatu. Every week there are three flights between New Zealand and Indonesia, three flights between New Zealand and Malaysia, and four flights between New Zealand and Thailand. From four flights a week in 1985, there are now 10 flights between New Zealand and Singapore. There are four weekly services between New Zealand and Hong Kong. There are seven services a week between New Zealand and Japan and an additional three to the new point of Nagoya as of April 1991. In the twelve months from March 1984 to March 1985, there were 72,405 visitors to New Zealand from Asia. In the same period between 1988 and 1989, there were 160,448 visitors from Asia (source: New Zealand Ministry of External Relations and Trade).

2. The value of Japanese direct investment in New Zealand fell from US$121 million in 1987 to US$101 million in 1989. In the same period, Japanese global direct investment increased by 40 percent (Japan–New Zealand Business Council 1990: 18, fig. 5.2.1).

9

U.S. Economic Relations with the Asia-Pacific Region: Confrontation or Cooperation?

THOMAS A. LAYMAN AND RICHARD W. BAKER

The decade of the 1980s, particularly the latter half, saw a more integrated world economy than any previous period. This was due to a combination of economic growth, deregulation, and market opening in many countries, and remarkable advances in technology and communication. These changes in turn mean that the transmission of economic developments from one country to another can now occur almost instantaneously. The combination of greater interaction and more rapid communications also means that there is now a greater potential for volatility than in previous periods of history.

The 1980s were generally characterized by world economic expansion and a relatively stable inflationary environment. However, the expansion was also accompanied by growing trade and current account imbalances on the part of many countries. Serious continuing imbalances were experienced not only within the industrialized world, but also on the part of a number of developing economies, including the newly industrialized economies (NIEs) of East Asia (Ogata, Cooper, and Schulmann 1989: 3-4). These imbalances underlay a series of significant and often sudden fluctuations in foreign exchange and financial markets (most dramatically illustrated in the global stock market crash of October 1987) demonstrating the increased volatility of the more integrated international economic order.

The advent of a truly global economy has contributed to a general recognition that economic stability is now a shared responsibility. This in turn led to the first concerted attempts at macroeconomic policy coordination among the major industrialized countries, particularly the G-7 group. It has also been reflected in the effort to expand the scope of international trade negotiations through the General Agreement on Tariffs and Trade to cover previously excluded areas such as agriculture, services, and investment. It has also given further impetus to efforts to organize closer economic cooperation at the regional level in many parts of the world, including the Asia-Pacific region.

However, there have been countertrends as well. While most governments profess a commitment to a liberal international trade system, they also face strong demands for protection from sectors of national economies that are threatened by the processes of change. This has led to an increasing resort to unilateral measures, and thus to rising contention and conflict at the international level. As a major beneficiary of the previous order, with multiple vested interests, the United States has been one of the major exemplars of these countertrends.

The purpose here is to explore these trends and issues as they affect the economic policies of the United States toward the countries of the Asia-Pacific region. The first section looks at the changing U.S. economic relationships in the region, with the focus on trade relationships. We then consider the U.S. policy response to these changes, which has been a mix of bilateral, multilateral, and regional elements. We argue that, because of the way U.S. policy has evolved and the multiplicity of interests involved, U.S. economic policies in the region have not been integrated into a cohesive whole. We also point out various internal conflicts and inconsistencies that create uncertainties for U.S. economic partners in the region. Finally, we discuss the outlook for U.S. policy, concluding that major departures from the current pattern, including an element of unpredictability, are unlikely.

U.S. TRADE WITH THE ASIA-PACIFIC REGION

The seven-year period of sustained economic growth in the United States, beginning in 1983, was accompanied by a further opening up of the U.S. economy to external trade. By the end of the decade, foreign trade (exports plus imports) accounted for over 15 percent of the U.S. GDP, compared to less than 5 percent two decades earlier.

This period of U.S. economic expansion probably benefited the countries of the Asia-Pacific region more than any other group of countries in the world. A majority of the growth in U.S. consumption was satisfied by imports of manufactured goods from East Asia, in particular Japan. This was partly due to price effects associated with the strengthening of the U.S. dollar through the mid-1980s, which allowed many Asia-Pacific exporters to gain a competitive edge and increased market shares. The majority of these countries, particularly the NIEs, were also able to capitalize on their labor-intensive manufacturing base to produce high quality products desired by U.S. consumers.

The extraordinarily rapid growth of U.S. imports from the Asia-Pacific region shows clearly in a variety of trade statistics. In 1983, over 30 percent of total U.S. imports, excluding trade with OPEC countries, came from countries in Western Europe, compared with 22 percent from Japan and the major developing countries of East Asia. One year later, those percentages had reversed, and by 1992 the Asia-Pacific region accounted for 44 percent of total non-OPEC imports by the United States.

As Table 9.1 shows, in 1978 some 23 percent of the region's exports, including those from Japan, Australia, New Zealand, and most developing countries, were destined for the United States. By 1985, with the substantial rise in value of the U.S. dollar and accelerating demand by U.S. consumers, that proportion had risen to over 30 percent, representing a compound annual growth rate of over 12 percent. Almost 40 percent of all Japanese exports in 1985 went to the U.S. market, compared to just under 26 percent in 1978. For the developing countries of the region, the growth in exports to the United States over the period was equally strong. The United States had become the largest export market for Japan and almost every developing country in the region.

Since 1985, exports from the region to the United States have continued to grow rapidly, but growth has tapered off somewhat from the double-digit pace of the mid-1980s. The combined effects of slower U.S. economic growth and efforts by many countries in the Asia-Pacific region to diversify their external market base caused the growth of the region's exports to the United States to decline to an average annual rate of 8.5 percent in the six years through 1991. As a result, the share of total regional exports going to the United States declined to 23 percent, roughly back to where it was in 1978 (see Table 9.1). Only China, Thailand, Pakistan, and the Philippines continued to see a rising proportion of their exports go to the U.S. market during the latter half of the 1980s.

Of course, not all Asia-Pacific countries benefited equally from strong growth in the United States during the 1980s, and some did not benefit much at all. For example, most commodity-dependent exporters in the region experienced delays in sustained revival due to falling terms of trade through 1986. Others with large external debts suffered because high international real interest rates also accompanied improved world growth.

The greatest beneficiary in the region of American growth was clearly Japan, as exports were directly stimulated by the surge in U.S. demand and the rise in the dollar. The decline in raw materials prices also benefited Japan, given the high dependence of Japanese manufacturers on commodity imports. Finally, given Japan's net creditor status, the rise in real interest rates also benefited Japan, reinforcing the trend toward Japan becoming the largest net creditor nation in the world (Krause 1988: 41).

DEALING WITH THE TRADE DEFICIT

The counterpart to burgeoning U.S. imports from East Asia was a growing American trade deficit with the region. In 1984, the U.S. trade deficit with Japan reached $37 billion; just as important, the United States ran up trade

Table 9.1. Exports from East Asia to the United States, 1978–1991

Country	1978		1985		1991		Average Annual Growth Rate (%)	
	US$million	Share of Trade with World (%)	US$million	Share of Trade with World (%)	US$million	Share of Trade with World (%)	1978–85	1985–91
Total Exports	49,141	23.4	123,000	30.3	200,968	23.1	12.2	8.5
Japan	25,362	25.8	66,684	37.6	92,200	29.3	12.8	5.5
Australia	1,632	11.3	2,344	10.4	4,271	10.2	4.6	10.5
New Zealand	557	14.9	820	14.4	1,225	12.8	5.0	6.9
Developing Asia Total	21,590	23.1	53,152	26.4	103,272	20.5	11.9	11.7
Brunei	166	9.0	215	7.3	26	1.0	3.3	-29.7
China	271	2.8	2,336	8.5	6,192	8.6	30.9	17.6
Hong Kong	3,490	30.4	9,301	30.8	22,391	22.7	13.0	15.8
India	901	13.6	1,563	18.9	3,126	15.3	7.1	12.2
Indonesia	2,962	25.4	4,040	21.7	3,509	12.0	4.0	-2.3
Malaysia	1,379	18.6	1,970	12.8	5,808	16.9	4.6	19.7
Pakistan	99	6.6	274	10.0	742	11.4	13.6	18.0
Philippines	1,159	33.8	1,658	35.9	3,151	35.7	4.6	11.3
Singapore	1,626	16.0	4,830	21.2	11,674	19.7	14.6	15.8
South Korea	4,076	32.0	10,789	35.6	18,311	26.4	12.9	9.2
Taiwan	5,010	39.5	14,773	48.1	22,321	29.3	14.5	7.1
Thailand	451	11.0	1,402	19.7	6,021	21.8	15.2	27.5

Sources: IMF, *Direction of Trade Statistics* (various issues), and national sources.

Note: Columns may not add due to rounding.

deficits that year with every developing country in the East Asian region, with the exception of Brunei (Layman 1985).

Faced with persistent and increasing problems in its foreign trade balances, the United States launched a series of efforts designed to address the trade deficit starting in the mid-1980s. Although these policies were global in scope, they had a special salience for the Asia-Pacific region because of the size and visibility of the U.S. trade deficit with Japan.

Concerted efforts to correct the U.S. external deficit really began in 1985 when policymakers from the G-7 industrial countries agreed on a coordinated attempt to reduce the value of the dollar, now known as the Plaza Accord. The currency correction focused mainly on industrial countries, especially Japan, in hopes that a devaluation would help U.S. import-competing manufacturers and exporters alike.

While devaluation of the dollar did stimulate U.S. exports, imports remained stubbornly strong. Many foreign firms initially elected to absorb the impact of the declining exchange rate by keeping the U.S. dollar prices of their products relatively unchanged thereby avoiding loss of market share. Moreover, because in many cases trade restrictions (such as so-called voluntary export restraint arrangements) were in place that limited the quantity but not the value of imports, manufacturers of such products as automobiles were able to shift their product lines in the direction of higher-priced models, maintaining or even increasing profit margins. Also, many developing countries in the Asia-Pacific region whose currencies were linked with or weighted heavily toward the U.S. dollar allowed their currencies to depreciate between 1985 and 1986, remaining competitive and, in some cases, even gaining market share in the United States.

The Trend toward Bilateralism

The United States had long pursued a global policy of encouraging its economic partners to make their domestic economies more open to international competition. In response to the persistent balance of trade deficits in the mid-1980s, U.S. policymakers began to focus these efforts particularly on obtaining reciprocal access to the markets of countries that had benefited from exporting to the U.S. market. Bilateral negotiations were also stepped up to encourage various countries to purchase more U.S. agricultural products and to provide increased protection for copyrights and intellectual property rights. It was during this period that agricultural export subsidies, used by the United States to compete with European subsidies and to press the Europeans to cease subsidizing exports, became a contentious issue in bilateral relations between the United States and Australia.

The United States also took steps to limit access to the U.S. market when specific practices on the part of its trading partners were deemed unfair to American producers. These steps included invoking the so-called 301 clause of the U.S. Trade Act of 1974 (and subsequent years), mandating the imposition of sanctions in cases where obstacles could not be removed through negotiations, as well as the increasing use of antidumping procedures and sanctions.

In early 1987, U.S. bilateral measures were expanded still further to encompass exchange rate policy. The United States pressed Taiwan and South Korea to adjust their exchange rates upward. In response, both Taiwan and South Korea allowed their currencies to appreciate rapidly against the U.S. dollar. By 1989, the New Taiwan dollar had risen by over 50 percent from its average level in 1985 (see Table 9.2). Upward movement of the Korean won, at roughly 30 percent, was less pronounced but still significant. On a real effective basis, the appreciation was almost 10 percent for South Korea and 17 percent for Taiwan.[1]

Singapore, whose trade surplus with the United States had remained fairly low at around $2 billion per year, was not targeted for pressure on its exchange rate. However, it also allowed its currency to appreciate almost 13 percent against the dollar. The fourth NIE, Hong Kong, kept its exchange rate fixed at HK$7.8 per U.S. dollar, mainly for political reasons.

By the end of 1988, the United States also removed preferential tariff treatment under the General System of Preferences (GSP) from all of the NIEs, another measure aimed directly at reducing imports from the Asia-Pacific region. Although the loss of GSP privileges disadvantaged producers in the NIEs, the net impact on imports into the United States was, at least partially, offset by the increased competitiveness of the exports of the developing countries of Southeast Asia, which were allowed to retain GSP privileges. Moreover, exchange rate management in the developing countries concentrated not only on maintaining market share in the United States but also on accelerating export growth to other countries, including Japan and some of the NIEs of the region. This was reflected in the real effective devaluations of the developing countries' currencies that continued through 1989 (see Table 9.2).

In 1988, the U.S. Congress responded to increased calls from domestic American industries for trade protection and increased market access for exports by passing much stronger trade legislation, the Omnibus Trade and Competitiveness Act. This act reinforced the 301 clauses, now referred to as "Super 301," by requiring the U.S. trade representative to identify and initiate bilateral negotiations to reduce major barriers and trade distorting practices that restrict U.S. exports. During 1989, three countries were named under the Super 301 provision for restrictive trade practices — Japan for three practices, India for two, and Brazil for one. Other countries, including South Korea and Taiwan, were put on a watch list for various practices and trade barriers.

In part as a means of dealing with growing Japanese resistance to making concessions, or indeed, even negotiating on specific trade issues through

Table 9.2. Exchange Rate Changes: Asian Newly Industrialized Economies and Southeast Asian Countries

Country	Currency	Nominal Exchange Rate[a] (Units/US$)		Real Effective Exchange Rate[b] (1985=100)	
		% change 1985–89	% change 1989–92	% change 1985–89	% change 1989–92
Newly Industrialized Economies					
Hong Kong	HK$	0.0	1.2	-6.4	33.9
Singapore	S$	12.8	19.6	-9.2	10.5
South Korea	Won	29.7	-13.8	9.7	-2.3
Taiwan	NT$	50.8	5.2	17.2	-1.7
Southeast Asia					
Indonesia	Rupiah	-37.2	-12.5	-45.5	-3.6
Malaysia	M$	-8.5	6.3	-30.0	-2.5
Philippines	Peso	-14.3	-15.6	-22.3	-0.7
Thailand	Baht	5.8	1.2	-17.8	-1.0

Sources: WEFA Group, "World Economic Service," Bala-Cynwid, Pennsylvania, and national sources.

a. Negative change in nominal exchange rate = depreciation.

b. Decrease in real effective index = depreciation.

such high-pressure mechanisms as Super 301, the United States in 1989 proposed the Structural Impediments Initiative (SII). These U.S.–Japanese
talks focused on broader aspects of national economic policy and structure
that might impede trade or economic adjustment.[2] The SII marked a significant departure in U.S. trade negotiations and a venture into largely uncharted
waters involving politically sensitive areas of domestic policy-making and
even cultural traditions. In Japan the SII negotiations could ultimately lead
to a shift in the balance of economic-political power from producers to consumers. For their part, U.S. policymakers may have to make an international
commitment to solve structural problems plaguing the United States such as
the budget deficits.

Progress and Prospects

While these measures resulted in very little improvement in the global
U.S. trade deficit between 1987 and 1990, U.S. trade balances with a number
of countries in the Asia-Pacific region improved. As Table 9.3 shows, the
U.S. trade deficit with Japan declined by $15.2 billion to a level of $41 billion
in 1990. The combined U.S. deficit with the NIEs fell by $14.3 billion over
this three-year period, to just under $20 billion. Deficits with the four coun-
tries of Southeast Asia also shrunk to $6.4 billion between 1987 and 1990.
With the exception of India and Taiwan, annual U.S. export growth to all
countries in the region was in double digits. The slower growth rate for
exports to Taiwan mainly reflected extraordinary purchases of gold, by
Taiwan, during 1988 that inflated the figure for the base years.

Growth in U.S. imports from Japan and the NIEs was subdued during
1989 and 1990. However, by contrast and despite the chill in U.S. political
relations with the People's Republic of China after the 1989 Tiananmen
massacre, the U.S. trade deficit with the PRC nearly tripled between 1987
and 1990 to over $10 billion, making it the United States' third largest bilat-
eral trade deficit.

The recession that hit the U.S. economy in 1990–91 contributed to a marked
improvement in the balance of trade. Weak domestic demand caused total
imports into the United States to fall by 1.5 percent in 1991. By comparison,
export growth accelerated to over 7 percent that year, allowing the overall
U.S. trade deficit to decline to $66.2 billion. This was the lowest the deficit
had been since 1983. The trend toward narrowing trade imbalances also
continued with most countries in the Asia-Pacific region during 1991, as
U.S. export competitiveness in the region was aided by a slowdown and
even, in some cases, a reversal of the real effective depreciation of exchange
rates after 1989 (see Table 9.2). However, there have been some notable
exceptions. In the case of Japan, U.S. import growth continued to decline
in 1991, but a deteriorating Japanese economy also caused demand in Japan
for exports from the United States to slip by 1 percent that year. As a result,

the net U.S. trade deficit with Japan rose $2.3 billion from 1990 to $43.4 billion in 1991. Despite continued rapid export growth to Thailand, Malaysia, and China in 1991, the U.S. trade imbalances with those countries also rose, as did the deficits with both the Philippines and India, due mainly to their weak economic performance that translated into a decline in U.S. exports.

As the U.S. economy began to pick up slowly during 1992, import growth accelerated, causing the overall trade deficit to reverse its four-year decline. With the exception of Australia, New Zealand, Taiwan, and Hong Kong, U.S. trade imbalances worsened with every country in the Asia-Pacific region. The deepening recession in the Japanese economy coupled with rising demand by U.S. consumers resulted in a $6 billion increase in the U.S.-Japanese trade deficit for 1992 (see Table 9.3). U.S. imports from the countries of Southeast Asia were particularly strong, growing by an average of 31 percent above their 1991 levels, causing the cumulative deficit with Indonesia, Malaysia, Thailand, and the Philippines to widen to almost $11 billion. With China, a slight slowing of U.S. exports and a 35 percent surge in U.S. imports gave rise to an $18.2 billion trade deficit, allowing China to again post the second largest bilateral trade deficit with the United States, a ranking first gained in 1991.

Given that a continued U.S. economic rebound could reinforce these trends, it seems unlikely that the United States will soon abandon or even significantly soften its concerted effort to reduce these deficits. Correspondingly, it appears unlikely that trade frictions between the United States and countries of the region will abate significantly in the coming decade. The sharply rising deficit with China only reinforced calls for trade sanctions that first emerged after the crackdown on the student-led demonstrations during the summer of 1989.

Resistance to concessions by countries of the region may well also increase. Japanese resistance to direct pressures, especially under congressional mandates, has already been noted, but is not the only case. For example, domestic growth in both Taiwan and South Korea slowed markedly during 1990, and South Korea's current account actually swung into deficit. In response, Taiwan amended its application to join the GATT to make it less generous in reducing domestic protection. The South Korean government faced internal pressures to resume various export promotion policies, devalue the exchange rate, and generally slow the process of market liberalization.

THE UNITED STATES AND TRADE LIBERALIZATION

At the same time as the U.S. government has pursued an increasingly aggressive series of essentially unilateral actions targeted at reducing the U.S. trade deficit, however, the government has also continued to place heavy emphasis on broader efforts to achieve international trade liberalization.

Table 9.3. U.S. Bilateral Trade, 1987-1992

Country	Trade Balance[a] (US$billion)				Export Growth (annual percentage change)			Import Growth (annual percentage change)		
	1987	1990	1991	1992	1987-90	1990-91	1991-92	1987-90	1990-91	1991-92
Total	0.0	-101.7	-66.2	-84.3	12.8	7.2	6.2	5.2	-1.5	9.1
Canada	-11.3	-7.7	-6.0	-7.9	9.5	1.7	6.5	7.5	-0.3	8.1
Western Europe	-25.8	4.0	16.1	6.2	12.9	5.0	-1.4	2.1	-5.9	8.0
European Community	-20.6	6.3	16.7	8.7	12.7	5.2	-0.4	1.6	-5.9	8.8
Japan	-56.3	-41.1	-43.4	-49.4	16.4	-1.0	-0.6	3.4	2.1	6.1
Australia	2.5	4.1	4.4	5.2	14.7	-1.2	6.0	9.1	-9.1	-7.5
New Zealand	-0.2	-0.1	-0.2	0.1	10.4	-9.1	30.0	4.7	0.0	0.0
Newly Industrialized Economies	-34.1	-19.8	-13.6	-13.9	17.8	12.0	6.4	2.8	-2.1	5.2
South Korea	-8.9	-4.1	-1.5	-2.1	18.6	7.6	-5.8	5.1	-8.1	-1.8
Taiwan	-17.2	-11.2	-9.8	-9.4	15.1	14.8	15.2	-0.4	1.3	7.0
Singapore	-2.1	-1.8	-1.2	-1.7	22.2	10.0	9.1	12.8	2.0	13.0
Hong Kong	-5.9	-2.8	-1.1	-0.7	16.5	19.1	12.3	-0.5	-3.1	5.4

Southeast Asia	-5.0	-6.4	-7.1	-10.7	14.4	10.2	17.6	13.3	9.2	30.7
Indonesia	-2.6	-1.4	-1.3	-1.7	19.2	0.0	47.4	1.0	-3.0	40.6
Thailand	-0.7	-2.3	-2.4	-3.5	14.2	26.7	5.3	25.6	15.1	23.0
Malaysia	-1.0	-1.8	-2.2	-3.9	15.2	14.7	12.8	17.2	15.1	36.1
Philippines	-0.7	-0.9	-1.2	-1.6	11.2	-8.0	21.7	11.0	2.9	25.7
India	-1.1	-0.7	-1.2	-1.9	17.9	-20.0	-5.0	9.3	0.0	18.8
Pakistan	0.3	0.5	0.3	0.0	14.5	-9.1	-10.0	7.4	16.7	28.6
China	-2.8	-10.4	-12.7	-18.2	18.4	31.3	19.0	24.0	25.0	35.3
USSR (former)	1.1	2.0	2.8	2.8	42.7	16.1	0.0	18.1	-27.3	0.0
Eastern Europe	0.1	2.0	3.0	3.5	71.5	14.3	14.6	88.1	-18.2	11.1
OPEC[b]	-10.3	25.7	-12.6	-7.9	5.3	45.8	11.0	9.5	-14.4	-3.7

Sources: U.S. Department of Commerce, Bureau of Census, Foreign Trade Division, *FT900* and *FT990*, various issues.

a. Exports, f.a.s.; imports, customs basis.

b. Excludes trade with Indonesia.

Multilateral Approaches

U.S. initiatives and support were central to the launching in 1986 of the Uruguay Round of international trade negotiations under the GATT. This was probably the most ambitious undertaking in the 40-year history of the trade organization. Besides aiming to cut remaining world tariffs by 30 percent and to tighten existing rules in a number of areas, the round also tried to bring new and very significant areas under the multilateral umbrella. In addition to agriculture, the new areas include trade in services, intellectual property, and trade-related investment measures (TRIMS).

In agriculture, the United States worked with Australia, New Zealand, and the other members of the Australian-organized "Cairns Group" of nonsubsidizing agricultural exporting countries to gain agreement in the negotiations on a program of radical cuts in farm price supports and export subsidies by the year 2000. Agricultural trade proved to be the most contentious issue in the round, with European (and secondarily, Japanese) resistance to cuts in agricultural subsidies and increased market access being the principal stumbling blocks. In addition, difficulties also emerged in concluding agreements on revisions to the antidumping code, inclusion of TRIMS under the GATT umbrella, enhanced protection of intellectual property rights, and proposals to phase out textile quotas under the Multi-Fiber Agreement.

However, the United States was by no means totally pure in its approach to the round. Because of the importance of antidumping procedures in recent U.S. trade policy, U.S. negotiators were insistent on maintaining very vague and permissive language in the GATT antidumping code. The United States and Canada strongly resisted efforts by textile exporting countries, mainly in the Asia-Pacific region, to revamp and liberalize the quota arrangements under the Multi-Fiber Agreement covering textile trade. The United States also requested numerous exceptions to liberalizing trade in aviation and shipping, and threatened to reduce existing access to the U.S. telecommunications and financial services markets if other parties did not open their markets in these areas. The United States also did little to help a proposal by most primary commodity exporters, including Australia, to reduce and in some cases eliminate tariffs and controls on trade in natural resources.[3]

Disagreements on many of the issues in the Uruguay Round, and the resulting failure to meet successive deadlines for concluding the negotiations, partly reflected the inherent difficulty of expanding the scope of the negotiations into new and sensitive areas in which there are significant differences among national policies. They also reflected the large number of negotiating parties within the GATT, and the limits of the least-common-denominator approach inherent in this framework. Nevertheless, the United States persisted in pushing for a successful and significantly liberalizing conclusion to the round.

Regional and Bilateral Approaches

Frustration over the extended and seemingly unproductive GATT process, however, has been one of several factors behind a growing interest in recent years in trade liberalization on a more limited basis, either regional (e.g., the European Community) or bilateral (the Australia–New Zealand Closer Economic Relations [CER] model). The highly inward-oriented, protectionist approach of the European Community also stimulated consideration of regional or subregional approaches as a defensive measure or a fallback in case of a complete collapse of the multilateral framework. This was certainly one of the motivations behind the U.S. move to establish a North American Free Trade Area (NAFTA) and the projected expansion of this area to include the entire hemisphere.

Indeed, the conclusion of the free trade pact between the United States and Canada (the Canada–U.S. trade agreement [CUSTA]) in 1987, and the negotiation of the NAFTA agreement with Canada and Mexico in 1991–92, plus the prospect that similar agreements will be extended to include other Latin American countries in the near future, have reinforced the perception in the Asia-Pacific region of a turn by the United States away from the multilateral approach. Some in Australia and elsewhere have worried that pursuit of regional or bilateral arrangements would in fact detract from the effort put into the GATT negotiations, make a failure of the Uruguay Round even more likely, and contribute to a general slide into a world of trade blocs, anathema to the Antipodean countries among others.

Such anxieties seem exaggerated. There is no evidence that the CUSTA or NAFTA negotiations resulted in reduced U.S. interest or investment in the Uruguay Round. The fallback motive was not the only, or even the principal, driving force behind the North American negotiations or other bilateral arrangements such as the free trade agreement (FTA) with Israel. In each case other considerations, including the fact that Canada is the U.S.'s largest trade partner and the desire to encourage and lock in deregulatory economic reforms in Mexico, were more critical to the decision to negotiate an FTA.

During the 1992 campaign, President George Bush announced that the United States (at least under a second Bush administration) would pursue FTAs with a number of other countries including several in the Asia-Pacific region.[4] Australia and New Zealand were among the countries named as possible FTA partners.[5] Although the New Zealand government expressed interest in the proposal, the Australian government was critical on a number of grounds, including the unlikelihood that significant concessions would be forthcoming from the United States in the areas of most interest to Australia (especially agriculture).[6]

The Bush proposal seemed to reflect campaign imperatives (the need to put forward new ideas and proposals) rather than a fully considered policy initiative. Nevertheless, the proposal at least indicated that the administration was thinking in broader terms than a hemispheric trade block. Indeed, Bush administration officials argued that the pursuit of trade liberalization through multilateral, regional, and bilateral channels were not inconsistent but rather mutually reinforcing. If more progress toward free trade could be achieved on a regional or bilateral level than was possible through GATT, such agreements both advanced the overall cause and could provide useful models for emulation or expansion. In the words of one U.S. official, the basic U.S. approach was to "take trade liberalization where we can find it" (Lavin 1992).

Throughout his own presidential campaign, and subsequently as President-elect, Bill Clinton appeared to distinguish himself from the Bush approach by calling for a tougher and more aggressive policy of promoting American industry and American exports. However, Clinton also presented himself as an economic internationalist opposed to narrowly protectionist approaches. For example, in his most detailed speech on foreign policy during the campaign, his address to the World Affairs Council of Los Angeles on 13 August, Clinton called for "championing open world trade that benefits American workers as well as American businesses" (Clinton 1992a). In his major statement on the NAFTA agreement on 4 October, he said "I support the North American Free Trade Agreement. . . . If it is done right," but that he would not sign the implementing legislation "until we have reached additional agreements to protect America's vital interests" (Clinton 1992b). These statements preserved a good deal of room for flexibility in specific decisions, but at least indicated a clear awareness of the advantages of a liberal, multilateral trade order.

THE UNITED STATES AND ASIA-PACIFIC REGIONALISM

For a variety of reasons including its own origins as a federation, the United States has generally been a strong supporter of regional cooperation and the establishment of regional communities around the world. The United States welcomed and encouraged the movement toward European integration from its earliest stirrings after the Second World War, and despite numerous and sometimes heated disagreements with the European Community over economic issues, U.S. support for the process and goal of European integration has not wavered.

Consistent with this broad orientation, the United States has generally supported regional cooperation in the Asia-Pacific region. The United States was an early and consistent supporter of ASEAN as a vehicle for both foreign policy coordination and economic cooperation among the Southeast Asian states. Similarly, the United States welcomed the creation of a single market between Australia and New Zealand through CER, and has supported and worked with the Pacific Island states' regional organization, the South Pacific Forum.

The American attitude toward broader initiatives for Asia-Pacific regional cooperation, however, has been more guarded. U.S. officials have been particularly wary of proposals for security cooperation that might reduce the ability of the United States to meet its security commitments in the region, and of any proposals for regionwide organizations that appeared to exclude the United States. The first concerns were the basis for the consistent American rejection of proposals from the former Soviet Union for regional security or arms control arrangements, and of general American opposition to proposals for nuclear free or neutral zones in the region. U.S. objections to Malaysian Prime Minister Mahathir's proposal for an East Asian Economic Group (later renamed Caucus) were based on the exclusion of the United States and the resulting concern that the grouping might harm American economic involvement and interests in the region.

Although various American individuals and institutions have played important supportive roles, the United States has essentially been a passenger in the movement toward economic cooperation in the Asia-Pacific. There is regular American participation at the meetings of the nongovernmental regional organizations such as PBEC and PECC, and U.S. national committees coordinate American involvement. However, U.S. representation at the meetings of these organizations, from both the private sector and the government, by and large has not been at a level commensurate with that of the delegations from other major countries. (This is certainly true by contrast with both Australian and New Zealand representation.)

On the government side, the initiative to commission the Drysdale-Patrick study of OPTAD in 1979 was the action of one American legislator, with no significant involvement or interest from the executive branch.[7] The U.S. response to the APEC initiative is covered in greater detail below, but it should be noted at this point, that following the first APEC meeting in 1989, American participation at APEC ministerials has frequently been at sub-ministerial level at least for most of the sessions. (In fairness, it should be noted that the distractions of sudden crises elsewhere and changes of personnel have been partially responsible for the lack of ministerial-level attendance at some APEC meetings; however, this in itself is a measure of the level of priority that top-level American policymakers are able to give to efforts such as APEC.)

The U.S. attitude toward APEC has evolved significantly over the short lifetime of this initiative. The initial Hawke proposal did not mention the United States among the projected core APEC membership. Although Japan and others quickly confirmed that U.S. participation was essential, U.S. officials were privately irritated by what they saw as a deliberate slight. Publicly, the State Department announced that the United States would await ASEAN's response to the proposal before making its own decision regarding participation. This position both provided a plausible explanation for the lack of an immediate U.S. embrace of Hawke's initiative, and was a useful gesture toward the ASEAN states who were concerned that APEC might detract from their organization's position in the region.

Once the ASEAN states agreed to participate in the Canberra meeting, however, the United States also accepted, and it has been a regular and increasingly committed participant in the subsequent meetings. The Americans have been actively involved in the elaboration of a series of APEC working groups examining such issues as trade promotion, technology transfer, and the development of a common regional data base. The United States offered to host the 1993 ministerial, and by 1991 U.S. officials were referring to APEC as the premier economic forum of the Asia-Pacific region. By agreeing to host the 1993 meeting, the United States created both an opportunity to assert leadership and a clear test of the seriousness of the American commitment.

Reflecting the cautious U.S. attitude toward the establishment of new security institutions in the region, American officials have emphasized the essentially economic focus and mandate of APEC. They distinguish in this way between the functions of APEC and those of the annual ASEAN Post-Ministerial Conference involving the United States and other developed country "dialogue partners," whose agenda is seen to be broader, including political-security topics such as the Cambodian problem. The importance of this distinction, at least to the Bush administration, appeared to be confirmed in the U.S. reaction to the 1992 proposal of Hawke's successor as Australian Prime Minister, Paul Keating, for a summit meeting of APEC members. Although the Americans expressed support in principle, some in Washington were concerned over the possibility that a summit meeting might venture into political and security subjects (*Pacific Research* 1992). (When Clinton took up the summit idea in 1993, he stressed its purely economic agenda.)

U.S. POLICY: ECLECTIC

The preceding discussion enables us to deal directly with the specific questions about U.S. economic policies in the region posed in this section of the study.

The fundamental point is that the United States does not have a single, integrated economic policy toward the Asia-Pacific region per se. Rather, U.S. economic policy in this region is a set of policies that reflect global U.S. interests and domestic economic circumstances as well as specific U.S. interests and involvements in the region. The resulting mix has a number of strands, not necessarily fully consistent with one another but nevertheless coexisting. Elements of multilateralism, regionalism, and bilateral policy approaches can be identified. It is also possible to distinguish between collaborative and unilateral approaches to decision-making and policy implementation, unilateral action often being the trump card in U.S. policy in the event negotiations or consultative efforts fail to meet fundamental U.S. objectives.

Although the United States has become increasingly supportive of APEC as the major vehicle for regional economic cooperation, it is also clear that regional economic cooperation as such does not have a significantly higher priority in U.S. policy than efforts at the global, subregional, or bilateral-unilateral levels. Further, U.S. support for APEC or any other regionwide mechanism for economic cooperation or consultation is clearly conditioned on the requirement of U.S. participation.

There is very little prospect of any early movement toward the creation of an Asian or Asia-Pacific regional arrangement parallel to the European Community. However, it seems highly unlikely, at least under present conditions, that the United States would be supportive of such an effort. Unlike the early postwar period when the concept of a European community was first launched, the United States is not now the overwhelmingly dominant economic power and is not as confident in its competitiveness. It is preoccupied with concerns over slow economic growth and high unemployment at home. Thus, the American stance on any international economic question now gives far greater priority to the immediate economic self-interest of the United States than was the case in the early decades following the Second World War. This is not to say that U.S. interests and those of other regions or the international system are seen as conflicting, only that the former considerations have greater weight in the policy equation today.[8]

Given the lack of an integrated regional economic policy or strategy on the part of the United States, it is hardly surprising that the U.S. approach to cooperation with Australia and New Zealand on regional economic issues is also essentially ad hoc. Again, this is not to say that cooperation does not take place. Cooperation clearly occurs, regularly, on issues as varied as the effort to reform agricultural export subsidies in the Uruguay Round, attempts to gain greater opening of markets in the region, and economic development assistance to the Pacific Islands. The broad interests of the three are sufficiently similar that there are far more issues on which there is cooperation than conflict.

Nevertheless, it could not be said that the U.S. government attaches more importance to cooperation with either or both of its ANZUS partners on such matters than with a large number of other economic partners in the Asia-Pacific region or elsewhere. It is hard to identify any "special" role for cooperation with Australia and/or New Zealand in U.S. economic policy, regional or otherwise, now, prospectively, or in fact earlier in the alliance period.

Problems for Partners

From the perspective of America's regional trade partners, including Australia and New Zealand, the trouble with an essentially eclectic U.S. economic policy is that it is frequently difficult to anticipate the U.S. position on specific issues. Because of the influence of the United States in the international system as a whole, uncertainty about U.S. decision-making reduces the overall predictability of the system that is central to the stability of an interdependent global economy. Countries, such as Australia and New Zealand, that have very limited influence of their own are particularly dependent on a reliable, rule-and-principle–based international system to protect their interests.

In addition, bilateralism or unilateralism in American policy can directly harm the interests of individual partners. For example, it is the stated American policy that when it negotiates market opening with its trading partners, the resulting opportunities are available to all countries; however, given the bilateral nature of the negotiations it has been difficult for the United States to convince others interested in these markets that the resulting agreements are genuinely nondiscriminatory. In another example, although subsidized U.S. agricultural sales under the Export Enhancement Program are targeted at Europe's subsidized exports, they have the effect of lowering the international market prices for the commodities involved, and can also directly reduce the sales of other countries in their traditional markets. It is hardly surprising that other countries should not be convinced that in such essentially unilateral undertakings the Americans really have their interests at heart or even in mind.

THE OUTLOOK

There has been a continuous and frequently contentious debate within the United States in recent years over the direction of American international economic policy. Some trade policy analysts such as Clyde Prestowitz (1988) argue essentially for "managed trade" approaches. Numerous members of Congress have proposed specific protectionist measures such as domestic content requirements. In the 1992 presidential primaries Democratic candidate Tom Harkin espoused openly protectionist policies, and Republican challenger Pat Buchanan used the only slightly more subtle slogan of "America First." Nevertheless, the voices calling for radical change remain in a distinct minority. President Bush successfully vetoed the few protectionist measures that actually emerged from Congress during his term, and the protectionist candidates were soundly defeated in the presidential primaries.

The first few months of the Clinton administration provided no signs that there would be major changes in the previous eclectic, multitrack approach. In his first major speech on international trade, at American University on 26 February, the new president explicitly rejected the idea that multilateral, regional, bilateral, and unilateral approaches were somehow alternatives, asserting that "each of these efforts has its place" (Clinton 1993). He specifically reaffirmed his commitment to a successful conclusion of the GATT Uruguay Round, and his more conditional support for the NAFTA agreement. However, he also took a tough line on reciprocity and equal treatment, and White House officials indicated that the bilateral and unilateral provisions of U.S. trade legislation (antidumping, Super 301) would be used aggressively to ensure that American exporters are treated as fairly in foreign markets as foreign exporters are in U.S. markets.

Thus, although there are bound to be some differences of emphasis and packaging, it seems unlikely that the Clinton administration in practice will depart dramatically from the broad lines of international economic policy under the Reagan and Bush administrations. The multiple U.S. interests and the difficult trade-offs involved in international economic policy all work in this direction. This prospect of fundamental continuity extends to those policies that affect the Asia-Pacific region.

The result will not be a neat or theoretically elegant package; there are bound to be inconsistencies as well as twists and turns on specific matters. In fact, the high priority accorded by Clinton to domestic economic recovery and reform will probably result in somewhat less attention, at least at the presidential level, to issues of the international system. The essentially eclectic and more self-interested focus of American policy-making will continue to be a source of concern for U.S. trade partners in the region. Such a policy mix certainly contains the possibility of increased confrontation between the United States and countries of the Asia-Pacific region. However, the realities of economic interdependence are such that the broad pattern is more likely to be one of cooperation.

NOTES

1. The real effective exchange rate is an index of a country's bilateral exchange rates with its major trading partners (in this case, six) weighted by the total trade with those partners and adjusted for relative price differences between the country and the partners. A negative movement in the index would represent a devaluation and improve the country's competitive position for its exports.

2. The United States identified six areas of concern. These were: the mismatch of savings and investment that limits growth in the Japanese standard of living; land-use policies that keep real estate prices high and constrain new construction; pricing mechanisms that keep domestic prices higher than those often found for the same Japanese product in the United States; the distribution system that contributes to these pricing discrepancies and limits access to the local market; antitrust policies that are not rigorously enforced; and so-called keiretsu relationships that allow cross ownership of stock between firms and limit shareholder rights. The Japanese government, for its part, principally raised points about the U.S. economy that affect export competitiveness, such as the low U.S. saving rate, the lack of investment and export promotion incentives, and the increased need for work force training and education.

3. It is interesting to note that early on, Krause (1988: 47) predicted that the approach taken by U.S. trade policymakers in the GATT round was a "high-risk venture and may fail."

4. The announcement was made in remarks by President Bush in Detroit on 10 September 1992 (Bush 1992), and was further elaborated in a document released that

day, *Agenda for American Renewal,* and other subsequent statements by administration spokesmen.

5. The fact that Japan was left off the list caused concern for some, such as Australian Prime Minister Paul Keating, as being unnecessarily confrontational with Japan. The failure to mention Japan is largely explained by domestic political considerations having to do with the campaign. But it is also true, as Bush advisers subsequently explained, that as a practical matter it was very unlikely that the Japanese government would be in a position in the near-term future to consider the kinds of concessions necessary in a free trade agreement.

6. The Australian position on the FTA proposal was prefigured in a response by Prime Minister Keating to a question from Harry Woods, M.P., concerning Australia's position on joining a free trade area with the United States, during Question Time in the Australian House of Representatives on 8 September 1992.

7. One of the authors (Baker) was working on the staff of Senator John Glenn, who sponsored this study, during the time the Drysdale-Patrick report was submitted and released, and thus has first-hand knowledge of the general lack of wider interest or follow-up to the study elsewhere in the U.S. government.

8. A report issued in early 1993 by a working group convened by the Asia Foundation, in which one of the authors (Layman) participated, makes many of the same points in the context of an argument for greater attention to the Asia-Pacific region by the Clinton administration. (See Asia Foundation 1993: esp. 13–15.)

Comment

RICHARD W. BAKER AND GARY R. HAWKE

Viewed from the perspective of the evolution of relations among the ANZUS states, a comparison of the preceding analyses of the Australian, New Zealand, and U.S. approaches to economic cooperation in the Asia-Pacific region yields some good news and some bad news. The good news is that there is, unsurprisingly, a high degree of congruence in the basic objectives of all three governments and the principles of international economic policy they espouse. The bad news is that their individual national interests and strategies within this context diverge in important respects. This does not preclude a substantial amount of cooperation among them, but it does mean that all three governments will look first to their own agendas and that on many practical questions there will only be a limited area of clear consensus.

On the level of principle, all three embrace the ultimate goal of an open, liberal international economic order as well as the proximate objective of reducing existing barriers to the free flow of trade and investment. They share the conviction that their individual national economies would be able to prosper best over the long run under such an economic order. A corollary of this belief is a shared preference for a nondiscriminatory or most-favored-nation approach to trade liberalization—if barriers are lowered to one or a group of countries, the same terms should be granted or at least offered to others as well. A second corollary is that the formation of protective trade blocs and any return in the direction of the beggar-thy-neighbor policies of the 1930s are anathema.

There are voices in all three countries that challenge this prevailing economic orthodoxy. Particularly in the United States, but echoed to some degree in the other two countries, a small but vocal group of trade economists argues that differences in business culture between countries and regions are such that it will never be possible to achieve truly open and even competition. These individuals tend to advocate that their governments should follow what they perceive to be the Japanese example and take a more active and direct role in supporting innovation and investment at home and negotiating specific market access arrangements abroad. (It is worth noting, however, that their understanding of the Japanese example is often limited, especially its careful delineation of the appropriate spheres for cooperation and competition, its general subordination of government agencies to business leadership, and its avoidance of protection for uncompetitive Japanese enterprises.)

However, these voices remain a small minority. For the most part, even those economic interests that believe they will be harmed by reductions in trade barriers do not directly attack the long-term objectives. Instead, they couch their pleas for special consideration in terms of the same basic principles, arguing for example that their international competitors do not play by the rules of fair trade, or that their industry should be given a reasonable time to prepare for and adjust to a major change in the conditions under which they must do business.

A different challenge to the prevailing consensus in all three countries comes from parts of the environmental movement that believe that the concept of international free trade is too closely tied to old ideas of development with their single-minded emphasis on the objective of economic growth, and this is antithetical to the new, ecologically conscious focus on sustainable development. This challenge is still incipient rather than prominent in public debate, however. Policy circles in all three countries expect that, provided GATT survives the Uruguay Round, there will be an intelligent and well-formulated discussion of how environmental considerations can be built into the international trading order along with proper consideration of competing national interests. The issues are difficult ones, and it will take several years for an international consensus to be built, but in appropriate forums, extremists of all kinds will be marginalized.

Thus, multilateral liberalization remains the order of the day, and all three governments consistently state that their first priority is the negotiation of global lowering of barriers through the GATT and specifically the embattled Uruguay Round. All three also assert that trade liberalization measures on a regional or bilateral basis are only acceptable if they are consistent with the GATT, and that ideally such agreements should be open to others or at least encourage wider liberalizing steps. All three countries are members of free trade areas: CER in the case of Australia and New Zealand, and CUSTA and prospectively NAFTA—plus a free trade agreement with Israel—in the case of the United States. However, all point to the lack of common external tariffs and to their records of reducing external tariffs as proof that these are not protective or trade-restricting arrangements.

This broad consensus clearly provides substantial grounds for the three countries to work together toward their mutual goals. In turn, it is arguable that the success of such efforts in the international arena would provide the only truly effective rebuttal of the critics in each country of the open liberalization approach.

Nevertheless, within this general agreement on principles and overall objectives there are clear distinctions among the order of priorities of each country and the way that each has approached its economic relations with the region. Of the three, Australia has given the highest and most consistent priority to the development of Asia-Pacific economic cooperation and an institutional framework for this cooperation. Australia has enthusiastically welcomed and helped lead the movement toward regional cooperation, for a number of reasons including the belief that Australia's economic future depends increasingly on integration with the Asia-Pacific region.

As Jenelle Bonnor points out, Australia's view of the appropriate agenda for APEC has shifted somewhat from an emphasis on mounting a concerted lobbying effort on behalf of the region in the GATT Round to organizing the region to deal with the results of the round. This includes a growing sense that the region could provide an effective alternative vehicle for further trade liberalization in the event that the round leaves GATT with little capacity or stomach to have another go. Thus Australia, at least under the Labor government now in office for some time and returned in early 1993 for a further term, sees the region, and specifically APEC, as having a major priority in Australia's international economic strategy regardless of the fate of the global trade negotiations.

New Zealand has also been actively involved in the movement for regional cooperation. But New Zealand's support for the regional movement is clearly predicated on its compatibility with New Zealand's broader interests in an open international system and economic ties with other regions as well. As indicated by Alastair Bisley, New Zealand recognizes that in the event of the failure of the GATT Round or other setbacks to the process of global liberalization, regional approaches may provide a sort of firebreak to limit the further disintegration of the multilateral system. Nevertheless, this is clearly regarded as not even a second-best outcome, and one fraught with danger of further deterioration into a world of discriminatory trade blocs that historically, Bisley notes, are even quite costly to their members.

The New Zealand government has, however, moved toward a more positive reception of regional arrangements, while reiterating the importance it attaches to their being GATT-compatible. It welcomed a 1992 academic study that argued for linking CER and NAFTA in order to accelerate whatever reductions of barriers to trade in goods and services are possible through GATT, not as an exclusive arrangement but as one of a number of such linkages within the Asia-Pacific region (Holmes and Falconer 1992). The linkage would have to be genuinely open to membership by others who are able and willing to meet the obligations involved. The New Zealand government specifically noted that it was interested only in arrangements that included agricultural trade, and that were "Pacific friendly," that is, would have the effect of bringing countries in the region closer together (Bolger 1993).

The U.S. position presents an even more mixed picture. At least through the end of the Bush administration, there has been a palpable element of defensiveness in U.S. responses to Asia-Pacific regional initiatives. American policymakers have often seemed more concerned over the possibility that the United States might be excluded from, or made the principal target of, regional cooperative efforts, than over the possible benefits the United States might derive from participation. Also, from the American perspective, Asia-Pacific regional economic cooperation in itself does not appear to offer any early prospect of helping ease U.S. economic difficulties; one of the reasons for this is that the U.S. government sees no indications that the Asian nations with which it has the largest bilateral deficits would be any more willing to reduce trade barriers on a regional basis than they have been in the GATT or bilateral negotiations.

In pursuit of its own priority international economic objective of reducing its persistent trade deficits by gaining increased access for American exports in other markets, the United States is also clearly determined to use a variety of instruments, unilateral and bilateral as well as regional and multilateral, and to be the judge of which of these instruments to employ and when and how to employ them. In the eyes of Australia and New Zealand, and other trading partners as well, there is a growing emphasis in U.S. policy on bilateral or unilateral actions which detract from or directly conflict with the interests of an open multilateral system. So Asia-Pacific economic cooperation has a place in U.S. international economic policy, but it does not stand very high up on the priority list.

The reasons for these differences in approach and priorities are also clear enough. A self-described "middle power," Australia has distinctly limited reach and influence on the global scene, although in practice it has had far greater impact on a number of international issues (arms control, Cambodia) than its size and location alone would have led one to predict. In regional terms, however, Australia has considerably more potency. Its economy is as large as those of the ASEAN countries combined, and its infrastructure and cutting-edge technology give it more than equal standing with all but the region's giants. Australia's principal drawback as a regional player is rather that, for historical and ethnic reasons, many Asian countries do not regard it as a natural part of the region or a rightful member of the Asian club. The movement toward regional economic cooperation essentially coincided with the growing recognition and acceptance in Australia of its destiny and identity as an Asian-Pacific rather than a European state. For Australia, then, the opportunity to play a leadership role in building the first truly regional institutional structure offered the possibility of achieving several major national objectives at the same time.

For New Zealand, despite the CER agreement creating a single market with Australia, the balance of interests is rather different from that of its trans-Tasman partner. In contrast to Australia, whose minerals and energy exports weight its trade heavily toward the growing industrial economies of Asia, New Zealand's exports, particularly the traditional mainstay food products, are more evenly distributed among the world's major regions. In 1991, 17 percent of New Zealand's merchandise exports were to NAFTA countries and 3 percent to elsewhere in the Americas; 27 percent went to North Asia and 6 percent to Southeast Asia; and 18 percent went to Western Europe. The remainder was widely scattered, with some concentration on the Pacific Islands and the Middle East. Leaving Australia to one side, the three poles of North America, Japan and the EC are all important markets.

New Zealand is hardly a shrinking violet in international councils, but it has no illusions that it can on its own exert major influence even in the Asia-Pacific region. Thus, New Zealand has little to gain, and potentially much to lose, by putting too many eggs in any one regional basket. Although New Zealanders recognize that regional markets offer bright prospects and welcome the chance to develop the regional ties that can help open these markets, it is important to New Zealand that this regional affiliation should not detract in any way from the ability to maintain and develop markets in other regions as well.

The United States is and, barring catastrophic failure, will remain a global economic actor with global interests. The statement that U.S. trans-Pacific trade now exceeds its trans-Atlantic trade has become a cliché among Asia-Pacific hands in the United States and elsewhere. Nevertheless, the fact remains that trans-Atlantic trade is still just as critical to the U.S. economy as trans-Pacific trade, and that trade within the Americas (where Canada is the United States' largest single trading partner) is essential also.

There is simply no prospect that the United States will devote the same level of attention and enthusiasm to the affairs and institutions of any world region as the countries for whom that region is their only or principal affiliation. The United States has attached considerable importance to ensuring that it is not excluded from Asia-Pacific councils, just as it moved quickly to ensure that its major institutional affiliations with Europe were continued in the post–Cold War period through the perpetuation of NATO and the CSCE. This does not mean, however, that the U.S. government will necessarily seek to play a major role, much less the leading role, on many of the issues that come up within these institutions. No less than Australia and New Zealand, and particularly in a period of serious resource constraints, the United States has to budget its influence and attention. Other concerns have equal or greater call on that attention than Asia-Pacific regional cooperation.

However, it is also true that certain issues in U.S. economic relations with the Asia-Pacific region, particularly the U.S.–Japan trade relationship, will remain very high on the U.S. agenda. While bilateral negotiations are an important part of these relationships, some aspects and issues can actually be pursued more fruitfully in wider forums. As noted by Alastair Bisley, one of the reasons that other countries are interested in APEC is that it gives them a voice in discussions that affect how the U.S.–Japan relationship develops; but this forum serves the U.S. interest also.

The basic approaches of the three to regional economic cooperation are not incompatible. In fact, in most respects they are mutually reinforcing. But they are different, and have evolved differently based on the individual positions and interests of each.

There is one respect in which the approaches may be incompatible, however. This is the perception on the part of Australians, New Zealanders, and others that the United States is putting such high priority on achieving reductions in its trade deficit, but is still sufficiently reluctant to make the more difficult and uncongenial domestic adjustments, that it is willing to take actions that hurt its trade partners and even undermine the international system in the process. This is a heavy charge and, if true, has implications for the larger international framework as well as for U.S. relations with partners such as Australia and New Zealand. U.S. government spokesmen and most American analysts would deny that U.S. policy has veered this far off the responsible internationalist track. But the movement toward a more aggressive, unilateralist approach is clear, as are the specific actions (e.g., Section 301, or the EEP) that have affected and/or offended individual U.S. trade partners. This is the more difficult at a time when most of the economies involved have been in recession or restructuring or both. In such a period any additional economic injury is all the more insulting, and the political reaction is all the more immediate and intense. One can only argue — and hope — that this situation is a temporary aberration rather than a harbinger of a more permanent reality. Regrettably, that proposition is not readily susceptible to ex ante proof.

Implications for Relationships

RICHARD W. BAKER

In this final section we return to the basic questions posed at the start of this volume. We want to assess the broad implications of the preceding analyses for cooperation among the three countries in the 1990s and beyond. The most fundamental question is whether coordinated, parallel, or individualistic approaches are more likely to characterize their regional policies.

The conclusions and argument of this section can be summarized as follows. All three countries attribute increasing importance to the Asia-Pacific region and their involvements with the region. In most areas of regional policy, there is a continuing fundamental compatibility in their overall interests and objectives. However, each has adopted increasingly distinctive individual positions in the three policy areas studied. And there are important differences on some issues. Behind the specific policy differences there is, in some respects, a broader trade-off for each country between its interests in developing its regional relationships and its identity as a member of an Anglo-Saxon Cold War alliance. These signs do not point to an imminent crisis; they do point to a continued trend toward less "special" relationships.

SECURITY POLICIES

Given their security alliance, it is somewhat ironic that the most significant differences in the evolution of regional policies among the three have come in the security area. On the other hand, this is perhaps the most natural consequence of the changed conditions, particularly the development of more distinctive self-images and independent political-diplomatic agendas on the part of the two Antipodean partners.

As indicated in Section I, barring major new crises that galvanize common interests and efforts, present trends suggest that the future is likely to see a more diverse set of regional security policies and priorities among the three. The continuing primary focus of the United States is on global concerns. In the Asia-Pacific region it is on Northeast Asia where the primary security problems and American forward troop deployments are located. Australia's security focus is on Southeast Asia, and as Stewart Woodman points out, there are some potential conflicts between Australia's regional identity and its image and role as an ally of the United States. New Zealand's position on nuclear weapons was clearly incompatible with the U.S. view of the requirements of an alliance relationship. Its concentration in defense policy and procurement on the South Pacific carries with it the potential for conflicts with Australia's priorities.

Despite the changes and these differences in focus, however, it is virtually certain that security cooperation among the ANZUS allies will continue for the foreseeable future. This will, at least, be the case bilaterally between Australia and the United States, on the one hand, and between Australia and New Zealand, on the other. Following the pattern of the Gulf War, there is a high probability that all three countries would be involved in responding to future crises, at least in the extended Asia-Pacific region.

The end of the Cold War changes but does not completely transform the regional security situation. It removes the most compelling common threat, the glue that sustained the alliance over most of its history, but many regional security concerns remain — including instability in Indochina and uncertainty on the Korean peninsula. Multipolar orders in the past have not been particularly noteworthy for stability or even for responsible conduct on the part of the individual players. Further, no alternative institutional framework for assuring security in the region exists or is in prospect. ASEAN's annual post-ministerial consultations or the APEC process could become vehicles for regional political-security dialogue, but it will take some time before either of these mechanisms could take on any kind of action-oriented role. Other proposals for regional mechanisms have been bruited but as yet are only in the talking stages. U.S. skepticism toward such ideas, although waning, has been one major factor inhibiting movement in this direction. Despite the UN role in the Gulf War and the Cambodian settlement effort, it remains to be demonstrated that the UN system would be able to respond effectively to conflicts in the Asia-Pacific region unless the United States and its allies take the lead in practice.

Thus, mechanisms for consultation, coordination, and the assertion of leadership by like-minded states will retain their value, and in some respects may become even more important in the new era than under the previous, more clearly defined international structure. At a minimum, the alliance will remain a useful insurance policy against a reversion to a more confrontational era and/or the failure of the new mechanisms. Numerous practical elements of security cooperation, including the joint defense facilities in Australia, will continue to play important roles in maintaining stability and deterring threats. A topical example was the contribution of the Nurrungar facility to defense against Scud missile attacks during the Persian Gulf War.

Alliance with the United States continues to be particularly important for Australia, both in its own security policies and defense planning, and in the security perceptions of significant portions of the Australian public. ANZUS also provides the legal framework for Australia's continuing and even closer defense relations with New Zealand. As a practical matter, and even more so following the U.S.–New Zealand break, ANZUS is an Australia-centered alliance. As such, security cooperation under the alliance will last as long, and be as intensive, as Australian governments find useful.

There is a whole new agenda of "security" issues in the region that could engage cooperation on the part of the three ANZUS governments. These include the strengthening of democratic institutions and human rights in the region, threats to the environment, organized crime (including drug trafficking), terrorism, refugee problems, and so forth. Since the resource pinch is, if anything, worse now than in earlier periods for all three, the attractiveness of collaborative efforts increases if these show any promise of reducing individual costs.

However, in practice there appears to be relatively little likelihood of explicit bilateral or trilateral coordination of policies and actions in most of these areas. Each of the three countries has a different set of regional relationships, interests, domestic constraints, strengths, and liabilities. Combined efforts often risk magnifying the liabilities without increasing the effectiveness of the action. There is no convincing evidence that joint approaches would be likely to advance the fundamental political principles and other values that they share—for example, press freedom in Indonesia or constitutional democracy in Fiji—partly because the domestic political constraints and the bilateral relationships with which each comes to these situations inevitably differ.

Thus, in this area, their generally shared or at least complementary goals are most likely to be pursued through individual action, supported by a discreet consultation process rather than overt collaboration. This point is reinforced by necessity in the case of U.S.–New Zealand relations, due to the absence of a structured process for regular cooperation such as existed prior to the break in their security relations under the ANZUS treaty.

THE PACIFIC ISLANDS

In the Pacific Islands subregion, despite close common interests, the three countries face very different specific problems and, correspondingly, their policies and actions will be determined in a largely individualistic manner.

New Zealand perforce devotes primary attention in its security policies to the island region, although resource constraints limit its actual capabilities even in this subregion. Although its economic interests are far more broadly spread and other regions rank considerably higher in priority as markets and trading partners, in a political and even cultural sense, New Zealand is increasingly projecting itself as a member of the island region. As such it tends to assert a proprietary claim to the status of interpreter of island interests and even intermediary to the outside world. On ecological and environmental issues of concern to the islands, from global warming to driftnet fishing to the threats of nuclear and chemical pollution, New Zealand is at one with the island states and almost always in or at a minimum close to the lead. That New Zealand's assertions and exertions on their behalf are not always fully appreciated in the islands does not lessen their growing importance in New Zealand's sense of geopolitical identity.

Although Australia for the most part carries more weight in the islands than does New Zealand, simply by virtue of its much greater size and therefore capacity in most fields (including development as well as security assistance), for Australia the islands remain a secondary policy theater. Australia's reorientation of its national identity has focused almost exclusively on the Asian part of the Asia-Pacific region. It is in Asia, primarily Northeast and Southeast Asia, that Australia sees its future, both economically and in terms of leadership on regional issues. As an activist "middle power," Australia also has broader international policy interests. Its involvement in such issues as arms control means that Australia sometimes must choose between island interests and its global interests, as in the case of the U.S. program to destroy chemical munitions in the islands region.

For the United States, with its truly global role, the Pacific Islands, even those that are American territories, rarely even rank as a secondary policy priority, and do not seem likely to assume significantly greater importance in the foreseeable future. It seems to take a near-crisis atmosphere—Soviet overtures in the islands in the mid-1970s or seizures of American tuna boats in the mid-1980s or an uproar over a chemical weapons destruction facility in 1990—to catch the attention of senior American policymakers. This does not mean that the United States pays no attention to the islands (indeed, in the past the problem has sometimes been of overreaction in an effort to make up for lost ground), but rather that it is difficult to sustain the interest of top officials over time, and that in decision-making on issues not perceived as directly affecting the islands their interest is all too easily overlooked. In these circumstances, the most assiduous efforts of the small cadre of dedicated island experts in the U.S. government are frequently rewarded only by frustration.

The three countries share obvious common interests in supporting island economic and political development, stability and security. The three governments also recognize that it is desirable to maintain complementarity and avoid redundancy in their various programs in the island region. However, despite these areas of agreement it is, frankly, difficult to portray any aspect of the region's evolution over the postwar period as reflecting a conscious common or coordinated effort on the part of the three ANZUS states. At best there is a tenuous division of labor, with each giving primary support to the island entities with which each has historical links, and some joint activities such as the Australian–New Zealand air surveillance of EEZs. Beneath the high-minded rhetoric of ministerial meetings, this is the practical reality. The experience of Pacific Islands policy does not provide any solid evidence that a habit of cooperation has developed among the ANZUS states in areas of common interest not directly related to defense.

REGIONAL ECONOMIC COOPERATION

All three countries are and can be expected to continue to be supporters of the budding effort to enhance Asia-Pacific economic consultation. As indicated in the preceding section, the Asia-Pacific region is of increasing economic importance to all three.

The basic approaches of the three to regional economic cooperation are certainly compatible. In fact, in most respects — certainly in their common support of an open rather than protective approach to economic regionalism — they are mutually reinforcing. But there are a variety of individual views among them as to the desirable scope, agenda, and objectives of regional economic cooperation, each view reflecting the individual national interests and priorities of each country.

Of the three, Australia has given the highest priority to efforts to organize regional economic cooperation, in keeping with its overall interest in establishing an accepted and significant place for itself in the region. New Zealand has been a consistent and interested participant, although it has had somewhat mixed emotions on the subject because of its concern that Asia-Pacific economic regionalism not detract from its equally important trade relationships with other parts of the world. The United States has, to date, been more of a passenger on the regional bandwagon, more concerned over losing its seat than committed to forward progress. None of the three wish to see the world divided into regional trading blocs, much less to be forced to affiliate with one at the expense of ties with the others. But they seem to have adopted very different strategies in this regard.

At only a modest risk of oversimplification, the respective strategies appear to be the following. Australia under Labor has been increasingly looking to Asia as a major vehicle through which to both lobby for the maintenance of an open world system and cushion the impact of setbacks on this path. The United States under the (now former) Republican administration has been preparing a fall-back position in the Americas while attempting to discourage the development of anything resembling a separate trade bloc in Asia. New Zealand under both Labour and National governments has been energetically casting about for any available means of hedging its bets on a liberal international order by securing its relationships to a number of regions. All of these approaches have a rationality of their own given the circumstances of each party, but they can hardly be described as reflecting a common strategy in pursuit of the agreed common objective.

Further, there are at least some indications of a potential for competition or conflict between these approaches. Australia's original formulation for APEC did not include U.S. membership, apparently due, partially, to momentary stresses in the bilateral relationship but also because in making the APEC proposal the Australian government wanted to emphasize its own identity with the Asian economic region. The cautious American response to the initiative in part simply returned the compliment but more importantly reflected the importance the United States attached to its relations with the ASEAN grouping and its desire to be certain the ASEAN states did not view APEC as a threat to their interests. New Zealand's interest in exploring possible links with the North American free trade area may be frustrated because Australia, with which it is now economically linked through CER, sees such a move as potentially detracting from the pursuit of its priority objective of strengthening its ties with and acceptance by the major Asian economies. Finally, the Malaysian proposal for an East Asian Economic Grouping did not include any of the ANZUS countries, suggesting that all three have legitimate reason to give priority to ensuring their own acceptance in regional councils.

The available evidence thus strongly suggests that individual and, to some degree, competitive interests will predominate in national policy-making in this field over considerations of mutual interest or solidarity.

THE FUTURE

The broader conclusion that emerges from these assessments of the outlook for cooperation in the three policy areas is that, in the future, the regional policies of the three countries are more likely to be characterized by individualistic approaches than by coordination or even cooperation. As indicated in each case, their interests and objectives are and will continue to be broadly parallel, but operationally their positions and strategies are likely to display considerable variation.

Should this conclusion surprise anyone? Probably not. The more natural assumption about national interests and policies is that they will reflect the individual situations and perspectives of the countries involved, and that these are bound to differ in degree if not more fundamentally. But in the case of the ANZUS states, there has been a tendency (certainly in the United States) to assume that the fundamental congruence in their historical backgrounds and values, coupled with the fact that the rest of their region is characterized by very different peoples, cultures, and systems, would produce a significant commonality of interests across a wide range of fields. The existence of the ANZUS defense alliance reinforces the presumption of commonality. This assumption in turn can easily lead to exaggerated expectations on all sides as to the degree of agreement and support that will be forthcoming, and to a correspondingly exaggerated sense of disappointment, even betrayal, when these expectations are not fulfilled.

So it is instructive (or should at least have some cautionary value for all concerned) to document the differences that exist or have developed among the three in these important policy areas. Similarities of origin, ethnic composition, culture, language, and political and economic systems may make for a degree of natural affinity between peoples and governments and facilitate working together toward shared objectives, but they do not in and of themselves ensure any generalized congruity of interests or policy approaches.

An additional point is worth highlighting. To some degree, the similarities among the three countries may actually inhibit practical cooperation and even lead to competition among them. All three countries attribute increasing importance to the Asia-Pacific region and their involvements with the region. But, precisely because of their differences in background and culture from most of the rest of the Asia-Pacific countries, they all face problems in gaining acceptance as bona fide members of the regional community. To the degree that they are perceived in the region as coordinating their efforts to this end (or otherwise pursuing a common policy agenda), this merely serves to emphasize their distinctiveness from the rest of the region — Anglo-Saxon outsiders seeking membership in an Asian club. For each of the three countries, then, there is a degree of conflict between its interest in establishing its Asian-Pacific credentials and its identity as a member of an alliance of Western, European-origin states. When such conflicts arise, all three governments, not surprisingly, have tended to give higher priority to their individual interests in the region rather than to the interests of trilateral cooperation or harmony. The dilemmas and trade-offs involved would be raised in acute form in the event of a collapse of the GATT Round and/or an accelerated drift toward regional trade blocks.

Nevertheless, a basic commonality of interests and objectives among the three states does exist, and cooperation will be mutually advantageous on a whole series of regional issues including many major aspects of the policy areas we have examined. But this analysis suggests that such cooperation faces an additional challenge. If it is not to detract from the standing and credentials of the three governments as members of the region, policy coordination among the ANZUS states must be seen by the other involved states as clearly supportive of the region's interests (security and otherwise) and institutions rather than the more self-centered or idiosyncratic interests of the three. As a practical matter, for the most part it will probably be easier for the three governments to achieve such perceptually correct collaboration by operating openly and within larger groupings and forums rather than through private consultations in bilateral or trilateral mechanisms. This point may help explain why there has not been more intensive consultation and coordination of positions among the three on such sensitive issues as political change in the Pacific Islands.

Two exceptions to the preceding generalizations should be noted. First, the relationship between Australia and New Zealand is qualitatively different from the relationship of either with the United States. The combination of physical proximity, the increasing integration of the two economies under CER, and a growing practical interdependence between the two military establishments creates a series of links and common interests that belies the rivalry and colorful exchanges characterizing the superficial aspects of the bilateral relationship. This does not necessarily make for any more immediate or inevitable congruity of perspective between the two governments on specific issues such as those examined in this study. It does mean that the two are, to a degree, locked into a partnership that more often than not will end them up in similar positions despite differences in their initial preferences or priorities.

The second important exception, for the foreseeable future, is U.S.-Australian security cooperation. The U.S.-Australian security relationship is extraordinarily close, with a wide range of joint activities, exchanges of personnel, etc. This practical, operational collaboration serves important interests on both sides — interests that appear likely to continue for as long as projections can reliably be made and are to a large degree impervious to policy differences between the two governments on the handling of regional and other security issues. Therefore, in this area the question is not whether the basis for cooperation in this field will deteriorate, but rather whether differences and problems in other aspects of the bilateral relationship will erode the atmosphere for security cooperation. Present evidence does not create any presumption that such an erosion will occur, but neither can it be excluded.

Finally, none of this discussion is intended to suggest that some fundamental crisis in the relationships is imminent. Indeed, the fact that the broad U.S.-New Zealand relationship has survived so well, despite the effective severing of alliance ties, could be taken as evidence to the contrary. Our study does suggest that, despite their long security alliance and other basic affinities between them, the relationships between Australia and New Zealand, on the one hand, and the United States, on the other, for the most part resemble those between any other pair or group of fundamentally friendly states. The relationships are not moving toward serious conflicts. But neither are they becoming more "special" in any operationally meaningful sense of that term.

Bibliography

GENERAL

ASEAN Heads of Government. *Singapore Declaration of 1992*. ASEAN Heads of Government Meeting, Singapore, 27–28 January 1992.

Baker, Richard W. *Australia, New Zealand, and the United States: Fifty Years of Alliance Relations*. Report of a Study Project. Honolulu: International Relations Program, East-West Center, September 1991(a).

———, ed. *Australia, New Zealand, and the United States: Internal Change and Alliance Relations in the ANZUS States*. New York: Praeger, 1991(b).

———. *The International Relations of the Southwest Pacific: New Visions and Voices*. Occasional Paper 4. Honolulu: International Relations Program, East-West Center, August 1992.

———, and Gary R. Hawke, eds. *ANZUS Economics: Economic Trends and Relations Among Australia, New Zealand, and the United States*. Westport, Connecticut: Praeger, 1992.

The Economist. Various issues.

Fairbairn, Te'o I. J., Charles E. Morrison, Richard W. Baker, and Sheree A. Groves. *The Pacific Islands: Politics, Economics, and International Relations*. Honolulu: International Relations Program, East-West Center, 1991.

Grant, F. L., A. A. Jordan, E. H. Preeg, and J. Wanandi. *Asia Pacific Economic Cooperation: The Challenge Ahead*. Washington, D.C.: The Center for Strategic and International Studies, 1990.

Islands Business. (Also *Islands Business Pacific, I B Pacific* for various periods.) Suva, Fiji. Various issues.

Japan Center for International Exchange (JCIE). *The Pacific Community Concept: Views from Eight Nations*. Proceedings of the Asian Dialogue at Oiso, Japan, January, 1980. The JCIE Papers. Tokyo: The Japan Center for International Exchange, 1980.

———. *The Pacific Community Concept: A Select Annotated Bibliography*. The JCIE Papers. Tokyo: The Japan Center for International Exchange, 1982.

Joint Statement. Canberra Ministerial-Level Meeting on Asia-Pacific Economic Cooperation, 5–7 November 1989.

Joint Statement. Asia Pacific Economic Cooperation Ministerial Meeting, Singapore, 29–31 July 1990.

Joint Statement. (Referred to as the "Seoul APEC Declaration.") Third Asia Pacific Economic Cooperation Ministerial Meeting (APEC III), Seoul, 12–14 November 1991.

Joint Statement. Fourth Asia Pacific Economic Cooperation Ministerial Meeting (APEC IV), Bangkok, 10–11 September 1992.

Hooper, Paul F., ed. *Building a Pacific Community: The Addresses and Papers of the Pacific Community Lecture Series.* Honolulu: The East-West Center, 1982.

Kojima, K. *Japan and a Pacific Free Trade Area.* London: Macmillan, 1971.

———. *An Organisation for Pacific Trade, Aid and Development: A Proposal.* Australia-Japan Economic Relations Research Project no. 40. Canberra: Australian National University, 1976.

Ministry of International Trade and Industry (MITI), Government of Japan. *Toward New Asia Pacific Cooperation: Promotion of Multilevel Gradually Advancing Cooperation on a Consensus Basis.* Tokyo: MITI, 1983.

Scalapino, Robert A., Seizaburo Sato, Jusuf Wanandi, and Sungjoo Han, eds. *Pacific-Asian Economic Policies and Regional Interdependence.* Research Papers and Policy Studies 27. Berkeley: Institute of East Asian Studies, University of California, 1988.

Soesastro, M. Hadi. "Institutional Aspects of Pacific Economic Cooperation." In Soesastro and Han 1983.

Soesastro, M. Hadi, and Sungjoo Han, eds. *Pacific Economic Cooperation: The Next Phase.* Jakarta: Center for Strategic and International Studies, 1983.

Wanandi, Jusuf. "Asia-Pacific Economic Cooperation: Ideas About Substance." In Grant, Jordan, Preeg, and Wanandi 1990.

AUSTRALIA

Alley, Roderic. "The 1987 Military Coups in Fiji: The Regional Implications." *The Contemporary Pacific* 2, no. 1 (1990): 37–58.

Alves, Dora. "Patrol Boats Foster Regional Stability." *Pacific Defence Reporter* 15, no. 12 (June 1990): 18–19.

Australian Broadcasting Corporation. "Blood on the Bougainvillea." Documentary, *Four Corners* program, 24 June 1991.

Australian Foreign Affairs Record (AFAR). Various issues.

Australian International Development Assistance Bureau (AIDAB). *Australia's Relations with the South Pacific.* AIDAB International Development Issues paper no. 2. Canberra: Australian Government Publishing Service, 1987.

Australian Parliament. Joint Committee on Foreign Affairs and Defence. *Threats to Australia's Security—Their Nature and Probability.* Canberra: Australian Government Publishing Service, 1981.

———. Joint Committee on Foreign Affairs and Defence. *The ANZUS Alliance.* Canberra: Australian Government Publishing Service, 1982.

———. Joint Committee on Foreign Affairs, Defence and Trade. *Australia's Relations with the South Pacific.* Canberra: Joint Committee on Foreign Affairs, Defence and Trade, March 1989(a).

———. Joint Committee on Foreign Affairs, Defence and Trade, Working Group on Asia-Pacific Economic Cooperation. "Submissions." Canberra: Commonwealth of Australia, 1989(b).

Australian Senate. Standing Committee on Foreign Affairs, Defence and Trade. *United Nations Peacekeeping and Australia.* Canberra: Australian Government Publishing Service, May 1991.

Australia's Overseas Aid Program 1990–91. 1990–91 Budget Related Paper no. 4. Canberra: Australian Government Publishing Service, 1990.

Australia's Overseas Aid Program 1992–93. 1992–93 Budget Related Paper no. 4. Canberra: Australian Government Publishing Service, 1992.

Ball, Desmond. *Building Blocks For Regional Security.* Canberra Papers on Strategy and Defence no. 83. Canberra: Strategic and Defence Studies Centre, Australian National University, 1991.

Beazley, Kim C. "South Pacific Defence Initiatives." Statement by the Minister for Defence to the House of Representatives, Australian Parliament. *House of Representatives Hansard,* 20 February 1987: 433–436.

———. "Self-Reliance and Cooperation: Australia's Regional Defence Policy." Statement by the Minister for Defence to the House of Representatives, Australian Parliament. *House of Representatives Hansard,* 23 February 1988: 499–506.

———. "Australian Defence Policy." In Desmond Ball, ed., *Australia and the World: Prologue and Prospects.* Canberra Papers on Strategy and Defence no. 69. Canberra: Strategic and Defence Studies Centre, Australian National University, 1990.

Berry, Ken. "APEC: Seoul Report." *Backgrounder* 2, no. 21. Canberra: Department of Foreign Affairs and Trade, 1991.

Bonnor, Jenelle. "The Politics of Asia-Pacific Economic Cooperation." Masters thesis, Australian National University, Canberra, 1990.

Burnett, Alan. *The A-NZ-US Triangle.* Canberra: Strategic and Defence Studies Centre, Australian National University, 1988.

Byrne, Michael. "Evans floats his vision of EC-type APEC." *Australian Financial Review,* 14 September 1992.

Cheeseman, Graeme. "The Military Dimensions of Australia's Regional Security Posture." In Greg Fry, ed., *Australia's Regional Security.* Sydney: Allen & Unwin Australia, 1991: 85–95.

———, and St. John Kettle, eds. *The New Australian Militarism: Undermining Our Future Security.* Sydney: Pluto Press Australia, 1990.

Connell, John. "Island Microstates: the Mirage of Development." *The Contemporary Pacific* 3, no. 2 (1991): 251–287.

———, ed. *Migration and Development in the South Pacific.* National Centre for Development Studies, Pacific Research Monograph no. 24. Canberra: Research School of Pacific Studies, Australian National University, 1990.

Cooper, A. F., and R. A. Higgott. "Middle Power Leadership and Coalition Building:

The Cairns Group and the Uruguay Round." Working Paper 1990 no. 1. Canberra: Department of International Relations, Research School of Pacific Studies, Australian National University, 1990.

Crawford, J., and S. Okita. *Australia, Japan and Western Pacific Economic Relations.* Canberra: Australian Government Publishing Service, 1976.

——, eds. *Raw Materials and Pacific Economic Integration.* London: Croom Helm, 1978.

The Defence Force and the Community. Report of the Interdepartmental Committee on the Wrigley Review, tabled in Parliament by the Minister for Defence, May 1991. Canberra: Australian Government Publishing Service, 1991.

The Defence of Australia 1987. Policy Information Paper presented to Parliament by the Minister for Defence, the Hon. Kim C. Beazley, M.P., March 1987. Canberra: Australian Government Publishing Service, 1987.

Defence Report. Annual report of the Department of Defence. Canberra: Australian Government Publishing Service, 1963–1991.

Department of Defence. "Key Elements in the Triennial Reviews of Strategic Guidance since 1945." Submission to the Joint Parliamentary Committee on Foreign Affairs and Defence, April 1986. *House of Representatives Hansard,* 17 February 1987(a): 303–318.

——. "Submission to the Joint Committee on Foreign Affairs and Defence Enquiry into Australia's Relations with the South Pacific." Canberra: Department of Defence, March 1987(b).

Department of Foreign Affairs (DFA). "Submission to the Joint Committee on Foreign Affairs and Defence Enquiry into Australia's Relations with the South Pacific." Canberra: Department of Foreign Affairs, March 1987.

Department of Foreign Affairs and Trade (DFAT). *Backgrounder.* Various issues.

——. *Insight.* Various issues.

——. *The Monthly Record.* Various issues.

——. Unclassified Outward Cablegram, 15 September 1989.

——. *The Australia New Zealand Closer Economic Relations Trade Agreement (CER): Background and Guide to Arrangements Arising From the 1988 Review, Status Report.* Canberra: Department of Foreign Affairs and Trade, August 1991.

——. *Composition of Trade: Australia 1991–92.* Canberra: Trade Analysis Branch, Economic and Trade Development Division, Department of Foreign Affairs and Trade, 1992.

Dibb, Paul. "New Directions in Australian Defence Policy." Presentation to the Asia-Pacific Security Conference, Singapore, February 1990.

Downer, Alexander. "Liberal Trading Arrangements for the Asia-Pacific Region: A Coalition Policy Statement." Statement by the Shadow Minister For Trade. Canberra, 26 April 1991.

Drysdale, Peter. *International Economic Pluralism: Economic Policy in East Asia and the Pacific.* Sydney: Allen & Unwin Australia, 1988.

——, and Ross Garnaut. "NAFTA and the Asia Pacific Region: Strategic Responses." Paper presented at the Conference on "NAFTA, The Pacific and Australia/ New Zealand," The Edward A. Clark Center for Australian Studies, University of Texas at Austin, 1–2 October 1992.

————, and Hugh Patrick. *An Asian-Pacific Regional Economic Organization: An Exploratory Concept Paper.* Prepared for the Committee on Foreign Relations, United States Senate, Library of Congress Congressional Research Service. Washington, D.C.: U.S. Government Printing Office, 1979.

Dupont, Alan. *Australia's Threat Perceptions: A Search For Security.* Canberra Papers on Strategy and Defence no. 82. Canberra: Strategic and Defence Studies Centre, Australian National University, 1991.

Elek, Andrew. "The Challenge of Asian-Pacific Economic Cooperation." *The Pacific Review* 4, no. 4 (1991).

Evans, Gareth. "Australia's Regional Security." Ministerial Statement by Senator the Hon. Gareth Evans, Q.C., Minister for Foreign Affairs and Trade, December 1989.

————. "Ministerial Response." In Greg Fry, ed., *Australia's Regional Security.* Sydney: Allen & Unwin Australia, 1991(a).

————. "Australia, The Asia Pacific and Hong Kong." Address by the Minister for Foreign Affairs and Trade to the Hong Kong Foreign Correspondents Club, Hong Kong, 22 April 1991(b).

————. "Managing Australia's Asian Future." Address by the Minister for Foreign Affairs and Trade, Third Asia Lecture, Asia-Australia Institute, University of New South Wales, Sydney, 3 October 1991(c).

————. "Trade and International Investment: The Australian Government's Strategic Approach." Address by the Minister for Foreign Affairs and Trade to the Centre for International Business Affairs Forum on "Strategic Approach to Trade and International Investment," Melbourne, 13 August 1992(a).

————. Press conference, Bangkok, 10 September 1992(b) (Department of Foreign Affairs and Trade transcript).

————. Remarks to Senate Estimates Committee B. *Senate Hansard,* 24 September 1992(c).

————. "Australia, The U.S. and the Mid-East." Address by the Minister for Foreign Affairs and Trade to the Mid-American Committee, Chicago, 2 October 1992(d).

————, and Bruce Grant. *Australia's Foreign Relations in the World of the 1990s.* Melbourne: Melbourne University Press, 1991.

Force Structure Review. Report to the Minister for Defence, May 1991. Canberra: Australian Government Publishing Service, 1991.

Fry, Greg. "Peacekeeping in the South Pacific: Some Questions for Prior Consideration." Department of International Relations Working Paper 1990 no. 7. Canberra: Research School of Pacific Studies, Australian National University, 1990.

————, ed. *Australia's Regional Security.* Sydney: Allen & Unwin Australia, 1991(a).

————. "Australia's South Pacific Policy: From 'Strategic Denial' to 'Constructive Commitment.'" Department of International Relations Working Paper 1991 no. 8. Canberra: Research School of Pacific Studies, Australian National University, 1991(b).

Garnaut, Ross. *Australia and the Northeast Asian Ascendancy.* Canberra: Australian Government Publishing Service, 1989.

Grattan, Michelle. "Keating attacks US on trade." *The Age,* 23 September 1992.

Hamel-Green, Michael. *The South Pacific Nuclear Free Zone Treaty: A Critical Assessment*. Canberra: Peace Research Centre, Research School of Pacific Studies, Australian National University, 1990.

Harper, Norman. "Australia and the United States." In Gordon Greenwood and Norman Harper, eds., *Australia in World Affairs 1956–1960*. Melbourne: F. W. Cheshire, 1963.

———. "Australia and the United States." In Gordon Greenwood and Norman Harper, eds., *Australia in World Affairs 1961–1965*. Melbourne: F. W. Cheshire, 1968.

Harris, Stuart. "Regional Economic Co-operation, Trading Blocs and Australian Interests." *Australian Outlook* 43, no. 2 (1989).

———. "Economic Changes in the International System: Implications for Australia's Prospects." Department of International Relations Working Paper 1989 no. 5. Canberra: Research School of Pacific Studies, Australian National University, 1989.

Hawke, Robert. "Regional Cooperation: Challenges for Korea and Australia." Address by the Prime Minister to the Luncheon of Korean Business Associations, Seoul, 31 January 1989.

Hayden, William. "Review of ANZUS." *Australian Foreign Affairs Record* 54, no. 9 (1983): 512–517.

———. *Uranium, The Joint Facilities, Disarmament and Peace*. Canberra: Australian Government Publishing Service, 1984.

———. "The ANZUS Treaty: Its Value and Relevance." *Australian Foreign Affairs Record* 56, no. 5 (1985[a]): 389–396.

———. "ANZUS: Regional Defence Implications." *Australian Foreign Affairs Record* 56, no. 5 (1985[b]): 397–402.

———. "Australia and the United States." *Australian Foreign Affairs Record* 58, no. 7 (1987): 355–356.

Hegarty, David. "The South Pacific and Papua New Guinea." In Desmond Ball and Cathy Downes, eds., *Security and Defence: Pacific and Global Perspectives*. Sydney: Allen & Unwin Australia, 1990: 412–434.

Henningham, Stephen. *The South Pacific Amid the Waves of Change*. Brisbane: Centre for the Study of Australia-Asia Relations, Griffith University, 1991.

Hewson, John. "Time to put Australia back on the multi-track." *The Australian*, 10 September 1992(a).

———. "New Priorities for Australian Foreign Policy in a New International Era." Address by the Leader of the Opposition, 1992 Roy Milne Memorial Lecture, Adelaide University, Adelaide, 26 October 1992(b).

Higgott, Richard, Andrew Cooper, and Jenelle Bonnor. "Asia Pacific Economic Cooperation: an evolving case-study in leadership and co-operation building." *International Journal* 45, no. 4 (1990).

Hill, Robert. "Hill Initiates Inquiry Into Asia-Pacific Regional Economic Cooperation." Shadow Minister for Foreign Affairs Media Release. Canberra, 16 June 1989(a).

———. "Hawke Compromising Years of Work on Pacific Basin Concept." Shadow Minister for Foreign Affairs Media Release. Canberra, 5 July 1989(b).

———. "Hill Says Evans Must Push for Business Role in APEC." Shadow Minister for Foreign Affairs Media Release. Canberra, 29 July 1990.

——. "After the War—A New World Order? An Alliance Framework for the Asia-Pacific." Address to the 500 Club, Melbourne, April 1991(a).

——. "Regional Economic Cooperation: Whither APEC?" Address by the Shadow Minister for Foreign Affairs to the North Queensland Zone Conference of the Liberal Party, Cairns, 13 April 1991(b).

——. "Regional Diplomacy: Advancing Australia's Interests." Address by the Shadow Minister for Foreign Affairs to the Australian Institute of International Affairs (North Queensland) and the Department of History and Politics, James Cook University, Townsville, 1 September 1992.

House of Representatives Hansard. Australian Parliament. Various issues.

Hughes, Helen. "Too Little, Too Late: Australia's Future in the Pacific Economy." *Australian Economic Papers* 27, no. 51 (1988).

Jennings, Peter. *The Armed Forces of New Zealand and the ANZUS Split: Costs and Consequences.* Occasional Paper no. 4. Wellington: New Zealand Institute of International Affairs, 1988.

Keating, Paul. "Trade." Questions Without Notice: question by Mr. Harry Woods MP to the Prime Minister. *House of Representatives Hansard,* 8 September 1992(a).

——. "Visit by the Prime Minister to Japan, Singapore and Cambodia." Ministerial Statement by the Prime Minister. *House of Representatives Hansard,* 13 October 1992(b).

——. "Australia–United States Trade and Investment Framework Arrangement." Statement by the Prime Minister (media release). Canberra, 26 November 1992(c).

Kerin, John. "Outcome of the 1992 CER Review." Speech by the Minister for Trade and Overseas Development to the Australia–New Zealand Business Council Conference, Wellington, 7 October 1992.

——, and Philip Burdon. "1992 Review of CER." Joint Statement by the Australian Minister for Trade and Overseas Development and the New Zealand Minister for Trade Negotiations, Wellington, 7 October 1992.

Killen, D. J. "Australian Defence." Statement presented to Parliament by the Minister for Defence, November 1976. Canberra: Australian Government Publishing Service, 1976.

King, Peter. "Redefining South Pacific Security: Greening and Domestication." In Ramesh Thakur, ed., *South Pacific Security.* London: Macmillan, 1990: 45–63.

Kitney, Geoff. "Keating puts Japan first." *The Australian Financial Review,* 23 September 1992.

Knapman, Bruce. "Aid and the Dependent Development of Pacific Island States." *Journal of Pacific History* 21 (1986): 139–152.

May, R. J., and Matthew Spriggs, eds. *The Bougainville Crisis.* Bathurst, New South Wales: Crawford House Press, 1990.

Mediansky, Fedor A. "Defence Reorganisation 1957–75." In William J. Hudson, ed., *Australia in World Affairs 1971–1975.* Sydney: George Allen & Unwin, 1980.

Millar, Thomas B. "Australian Defence 1945–1965." In Gordon Greenwood and Norman Harper, eds., *Australia in World Affairs 1961–1965.* Melbourne: F. W. Cheshire, 1968.

―――. *Australia in Peace and War: External Relations Since 1788*. Second edition. Canberra: Australian National University, 1991.

O'Neill, Robert. "Defence Policy." In William J. Hudson, ed., *Australia in World Affairs 1971–1975*. Sydney: George Allen & Unwin, 1980.

Pacific Report. Helen Fraser, ed. Canberra. Various issues.

Piper, John. "'Don't sit under the coconut tree with anybody else but me!': Australian Policy Towards the South Pacific, As Reflected in a Recent Parliamentary Report, and Related Government Statements." *Australian Journal of International Affairs* 44, no. 2 (1990): 119–130.

―――. "Pacific Challenges: The Islands and New Zealand." In Coral Bell, ed., *Agenda for the Nineties: Studies of the Contexts for Australian Choices in Foreign and Defence Policy*. Melbourne: Longman Cheshire, 1991: 198–233.

Peacock, Andrew. "Islands in the Sun: Australia and New Zealand in World Trade." Address to the Australia–New Zealand Business Council, Melbourne, 27 July 1992.

Radio Australia South Pacific News Summary (RASPNS). Various dates.

Ray, Robert. "Defence Into The Twenty First Century." *Senate Hansard*, 30 May 1991(a): 3956–3963.

―――. Address to the Melbourne Press Club, 22 May 1991(b).

"Review of Australia's Defence Capabilities." Report to the Minister for Defence by Mr. Paul Dibb, March 1986. Canberra: Australian Government Publishing Service, 1986.

Richardson, James L. "Australian Strategic and Defence Policies." In Gordon Greenwood and Norman Harper, eds., *Australia in World Affairs 1966–1970*. Melbourne: Cheshire, 1974.

Scholes, Gordon. "Labor Rejects Bipartisan Defence Policy." *Pacific Defence Reporter*, September 1981: 12–13.

―――. "The Alternative Defence Policy." *Pacific Defence Reporter*, March 1982: 20–23.

Senate Hansard. Australian Parliament. Various issues.

Snape, Richard H. *Should Australia Seek a Trade Agreement with the United States?* Economic Planning Advisory Council, Discussion Paper 86 no. 1. Canberra: Economic Planning Advisory Council, 1986.

―――. "Working towards new trade relationships." *The Canberra Times*, 5 October 1992.

―――, Jan Adams, and David Morgan. *Regional Trade Agreements: Part I, Implications for Australia*. Melbourne: Department of Economics, Monash University, 1992(a).

―――. *Regional Trade Agreements: Part II, Options for Australia, Interim Report*. Melbourne: Department of Economics, Monash University, 1992(b).

Steeves, Jeffrey S. "Vanuatu: the 1991 National Elections and their Aftermath." *Journal of Pacific History* 27, no. 2 (1992): 217–228.

Taylor, Tom. "Australia's largest deficits are with the United States." *Insight* 1, no. 5 (1992). Canberra: Department of Foreign Affairs and Trade, 1992.

Watt, Alan. *The Evolution of Australian Foreign Policy 1938–1965*. London: Cambridge University Press, 1968.

Willis, Colin. "Australia's role in the OECD." *Backgrounder* 3, no. 3 (1992). Canberra: Department of Foreign Affairs and Trade, 1992.

Wolfers, Edward. "The Regional Security Environment: South Pacific." In Fry 1991(a): 68–82.

Woodman, Stewart, and David Horner. "Land Forces in the Defence of Australia." In David Horner, ed., *Reshaping the Australian Army: Challenges for the 1990s,* Canberra Papers on Strategy and Defence no. 77. Canberra: Strategic and Defence Studies Centre, Australian National University, 1991.

Woolcott, Richard. "APEC: The regional wave of the 1990s." Address by the Secretary of the Department of Foreign Affairs and Trade to the Sydney Institute, Sydney, 29 November 1991.

NEW ZEALAND

Bennett, Bruce S. *New Zealand's Moral Foreign Policy 1935–1939: The Promotion of Collective Security Through The League of Nations.* Wellington: New Zealand Institute of International Affairs, 1988.

Bolger, J. B., and D. A. Graham. "National's Foreign Policy." Statement released by Hon. J. B. Bolger and D. A. Graham, Wellington, 18 September 1990.

Bolger, Jim. "Towards a Global View." *New Zealand International Review,* November/December 1990.

Bureau of Industry Economics. *Trade Liberalisation and Australian Manufacturing Industry: The impact of the Australia–New Zealand Closer Economic Relations Trade Agreement.* Research Report 29. Canberra: Australian Government Publishing Service, 1990.

The Christchurch Star. Various issues.

Clements, Kevin. *Back From The Brink: The Creation of a Nuclear-Free New Zealand.* Wellington: Allen & Unwin New Zealand, 1988.

Cooper, Hon. Warren. "New Zealand Interests in the Pacific Basin." Speech delivered on 5 July 1983.

Defence and Security: What New Zealanders Want. Report of the Defence Committee of Enquiry (with Annex). Wellington: Government Printer, July 1986.

Defence of New Zealand: Review of Defence Policy 1987. Wellington: Government Printer, 1987.

The Defence of New Zealand 1991: A Policy Paper. Wellington: Government Printer, 1991.

Defence Review 1978. Wellington: Government Printer, 1978.

Defence Review 1983. Wellington: Government Printer, 1983.

The Dominion (Wellington). Various issues.

Glover, Rupert G. *New Zealand In Vietnam: A Study of the Use of Force in International Law.* Palmerston North: Dunmore Press, 1986.

Gordon, Bernard K. *New Zealand Becomes A Pacific Power.* Chicago: University of Chicago Press, 1960.

Graham, Kennedy. *National Security Concepts of States: New Zealand.* New York: Taylor & Francis for United Nations Institute for Disarmament Research, 1989.

Henderson, John. "New Zealand and the Other Pacific Islands." In Richard Kennaway and John Henderson, eds., *Beyond New Zealand II.* Auckland: Longman Paal, 1991.

Heylen Research Centre. "One Network News/Heylen Political Poll 91-D: Government's Handling of Nuclear Issues." Auckland: May 1991.

Hoadley, Steve. *New Zealand's Defence Policy and the ANZUS Dispute*. Singapore: Singapore Institute of International Affairs and Heinemann Asia, 1986.

——. "New Zealand-American Logistics Cooperation." *New Zealand International Review* 13 (January 1988[a]): 23-27.

——. "New Zealand's National Interests, Defence Capabilities, and ANZUS." In Jacob Berkovitch, ed., *ANZUS in Crisis: Alliance Management in International Affairs*. London: Macmillan, 1988(b).

——. "New Zealand and South Pacific Resource Sharing." In Bernard T. K. Joei, ed., *From Pacific Region Toward Pacific Community*. Taipei: Tamkang University Center of Area Studies, 1989.

——. "New Zealand's South Pacific Strategy." In Fedor Mediansky, ed., *Strategic Cooperation and Competition in the Pacific Islands*. Washington, D.C.: National Defense University Press, 1991.

Holmes, Frank, and Crawford Falconer. *Open Regionalism? NAFTA, CER and a Pacific Basin Initiative*. Wellington: Institute of Policy Studies, 1992.

——, Ralph Lattimore, and Anthony Haas. *Canada-Australia-New Zealand: Partners in the Pacific*. A study prepared by the Institute of Policy Studies for the New Zealand Trade Development Board. Wellington: New Zealand Trade Development Board, 1988.

——, ed. *Stepping Stones to Freer Trade? Canadian, Australian and New Zealand Perspectives*. Wellington: Victoria University Press for the Institute of Policy Studies, 1989.

Ihimaera, Witi. "New Zealand as a Pacific Nation." In Hyam Gold, ed., *New Directions in New Zealand Foreign Policy*. Auckland: Benton Ross, 1985.

Jamieson, Ewan. *Friend Or Ally: New Zealand At Odds With Its Past*. Sydney: Brassey's Australia, 1990.

Japan-New Zealand Business Council. *Japanese Direct Investment in New Zealand*. Task Force Report. Wellington: Japan-New Zealand Business Council, October 1990.

Kay, Robin. *The Australian New Zealand Agreement 1944*. Documents on New Zealand External Relations, Volume I. Wellington: Historical Publications Branch, Department of Internal Affairs, 1972.

——, ed. *The ANZUS Pact and the Treaty of Peace with Japan*. Documents on New Zealand External Relations, Volume III. Wellington: Historical Publications Branch, Department of Internal Affairs, 1985.

Kennaway, Richard. *New Zealand Foreign Policy 1951-1971*. Wellington: Hicks Smith, 1972.

Kidd, D. L. "National's Policy on Defence." Statement released by D. L. Kidd, Wellington, 18 September 1990.

Kirk, Norman. *New Zealand and its Neighbours*. Wellington: New Zealand Institute of International Affairs, 1971.

Lange, David. *South Pacific Security and Development: A Small State Perspective*. Address delivered 19 October 1987. Honolulu: East-West Center, 1987.

McIntyre, W. David. "Labour Experience in Foreign Policy." In Hyam Gold, ed., *New Directions in New Zealand Foreign Policy*. Wellington: Benton Ross, 1985.

McKinnon, Don. Interview on Radio New Zealand's "Checkpoint" program, 8 November 1990.

McKinnon, Malcolm. "From ANZUS to SEATO." In Sir Alister McIntosh, et al., *New Zealand in World Affairs*. Wellington: Price Milburn for The New Zealand Institute of International Affairs, 1977.

McMillan, Stuart. *Neither Confirm Nor Deny: The Nuclear Ships Dispute Between New Zealand and the United States*. Wellington: Allen & Unwin New Zealand, 1987.

Ministry of Foreign Affairs. *New Zealand Foreign Policy Statements and Documents 1943–1957*. Wellington: Government Printer, 1972.

Moore, Mike. *A Pacific Parliament*. Wellington: Asia Pacific Books, 1982.

———. "New Zealand and Asia." Speech delivered on 29 August 1985.

Muldoon, Robert. Speech given in Sydney, June 1982. Cited by M. J. C. Templeton, in *New Zealand Foreign Affairs Review* 33, no. 2.

Mullins, R. M. "Defence Outlook." In Ken Keith, ed., *Defence Perspectives*. Wellington: Price Milburn for the New Zealand Institute of International Affairs, 1972.

New Zealand Defence Force. *New Zealand Defence Force Contingents in the Gulf Region and Background Documents*. Wellington: Headquarters New Zealand Defence Force, February 1991.

Pearson, Mark. *Paper Tiger: New Zealand's Part in SEATO*. Wellington: New Zealand Institute of International Affairs, 1989.

Pomfret, R. "Trade Policy for the 1990s: Bilateralism or Multilateralism." *SAIS Review* 8, no. 1 (1988).

South Pacific Policy Review Group (SPPR). *Towards a Pacific Island Community*. Wellington: Government Printer, May 1990.

Vautier, K. M. "ANZCERTA and the Pacific Basin: The Challenge of the 1990's." Address to the Australia and New Zealand Business Council Conference, 15 November 1990.

UNITED STATES

Armitage, Richard L. "U.S. Security in the Pacific in the 21st Century." *Strategic Review,* Summer 1990.

The Asia Foundation. *America's Role in Asia: Interests and Policies*. Report of a working group convened by the Asia Foundation's Center for Asian Public Affairs. San Francisco: The Asia Foundation, 1993.

Baker, James A. "America in Asia." *Foreign Affairs,* Winter 1991–92.

Blair, Clay. *The Forgotten War: America in Korea, 1950–53*. New York: Times Books, 1987.

Bush, George. "Remarks." Speech at the Economic Club of Detroit, 10 September 1992. *Weekly Compilation of Presidential Documents* 28, no. 37 (14 September 1992): 1614–1624.

Clinton, Bill (William J.). Address to the Los Angeles World Affairs Council, 13 August 1992(a).

———. Remarks at North Carolina State University, Raleigh, North Carolina, 4 October 1992(b).

———. "Remarks on the Global Economy." Speech at American University, Washington, D.C., 26 February 1993. *Weekly Compilation of Presidential Documents* 29, no. 8 (1 March 1993): 319–328.

Darlin, Damon. "Japanese Learn Thrills of Bargain Shopping from Mentors Abroad." *The Wall Street Journal,* 11 March 1988: 1, 12.

Department of Defense. "A Strategic Framework for the Asia-Pacific Rim: Looking toward the 21st Century." Report to the U.S. Congress, April 1990.

Dorrance, John C. *The United States and the Pacific Islands.* The Washington Papers no. 15, The Center for Strategic and International Studies, Washington, D.C. Westport, Connecticut: Praeger, 1992.

East-West Center. *The Summit of the United States and the Pacific Islands.* Honolulu: East-West Center, 1990.

Far Eastern Economic Review. "China: Testing the Waters." 12 March 1992: 8.

Fialka, John J. "North Korea May Be Developing Ability to Build Nuclear Weapons." *The Wall Street Journal,* 19 July 1989.

Goodman, Grant K., and Felix Moos, eds. *The United States and Japan in the Western Pacific: Micronesia and Papua New Guinea.* Boulder, Colorado: Westview Press, 1981.

Government of Guam. *Report of the Guam Commission on Self-Determination: Second Quarter 1990.* Agana, Guam.

Hamnett, Michael P., and Robert C. Kiste. *Issues and Interest Groups in the Pacific Islands.* A study commissioned by the U.S. Information Agency (USIA) Research Office. Washington, D.C.: USIA, December 1988.

Hamzah, B. A. *The Spratlies: What Can Be Done to Enhance Confidence.* Kuala Lumpur: Institute of Strategic and International Studies (ISIS) Malaysia, 1990.

Holbrooke, Richard. Statement before the Subcommittee on East Asian and Pacific Affairs of the Committee on Foreign Relations, United States Senate. In the report of a hearing on "The Emerging Pacific Community," 31 July 1978. Washington, D.C.: U.S. Government Printing Office, 1978.

Honolulu Star-Bulletin. "U.N. General Assembly admits 7 new members." 17 September 1991.

Kiste, Robert C. "The Fine Print of Compacts." *Pacific Islands Monthly,* November 1983.

————. "Termination of the U.S. Trusteeship," *Journal of Pacific History* 21, no. 3 (1986).

Krause, Lawrence. "Changing America and the Economy of the Pacific Basin." In Scalapino, Sato, Wanandi, and Han 1988: 24–50.

Kristof, Nicholas. "Hunger and Other North Korean Hardships Are Said to Deepen Discontent." *The New York Times,* 18 February 1992.

Lavin, Franklin L. "After NAFTA: Free Trade and Asia." The Heritage Lectures no. 418. Washington, D.C.: The Heritage Foundation, 1992.

Layman, Thomas A. "The Changing Nature of Pacific Rim Trade in the 1980s." San Francisco: Crocker Bank, Economics Department, September 1985.

Leibowitz, Arnold H. *Defining Status: A Comprehensive Analysis of United States Territorial Relations.* Boston: Martinus Nijhoff Publishers, 1989.

Meyers, Marilyn. "United States Policy Towards the Pacific Islands." Address by the Deputy Assistant Secretary of State, Bureau of East Asia and Pacific Affairs, U.S. Department of State, at the Pacific Islands Conference, Kona, Hawaii, 10 April 1990.

Oberdorfer, Don. "North Korea and Its Not-So-Secret Weapon." *The Washington Post National Weekly,* 2–8 March 1992.

Ogata, Shijuro, Richard N. Cooper, and Horst Schullmann. *International Financial Integration: The Policy Challenges.* A Report to the Trilateral Commission, 1989.

Pacific Research (a periodical of the Peace Research Centre, Australian National University) 5, no. 3 (August 1992): 23.

Prestowitz, Clyde V., Jr. *Trading Places: How America Allowed Japan to Take the Lead.* Tokyo: Charles E. Tuttle Company, 1988.

Ranney, Austin, and Howard R. Penniman. *Democracy in the Islands: The Micronesian Plebiscites of 1983.* Washington, D.C.: American Enterprise Institute for Public Policy Research, 1985.

Seib, Gerald. "U.S. Still Hopes That Diplomacy Can Press North Korea Into Dropping Nuclear Projects." *The Wall Street Journal,* 7 February 1992.

Takeuchi, Floyd. "Coleman's new Pacific Way." *Islands Business,* December 1990.

Tyler, Patrick E. "Pentagon Imagines New Enemies To Fight in Post–Cold-War Era." *The New York Times,* 17 February 1992(a).

———. "U.S. Strategy Plan Calls For Insuring No Rivals Develop." *The New York Times,* 8 March 1992(b).

United Nations Security Council. Resolution 683, 22 December 1990.

U.S. Congress. House of Representatives Armed Services Committee. *Report of the Delegation to the South Pacific.* Washington, D.C.: U.S. Government Printing Office, 1986.

———. House of Representatives Committee on Foreign Affairs. *Problems in Paradise: United States Interests in the South Pacific.* Report of a Congressional Delegation to the South Pacific, August 5–16, 1989. Washington, D.C.: U.S. Government Printing Office, April 1990.

Van Dyke, Jon M. "The Evolving Legal Relationships Between the United States and Its Affiliated U.S.–Flag Islands." Paper prepared for Pacific Basin Development Council, Honolulu, 1990.

Vasey, L. R., J. A. Kelly, and N. Levin. *Strategic Change in East Asia: A New U.S. Approach.* Honolulu: Pacific Forum/CSIS, January 1992.

Williams, Ian. "Freedom at last!" *Pacific Islands Monthly,* February 1991.

Wolfowitz, Paul D. "The ANZUS Relationship: Alliance Management." *Current Policy* (U.S. Department of State), no. 592, 1984.

Index

Agricultural export subsidies, 173, 186
Aid: Australian aid to South Pacific, 83–86; New Zealand assistance to Pacific Islands, 92, 100–2; TTPI aid by United States, 115–17; U.S. aid to South Pacific, 111, 113–14; U.S. Overseas Private Investment Corporation, 119
Air service agreements, 168 n.1
American Samoa: acquired by United States, 107; political status of, 73; U.S. fishing treaty with, 110
ANZAC Pact, 31
ANZUS Treaty: description of, 59–60; differences in participants security policies, 195–96; economic cooperation under, 151–52, 189–94; future cooperation by participating states, 200–2; New Zealand public opinion on, 38–39; New Zealand signing, 32–33; Pacific Island region under, 69–70, 89; signing by Australia, 11; U.S. combat support under, 16; U.S.–New Zealand nuclear ship disagreements, 36, 39–40, 43–45
APEC (Asia Pacific Economic Cooperation): activities, 134–35; Australia and, 140–45; benefits of, 155–57, 167–68; establishment, 133–34, 159;

APEC *(continued)*
New Zealand and, 155–59; priorities, 134–35; U.S. attitude toward, 183–84
ASEAN (Association of Southeast Asian Nations), formation of, 133
Asia-Pacific region: economic growth of, 130–35; MITI analysis of, 155; U.S. economic policy towards, 184–85; U.S. trade deficit with, 171–73, 176–77; U.S. trade with, 170–71
Australia: assistance to South Pacific, 83–88; bilateral trade agreements, 148–51, 178; constructive commitment towards South Pacific, 75–77; cooperation with New Zealand in Pacific Islands, 31, 104–5; future cooperation by, 200–2; and Pacific Islands, 75–90; regional economic cooperation and, 139–52, 199–200; security policies *(see* Australian security policy); strategic outlook of, 19–25; trade deficit with United States, 172, 177; U.S. security policy towards, 60–61, 66–68
Australian Defence Force (ADF), 13–14, 25, 86–87
Australian Federal Opposition, 141
Australian Labor Party (ALP), 12–13, 15, 144, 149
Australian security policy: constraints

220

About the Editor and Contributors

RICHARD W. BAKER is a senior fellow in the East-West Center's Program on International Economics and Politics (formerly the International Relations Program). He served as overall coordinator for the Australia–New Zealand–U.S. Relations Project. Mr. Baker holds a master's degree in public affairs from the Woodrow Wilson School, Princeton University. From 1967 to 1987 he was a career officer in the U.S. Foreign Service, serving in Singapore, Indonesia, and Australia, as well as at the Department of State in Washington, D.C. In 1978–79 he was a Congressional Fellow. Mr. Baker spent the academic year of 1983–84 at the East-West Center as a diplomat-in-residence, prior to a three-year posting as head of the Political Section at the U.S. Embassy in Canberra. His areas of interest and specialization include Southeast Asia, Australia–New Zealand, and Oceania, as well as Asia-Pacific regionalism.

ALASTAIR BISLEY is a career officer in the New Zealand Foreign Service. He earned a B.A. and an M.A. (with honors) from Victoria University of Wellington, and a B. Phil. in English literature at Trinity College, Oxford. He joined the Ministry of Foreign Affairs (now the Ministry of External Relations and Trade — MERT) in 1967, and has had postings in the Commonwealth and Asian divisions, the New Zealand High Commission in London, the administration division of the ministry, the New Zealand Embassy in Brussels and the New Zealand Consulate General in Sydney. He has also been seconded to the Department of Trade and Industry and served as a member of the Prime Minister's Advisory Group from 1978 to 1980. From 1987 to 1991 he was director of the economic division of MERT and in 1991 he was posted to Geneva as head of the New Zealand trade negotiations office.

JENELLE BONNOR is a foreign affairs adviser to Senator Robert Hill, shadow minister for foreign affairs of the Australian Federal Opposition. Ms. Bonnor obtained a B.A. (honors) degree from the University of Sydney and a masters degree in International Relations from the Australian National University. Her areas of special interest include Asia-Pacific regional economic cooperation, regional security, and Indochina. She was a co-author of "Asia-Pacific Economic Cooperation; an evolving case study in leadership and cooperation building," published in *International Journal* 45, Autumn 1990.

STEWART FIRTH is an associate professor in politics at Macquarie University where he teaches international relations and Pacific politics. Educated at Sydney and Oxford Universities, he received his Ph.D. from Oxford in 1973 for a dissertation on German colonial rule in the Pacific Islands. Professor Firth has taught at the University of Papua New Guinea, the University of California at Santa Cruz, the University of Hawaii in Honolulu (associate professor in Pacific Islands history from 1982–83 and visiting associate professor at the Center for Pacific Islands Studies 1988–89), and the University of Sydney. His publications include *Papua New Guinea: A Political History, New Guinea Under the Germans,* and *Nuclear Playground.*

GARY R. HAWKE is professor of economic history at Victoria University of Wellington, and was seconded from the beginning of 1987 to be director of the Institute of Policy Studies. He has written on the economic history of both New Zealand and the United States, and is an editorial adviser to the *Australian Economic History Review.* He was a member of the Economic Monitoring Group of the New Zealand Planning Council from 1980 to 1991, was a member of the council in 1985–91, and served as its chairperson between 1986 and 1991. He received his doctorate at Balliol and Nuffield Colleges in Oxford, England, and has been a visiting fellow at Stanford University, All Souls' College, and the Australian National University.

JOHN HENDERSON is a senior lecturer in political science at the University of Canterbury at Christchurch. He was formerly (1989–90) chairman of the South Pacific Policy Review, within the Office of the Prime Minister. Dr. Henderson is a graduate of the University of Canterbury (B.A. and M.A.) and Duke University, North Carolina (Ph.D. in international relations). He has held a number of positions in the New Zealand government including research officer in the Ministry of Defence (1969–71); director of the Opposition Research Unit in the Parliament (1980–82); director of the Advisory Group, Prime Minister's Department (1985–87); and director of the Prime Minister's Office (1987–89). From 1983–1985 he was deputy secretary general of the Commonwealth Parliamentary Association, London.

STEVE HOADLEY is an associate professor of political studies at the University of Auckland. He received his doctorate from the University of California at Santa Barbara. His current areas of research and teaching are New Zealand and South Pacific foreign affairs, development, and security; the foreign policies of Asia-Pacific states including trade and defense; and the politics of U.S. foreign policy decision-making, most recently regarding NAFTA. Professor Hoadley's professional experience includes participation in the Minister of Foreign Affairs' advisory committees on aid and arms control, presidency of the New Zealand Political Studies Association, corresponding editorship of the *New Zealand International Review,* and membership on the New Zealand National Committee for Pacific Economic Cooperation. His publications include *The New Zealand Foreign Affairs Handbook, Improving New Zealand's Democracy,* and *The South Pacific Foreign Affairs Handbook.*

JAMES A. KELLY is president of EAP Associates, Inc., which provides international business consulting services focused on East Asia and the Pacific for private and governmental clients. He served as a special assistant for national security affairs to President Ronald Reagan, and as senior director for Asian affairs of the National Security Council, from 1986 to 1989. From 1983 to 1986 he was deputy assistant secretary of defense for International Security Affairs for East Asia and the Pacific, responsible for managing defense policy matters involving the Pacific and Asia. He has traveled and worked extensively in East Asia, the Pacific, the Middle East, and Europe, including the Soviet Union. He holds an M.B.A. from Harvard University Graduate School of Business Administration and is a graduate of the U.S. Naval Academy and the National War College. From 1959 to 1982 Mr. Kelly was a career officer in the U.S. Navy Supply Corps, attaining the rank of captain.

ROBERT C. KISTE is a professor and the director of the Center for Pacific Islands Studies (formerly the Pacific Islands Studies Program) in the School of Hawaiian, Asian and Pacific Studies at the University of Hawaii, in Honolulu. He holds a B.A. degree from Indiana University, and earned his Ph.D. in anthropology in 1967 from the University of Oregon. Professor Kiste taught at the University of Minnesota from 1967 to 1978, becoming a professor of anthropology in 1976. In 1978 he was chosen to direct the University of Hawaii's Pacific Islands Studies Program. His areas of specialization and research interests include anthropology and linguistics of the Pacific islands, history of the Pacific and contemporary Pacific affairs; he has written extensively on these topics. Professor Kiste has also held a number of consultancy and advisory positions, including service on the Fulbright Board for Australia, New Zealand, and the Pacific Islands, and as a member of the advisory committee of the National University of Samoa, Apia.

THOMAS A. LAYMAN is a vice president of Visa International, heading the Business Research and Information Management Department. He was appointed to this position in 1991, following a year as head of Visa's Country Risk Department. Prior to joining Visa, Dr. Layman was director of the Asia-Pacific Department of the Institute of International Finance in Washington, D.C., which provides economic analysis to 185 member financial institutions and companies around the world. Before joining the institute in 1987, he was an international economist with Mellon Bank in Pittsburgh and Crocker Bank in San Francisco. He has also taught at Arizona State University and North Carolina State University. Dr. Layman has a B.A. from Vanderbilt University and a Ph.D. in economics from the University of North Carolina, where he specialized in international trade and finance and economic development. He has published numerous articles on Asia and development issues. He co-authored, with Robert Dickie, *Foreign Investment and Government Policy in the Third World: Forging Common Interests in Indonesia and Beyond* (Macmillan Press, 1988).

STEWART WOODMAN is a senior research fellow in the Strategic and Defence Studies Centre (SDSC) at the Australian National University (ANU). A graduate of Sydney University (B.A. honors) and the ANU where he received his Ph.D., he served in strategic and international policy areas in the Australian Department of Defence from 1980 until joining the SDSC in December 1990. Dr. Woodman's positions in the Department of Defence included service as assistant secretary for strategic policy and planning. In 1989 he was detached as a member of a small team preparing the policy review *Australia's Strategic Planning in the 1990s*. His research interests cover Australian defense strategy, regional security developments, and New Zealand's defense policy. His recent publications include "Defining Limited Conflict: A Case of Misunderstanding," in P. R. Young, ed., *Defence and the Media in Time of Limited War* (London: Frank Cass, 1992); "Land Forces in the Defence of Australia" (with D. Horner), in D. Horner, ed., *Reshaping the Australian Army: Challenges for the 1990s* (Canberra: SDSC, ANU, 1991); and "Home Alone? Australia–New Zealand Defence Relations in a Changing World," in *New Zealand's Defence and Strategic Policies in a Changing World* (Wellington: New Zealand Military Studies Centre, 1992).

Sponsoring Organizations

The East-West Center is a public, nonprofit educational institution located in Honolulu, Hawaii, with an international board of governors and staff. It engages in cooperative study, training, and research on major issues related to population, resources, development, the environment, culture, communication, and international relations in Asia, the Pacific, and the United States. The Center was established in 1960 by the United States Congress, which provides principal funding. Support also comes from more than twenty Asian and Pacific governments, as well as private agencies and corporations.

The Institute of Policy Studies was established by Victoria University of Wellington in 1983. Its purpose is to promote the study, research, and discussion of current issues of public policy, both foreign and domestic, important to New Zealand, and to strengthen links between academics, the public service, and the business community. It is funded by the university and by grants and other support from the public and private sectors.